YOU'RE HIRED!

YOU'RE HIRED!

UNTOLD SUCCESSES *and* FAILURES *of a* POPULIST PRESIDENT

CASEY B. MULLIGAN

REPUBLIC

BOOK PUBLISHERS

ISBN 9781645720133 (Hardcover) 9781645720126 (ebook)

For inquiries about volume orders, please contact:

Republic Book Publishers

501 Slaters Lane #206

Alexandria, VA 22314

editor@republicbookpublishers.com

Published in the United States by Republic Book Publishers

Distributed by Independent Publishers Group

www.ipgbook.com

Book designed by Mark Karis

Printed in the United States of America

To Julia, with love. Thank you for your unheralded sacrifice!

CONTENTS

Cast of Characters viii

Preface xi

INTRODUCTION xvii
Firsthand accounts of untold stories from President Trump's White House

1 NO LAFFING MATTER 1
How President Trump Surpassed the Technocrats

2 "I WISH THAT HE WOULD STAY OFF TWITTER" 14
POTUS Speaks Directly with Voters

3 "AMERICA WILL NEVER BE A SOCIALIST COUNTRY" 29
White House Analysis and Marketing Shifts the 2020 Campaign

4 "NO ONE IN OHIO CARES ABOUT BURMA" 42
The Washington Bubble and the Opioid Epidemic

5 "WE HAVE A LOT OF LOVE IN THE ADMINISTRATION" 64
Some Evidence on the Chaos Question

6 "OUR COMPANIES NEED HELP" 80
POTUS Begins Immigration Reform

7 RUNNING THE GOVERNMENT LIKE A BUSINESS 90
Perspectives on the Ukraine Call and Other Matters of State

8 "I AM A TARIFF MAN" 105
Comparing Presidents Reagan and Trump

9 "FAKE NEWS SHOULD BE TALKING ABOUT THIS" 130
How Deregulation Reversed the Trend for Prescription Drug Prices

10 INDUSTRY LOBBYISTS EXPOSED BY A ROBOT 144
The "Young Geniuses" Take on the Rebate and Car Rules

11 "DO I HEAR A CRY FOR HELP OUT THERE?" 165
Swamp Creatures Protect Putin's Bootleggers

EPILOGUE 180
What We Learn About Our President and Our Government

List of Acronyms 187
Acknowledgments 189
Bibliography of Social Media 191
Bibliography of Books and Articles 197
About the Author 231
Index 232

NAME	TITLE	NAME	TITLE
Acosta, R. Alexander	Secretary of Labor	Fitzgerald, Timothy	CEA Chief International Economist
Azar, Alex M. II	Secretary of Health and Human Services	Flood, Emmet	Acting White House Counsel
Barr, William	Attorney General	Furchtgott-Roth, Diana	Acting Assistant Treasury Secretary
Baxter, Andrew M.	CEA Staff Economist	Gottlieb, Scott	Commissioner of the FDA
Blase, Brian	Special Assistant to the President for Healthcare Policy (NEC)	Grogan, Joe	Director of the Domestic Policy Council
Bolton, John	National Security Advisor (NSC)	Haley, Vincent	Deputy Assistant to the President and Advisor for Policy, Strategy and Speechwriting
Bremberg, Andrew	Director of the Domestic Policy Council	Harrington, Kevin	Deputy Assistant to the President for Strategic Planning (NSC)
Burkhauser, Richard V.	CEA Member	Hassett, Kevin	CEA Chairman
Butterfield, Nicholas	Senior Associate Staff Secretary	Kenkel, Donald	CEA Senior Economist
Chao, Elaine	Secretary of Transportation	Kudlow, Larry	NEC Director
Cipollone, Pat	White House Counsel	Kushner, Jared	Senior Advisor to the President
Clarida, Richard	Vice Chair of the Federal Reserve	Larrimore, Jeff	CEA Senior Economist
Conway, Kellyanne	Senior Counselor to the President	Lighthizer, Robert	U.S. Trade Representative
Dolan, Anthony	Special Assistant to the President and Advisor for Planning	Matsumoto, Brett	CEA Senior Economist

NAME	TITLE	NAME	TITLE
McGahn, Donald	White House Counsel	Sanders, Sarah	White House Press Secretary
Menashi, Steven	Associate Counsel and Special Assistant to the President	Scavino, Dan	Senior Adviser to the President for Digital Strategy
Miller, Stephen	Senior Advisor to the President	Schlapp, Mercedes	Director of Strategic Communications
Mnuchin, Steven	Treasury Secretary	Sun, Eric	CEA Senior Economist
Mulligan, Casey B.	CEA Chief Economist	Trump, Donald J.	POTUS
Mulvaney, Mick	Acting White House Chief of Staff	Trump, Ivanka	Senior Advisor to the President
Navarro, Peter	Director of the Office of Trade and Manufacturing Policy	Urbanowicz, Peter	HHS Chief of Staff
Nordquist, D.J.	CEA Chief of Staff	Vought, Russell	Acting OMB Director
Parker, James	Senior Advisor to the Secretary for Health Reform	Willems, Clete	Deputy Director of NEC
Pence, Mike	VPOTUS	Wong, Anna	CEA Senior Economist
Philipson, Tomas J.	CEA Member	Worthington, Paula	CEA Senior Economist
Powell, Jerome H.	Chair of the Federal Reserve	Worthington, Ross P.	Deputy Assistant to the President and Advisor for Policy, Strategy and Speechwriting
Rollo, Andrew	Senior Director for International Trade (NSC/NEC)	Zinberg, Joel	CEA General Counsel
Rosen, Jeffrey	Deputy Attorney General	Weber, Jeremy	CEA Senior Economist
Ross, Wilbur	Secretary of Commerce		

PREFACE

FROM JULY 2018 TO JUNE 2019, I served as Chief Economist of the White House Council of Economic Advisers (CEA). This was a sabbatical from what (so far) had been a twenty-five year career as a University of Chicago economics professor teaching especially "public economics" topics such as regulation, taxes, social insurance, and the behavior of government officials. The people and policies I saw in the White House differed significantly from my expectations and conventional wisdom. The White House complex is a small place geographically, but it taught me about the "big picture," which is one reason this book's title alludes to President Trump's former television series, *The*

Apprentice. Because the White House belongs to, and is treasured by, the American people, I authored this book to supply them information and economic interpretation that nobody has yet provided.

Others serving, or who have served, in the Trump White House saw these things also but were probably too busy to prepare a user-friendly compilation of their observations. Others were understandably consumed by specific details and unable yet to see the broader landscape. Journalists and others outside the Trump Administration only learn about a fraction of these events and even then, mostly second hand. More importantly, significant changes, like those begun on November 8, 2016, are difficult to process and understand, because sparse and partisan information dominates the media.

An author's biography may be irrelevant for appreciating his or her book. It would be comfortable for me to embrace that conclusion. The problem is that events in this book take place in the Federal government, an organization so massive to defy the comprehension of any one person. Because my biography is vital to my understanding of the Trump administration, I owe the reader some further details.

During the Bush Administration I was asked first by CEA Chairman Ben Bernanke and later by Chairman Edward Lazear to serve as a CEA member. These appointments never happened due to circumstances both in Washington and Chicago. CEA membership during the George W. Bush administration would have been awkward for me because my research (separately) advised against privatizing social security and spilling of American blood overthrowing longstanding foreign dictators, because what fills their void is likely worse. Having no desire to begin a working relationship on distorted pretenses, I made sure that my West Wing interviewers knew about these publications (West Wing offices are closest in proximity to the President's Oval Office). Also, not being from Chicago, they (all Republicans) were perplexed as to why I would be voting in Democratic primaries. Moreover, back then CEA membership required Senate confirmation, and by the Lazear era the Senate was not confirming any Bush appointments partly due to the political legacy of the Iraq War.

Pursuant to the Employment Act of 1946, which founded the Council of Economic Advisers and the congressional Joint Economic Committee, in 2017 President Trump nominated Kevin Hassett as CEA Chairman and the U.S. Senate confirmed him. Kevin assembled an impressive CEA team, including Richard Burkhauser, a Chicago PhD. and Tomas Philipson, a lifelong Chicago professor, both appointed CEA members by President Trump. At first, I supplied them unofficial technical advice on corporate-income taxation, the opioid epidemic, and Obamacare, and then after a year joined as Chief Economist. Several other Chicago economists served at CEA during this time, including Kevin Corinth, Don Kenkel, Eric Sun, Anna Wong, and Paula Worthington. President Trump has more supply and demand analysis in his *Economic Reports of the President* than all other presidents combined, which reflects the unique combination of presidential policies that deregulate and cut marginal tax rates with several University of Chicago thinkers providing the analysis.

Economic thinking is omnipresent in the "Chicago" atmosphere. Any analysis lacking economic reasoning is considered fundamentally flawed. A number of those at President Trump's CEA were Chicago trained or affiliated and cherished that atmosphere and missed it after they earned their Chicago diplomas and took jobs elsewhere. They liked breathing that air again, which years ago none of us expected would be filling the White House. It was fun for me to see them enjoy it again, knowing that I was helping to make it that way.

Kevin did all the CEA television appearances, met often with the President, and with the sage assistance of Chief of Staff D.J. Nordquist, kept track of CEA's status in West Wing politics. Because the President as well as TV interviewers can cover a lot of often difficult ground in a brief period of time, these activities took a lot of Kevin's time and energy for preparation. (In the year before I arrived, Kevin miraculously also had time to engage in the details of CEA tax analysis and publications, which is a framework that continues to pay dividends).

As chief economist, my time was primarily spent in various stages of preparing Administration reports for the public, most of which were CEA products. This activity was strategically sequenced with the purpose of accumulating an inventory of results and tools that would propel later work. One example (among many): the measurement of prescription drug prices and FDA policy changes to entry barriers in that industry were the subject of thorough CEA analysis, which facilitated 18 months (and counting) of subsequent event-driven work as it became apparent to the rest of the Washington Bubble that prescription drug prices really were falling. As this book explains, these results often got the President's full attention and interest.

In terms of economics subfields, I estimate that regulation and health took most of my time at CEA (about one third each). Dissecting socialism took 12 percent of my time and labor economics and international trade each took a further 8 percent. My (infrequent) international trade work was about evenly divided between analysis of an import prohibition (see Chapter 11) and analysis of tariffs (Chapter 8). Events are recounted in this book in essentially the proportions cited above. The primary exception is that this book gives extra attention to international trade and immigration, at the expense of domestic labor economics. I did so to conform better to the topics of expected interest to readers. My regret is that the resulting book does not sufficiently reveal how I enjoyed working on labor issues with the people at the Department of Labor, which included then-Secretary Alex Acosta and his staff, experts from the Bureau of Labor Statistics, and the authors of several deregulatory actions.

When I was a student, like so many others, I was often lost in transactional details of my dissertation and forgot about its big picture. My advisers, especially Professor Robert E. Lucas, Jr., sometimes called me out of that fog by reminding me of the dissertation's fundamental importance and where it sat in the landscape of economic research. In the Lucas style, I would sometimes remind Presidential staff of the fundamental importance of their policy activities.

For example, I had published a book on the 2009 "stimulus"

law and another on the 2010 Affordable Care Act, and the Trump Administration was proposing (and executing) policies to reverse the disincentives created by those laws. Special Assistant to the President Brian Blase spearheaded many of the reversals related to health insurance, and (explained further in Chapter 1) I helped him remember, quantify, and articulate the large economic benefits of those efforts (we teased him that he better not take any vacation because his work was worth $1 billion per week to the nation). Deputy Policy Director Andrew Bremberg led the effort to push 16 statutes through Congress that reversed costly Federal regulations. Building on the *Chicago Price Theory* book I published in 2019 (with three other Chicago economists Jaffe, Minton, and Murphy), I showed Bremberg and others on President Trump's deregulation team how these accomplishments were lowering consumer prices, and how they fit into the overall history of U.S. deregulation (Chapter 8).

A unique part of my position is that I worked as an organizational entrepreneur, frequently crossing hierarchical boundaries. Sometimes, I was fully engaged in details, such as reading the Federal Register, writing my own code for scraping data from a website, or reading Congressional bills and testimony (this parallels my academic career where my reliance on research assistants has always been low, if usually zero). Other times, I was attending meetings with Cabinet members, Federal Reserve Chairman Powell, or the President himself, often as the only person in attendance who had seen the relevant details firsthand rather than having them communicated through subordinates. As explained in this book, various problems with Federal operations were found this way.

Simply put, my methods, conclusions, and the large majority of my activities were remarkably similar to what I had previously been doing at the University of Chicago, except that I saw the White House West Wing outside my office windows (nice) and always wore a suit and tie (yuck). And my findings had the world's best publicist: Donald J. Trump! The contents of many public CEA reports make it clear that we somehow missed the partisan memo instructing us to reverse long-held beliefs and practices in order to properly serve our evil master.

Frequently, I read online that the White House was in perpetual chaos, directly attributable to the President, which sapped everyone's productivity and encouraged back-stabbing as the primary way for colleagues to engage each other. This must have happened during my Chicago weekends, or perhaps the regular "White House in chaos" articles were belatedly referring to something that occurred long before I arrived. In my experience the opposite was true (Chapter 5). The Trump CEA has been historically productive, achieving feats to which earlier CEAs could only aspire. My last day at CEA was my only sad one, because I was saying goodbye to superb colleagues.

This book was not authorized by the Trump administration. No one in the administration knew that I was writing it; I was invited to serve as an economic policy analyst, not as a biographer. If you think otherwise, look especially at Chapter 4 and Chapter 11.

To avoid interrupting the intriguing and mostly untold stories about President Trump and his team working on economic matters, this book has no footnotes or endnotes. However, it was written based on precise and detailed records, many of which are shared at the end of each chapter in sections called "Further Watching and Reading." The end of the book also includes thorough bibliographies. Updated and hyperlinked versions of the bibliographies are available on this book's website, yourehiredtrump.com.

DECEMBER 2019, CHICAGO, IL

INTRODUCTION

FIRSTHAND ACCOUNTS OF UNTOLD STORIES FROM PRESIDENT TRUMP'S WHITE HOUSE

AMONG PRESIDENT TRUMP'S FAVORITE DUTIES is dealing with economic subjects. Each chapter of this book covers one of those subjects and how the President dealt with it. Read what President Trump had to say about auto companies, Senator Bernie Sanders, immigration, international aid, the 2016 election, Twitter, and much more. The news media usually neglected to report these events and what they tell us about the President's approach and capabilities, and our government.

Until 2016, Donald J. Trump had hardly any experience running for national office. Moreover, his candidacy for President of the United States was opposed by most leaders of the two political parties that dominate American politics. Nevertheless, later that year the American people told him, "You're hired!" Within months he would, among other things, direct the most momentous change in the Federal administrative state since the New Deal. Anyone wanting to understand, emulate, or oppose President Trump's "populist" methods and approaches will find this book's accurate, firsthand accounts beneficial.

Some of the chapters are about successes, and others about failures. If you are interested in reading about the failures first, begin with Chapter 11. The tragedies at the beginning of that chapter illustrate perennial flaws in at least a dozen presidential administrations, including the current one. Russian President Vladimir Putin is also part of that story. Chapter 4's description of the opioid epidemic has a similar flavor. Otherwise, enjoy this book in sequence, prepared to be as amazed and humbled as I was.

I

NO LAFFING MATTER

HOW PRESIDENT TRUMP SURPASSES THE TECHNOCRATS

"I like the mandate."

PRESIDENTIAL CANDIDATE DONALD J. TRUMP, FEBRUARY 18, 2016

"No person should be required to buy insurance."

PRESIDENTIAL CANDIDATE DONALD J. TRUMP, MARCH 2, 2016

FOR A FEW DAYS IN FEBRUARY 2016, Donald J. Trump echoed health-policy experts' advice, already enshrined in Federal law, to force everyone either to buy health insurance or pay a hefty tax penalty. By March, candidate Trump had already become the most vocal opponent of the tax penalty or "individual mandate," which he would soon repeal in the White House Oval Office.

Mr. Trump's political opponents complained that he was on both sides of the mandate issue in the span of a few days, and ultimately ignored the policy wonks. This constituted unmistakable evidence, they said, that he was dishonest, arrogant, and unscientific. But the pundits are now beginning to recognize their mistakes about the individual mandate. The most interesting part of the episode is how Mr. Trump quickly detects such errors, and in the process better appreciates the concerns of the general population than technical advisers typically do.

POPULIST EXPERIMENTER

For centuries scientists have appreciated the value of experimentation, especially in complex situations where smart people struggle to identify the important features of the situation and then understand how the pieces fit together. Take Guglielmo Marconi, who is credited with inventing wireless radio communication and received the 1909 Nobel Prize in Physics. He admitted that he had little understanding of how wireless radio waves worked, but trial and error had shown him that they do work before physicists understood why.

Mr. Trump experiments with skill, probably more often than Marconi. Knowing full well that he was beginning a process of trial and error, Mr. Trump advocated an individual mandate on February 18, 2016. We can assume that, as I have seen him do with various experiments since then, he closely watched the feedback. He was hearing from advisers, news media, businesses, and Republican party officials. He was also hearing from voters directly, and indirectly through pollsters, social media, elected officials, and candidates running for office. He understands the biases of the various commenters, but also how the technical advisers live in a Washington Bubble, insensitive to or unaware of public concerns.

Mr. Trump's critics can only see the experimental approach as proof that the President is unprincipled. However, the toughest practical situations are often those where theoretical principles are not yet developed enough to provide a clear understanding. Just ask Marconi.

Guglielmo Marconi's radio worked. Later physicists would explain why. Public domain photo from Wikipedia Commons.

The individual mandate was one of those situations. The technical challenges are large, even without political considerations. The Affordable Care Act (ACA), signed in 2010 by President Obama and containing the infamous individual mandate and its tax penalties, is a thousand pages long and supported by tens of thousands more pages of regulations promulgated by President Obama's Departments of Treasury, Labor, and Health and Human Services. Professional economists, including me, try to predict the effects of laws like this by using computers to build models of the various legal provisions and to connect those with measures of historical performance in affected markets. Technical predictions are fallible. To name a notable instance: the Congressional Budget Office significantly revised its modeling of the ACA four years after passage.

Formulating Federal policy is not just a technical problem of economics and law. There is a myriad of political pressures. Among them, insurance companies were supporting regulation of their business with the understanding that the Federal government would require people to buy their products. Hospitals expected to see reduced expenses for charity care and potentially changes in the number of emergency-room visits. Being unsure about the economic effects, policy experts had little reliable advice to offer in terms of the ACA's political success based on how diverse segments of the population engaged politically after experiencing the law.

A 2013 Cartoon Showing a Swamp Creature Demanding the Individual Mandate. Chip Bok Editorial Cartoon used with permission of Chip Bok and Creators Syndicate. All rights reserved.

Candidate Trump needed only a few days of experimentation to discover that repealing the individual mandate would be a political and economic success (actually the mandate was not repealed but rather the tax penalty enforcing it was set to zero, which is a distinction of interest only to attorneys; see also the end of this chapter). It would be at least three more years until the repeal was understood at a technical level.

The field of economics has experiments, but the experiments are often deliberately conducted in simplified environments. The President showed me how social experiments are useful in complex situations, at least for someone tasked with making decisions rather than evaluating a general theory.

As a second example, consider the late 2018 episode of the prescription drug "rebate rule," a complicated regulation proposed by Secretary of Health and Human Services Alex M. Azar II, which had a compelling narrative but was full of economic damage. With his economists offering the opposite opinion of Secretary Azar, the President asked CEA to study and evaluate the regulation (see Chapter 10 for more on the rebate rule). When our study was complete, CEA and other White House staff urged the President to stop the proposed rebate rule at the next Oval Office meeting, while Secretary Azar wanted the development of the rule to continue. (A Cabinet agency such as HHS is not considered part of the White House).

President Trump's experimental approach became plain to me when he did neither. Instead, the proposed rule should be put on the internet for the public comment period, at the end of which the White House would reconvene with Secretary Azar to plan a final rule. Unlike prior Administrations that viewed public comments as a nuisance along their path to imposing regulations, President Trump relished public comments as an abundant source of greater feedback on the results of his experiment.

MANAGING THE HAWTHORNE EFFECT

Marconi did not need to worry that radio waves would behave differently when they were part of his experiments. By contrast, the famous Hawthorne effect says that people may behave differently when they know they are involved with an experiment. President Trump accounts for the Hawthorne effect by keeping people, including his own staff, guessing as to whether his directive is genuine or experimental. Encouraging competing views among his senior staff also helps mitigate the Hawthorne effect.

As the April 3 "rebate rule" meeting approached, I further appreciated why he is President and the rest of us are just advisers: President Trump uses the Hawthorne effect to enhance the value of his experiments.

The public comment period gave Secretary Azar plenty of time to tout the rebate rule and the real problems it was intended to address with the news media, who (tellingly) admired the rebate rule more than truly beneficial health-related policies coming from the Trump Administration. A further delay in the rulemaking also gave the President more time to discuss the rule at rallies, as he did in Green Bay on April 27th.

Meanwhile, he had the White House economists thinking that the rebate rule would go into effect in the end. For example, in April in the presence of the more senior Secretary Azar, who regularly (and inaccurately) promoted himself as the only other "real businessman" in the discussions, the President urged the "young geniuses" in the White House to get to work finishing the Secretary's rule. At the last minute, in early July, the President ended the experiment. He told Secretary Azar to withdraw the rebate rule, citing both its costs to consumers and taxpayers and that voters would not find it appealing.

UNPREDICTABLE?

Opponents often criticize President Trump for being "unpredictable." After seeing a few decision processes play out, I learned to prefer that decisions end up in front of the President rather than his staff making less creative compromises among themselves. The President knows when and how to use unpredictability to obtain better results.

First, voters "hired" Mr. Trump to try something new rather than recycling the same old proposals. New proposals would include some surprises, and perhaps generate discomfort, or else they would not be new proposals. New proposals need to be critically evaluated and, if needed, discarded. Keeping an element of "unpredictability" counters the Hawthorne effect.

Second, President Trump typically tries ideas internally first. Sometimes the internal feedback is enough to end the experiment. Otherwise, the ideas reach the public at a time when they are already familiar to the staff. Indeed, the more serious challenge for the staff was to remember when a new idea was fresh to the public even while it was familiar to us. The Ukraine call (Chapter 6) is a good example.

Third, the President's experimentation is predictable once you understand how he operates. Much of the public has been confused about this, especially as relates to the President's Twitter messages (see also Chapter 2). *The New York Times Magazine* conveyed the conventional wisdom when it described the messages as "the unabridged representation of a singular man's impulses" and "daily electroshocks of presidential id." But this interpretation does not recognize experiments for what they are.

Take, for instance, the August 21, 2019, messages declaring that car company executives are "weak" and "foolish" for spending "more money on a car that is not as safe or good." Conventional wisdom would say that he was letting the world know that he decided against a regulatory request of the car companies. In fact, the President had been thinking seriously about the auto regulations for more than two years. Without any tweets on the subject, he decided early on to fully overturn the Obama Administration's regulations. By 2019, the American automobile manufacturers were tremendously pressuring him to change his decision (Chapter 10 of this book). The President was wondering how costly it would be to resist their pressure. How much would voters appreciate his resistance on their behalf? The August 21 tweets were part of his seeking answers to those questions. Properly understood, the tweets were *very* big news for auto consumers and auto companies. Within two months, the Administration announced that it would be allowing part of the Obama regulations to go ahead.

Some readers may think that Mr. Trump is not clever or strategic enough to make himself a capable experimenter. His intelligence (or, if you believe, lack of intelligence) is a topic for later chapters because it is hardly relevant here. The experimental method could have been an accidental discovery from earlier in his life. As explained on the following pages, other politicians practice it. As a 72-year-old President, Mr. Trump had many years before the White House to make such a discovery and to refine the method so that it better serves his purposes.

Indeed, I could tell that experimentation was not the least bit novel to him ("experiment" and "results" are my terms; he refers to "listening," "changing course," or "pivoting"). The events I saw, and recount in this book, are proof that Mr. Trump is by now a capable experimenter. Anyone not recognizing the method will find that Mr. Trump perpetually surprises them with actions that are in fact predictable.

A LEGENDARY LAFFER CURVE

Guided by Marconi's experimental results, theoretical physicists eventually caught up with him. Today, they can articulate the principles of physics that allow radio transmissions to cross the ocean. Mr. Trump's decision got us thinking more carefully about the individual mandate in the context of the ACA, which led to a more rigorous explanation of why its costs far exceed its benefits.

Consumers must be forced to buy health insurance, so goes the argument for the "individual mandate," or else they would only sign up when they are sick. Anyone who does not comply must be disciplined. Although too many pundits embrace this conclusion, as did the 111th Congress of the United States when it passed the 2010 Affordable Care Act (ACA), it is obviously incorrect when viewed in context.

Take Mr. Ben Winslett, a Baptist pastor, husband, and father of five from Alabama, who describes himself as "securely in the middle class earning nearly the exact average US income each year." His family's health insurance was "taken care of on my own in the previous system," but the ACA outlawed their $250-monthly policy, leaving them with far more expensive options. As he describes it, the ACA "has placed an enormous financial burden on normal, everyday people *quite literally forcing us onto government assistance* we didn't need before" (emphasis added). In other words, consumers are already encouraged to buy health insurance by the generous Federal subsidies intended to make it affordable. Consumers who turn down the government aid by failing, say, to buy a subsidized plan are owed gratitude by us Federal taxpayers. The ACA did the opposite with its "individual mandate," administering a financial punishment.

The Obama Administration saw consumers paying the individual mandate tax penalty for the "privilege" of purchasing a nonconforming (by Federal standards) plan they liked better even without subsidies. Instead of improving the ACA-compliant plans so that they would be more attractive to consumers, the Obama Administration doubled and tripled down on its punishment by prohibiting the nonconforming plans that were attracting consumers. Some of the prohibited plans were inexpensive "short term" plans and plans offered by groups of small employers. The major health insurance companies were overjoyed because not only did the Federal government penalize consumers who did not purchase its product, but it was also destroying competing insurance products that consumers preferred instead. President Trump's Secretaries of Treasury, Labor, and Health and Human Services ended these prohibitions, giving consumers more choices beyond Federally subsidized plans.

Arthur Laffer and his "Laffer curve" made famous the possibility that governments might lose revenue by increasing a tax because the higher tax discourages taxpayers from doing the things that are taxed. A sufficiently high cigarette tax, for example, could stop everyone from smoking legal tax-paying cigarettes and thereby reduce government revenue. The so-called discouragement effect of real world taxes, even in extreme cases, can provoke a vigorous debate among academics as to whether it is dominant enough to fit Mr. Laffer's description. The discouragement effect of the ACA's individual mandate tax was, by contrast, so large and obvious as to occupy an exclusive spot in the history of taxation. By pushing people, like Mr. Winslett, onto Obamacare plans that are tied to liberal tax credits, the individual mandate tax resulted in far more revenue lost to tax credits than revenue it collected from those who violated the individual mandate. Analysts ranging from the Trump Administration to the nonpartisan Congressional Budget Office (CBO) to M.I.T. economics professor Jonathan Gruber (perhaps the Obama Administration's most visible ACA consultant) all agree that the Treasury drain far exceeded the tax-penalty funds received. The individual mandate penalty is, from all perspectives, truly a tax unicorn.

What the experts did not realize until recently was the heavy economic costs associated with "successful" attempts to prevent consumers from turning down government assistance. Despite having featured Mr. Winslett's story in my 2015 book about the ACA, initially I did not appreciate the size of the economic damages from the individual mandate. When the Trump Administration tasked me with preparing a rigorous quantitative analysis, I could no longer gloss over the calculus of costs and benefits. Taxpayers were worse off because they were funding millions of involuntary participants in ACA insurance plans. Those same participants were also worse off because, as Mr. Winslett explained, they preferred to spend their own money on a non-ACA plan. In 2019, CEA released its quantitative analysis, three years after Mr. Trump had learned from his experiment that mandate repeal would be a winner.

TECHNOCRATS AND ELECTED OFFICIALS

Although the experts uniformly failed to recognize the size of the individual mandate's costs, candidate Trump was not the only politician to detect that something was seriously wrong. Many Republican members of the House and Senate were strongly opposed to the individual mandate. President Obama himself—seven times a candidate for elected office—was once opposed to the individual mandate. According to the memoirs of his communications director, President Obama privately acknowledged at the end of his term that the individual mandate may have been one of those details that he got wrong as he was bending "the arc of the moral universe ... toward justice."

Policy analysis many times suffers from groupthink, a.k.a., the Washington bubble. Only the elected officials, far outnumbered by the technocrats, must interact with people outside the bubble who are affected by Federal policies. Experiences with the individual mandate, the opioid epidemic (Chapter 4), and a host of Federal regulations (Chapters 7 and 8) supplied me with a profound new respect for our elected leaders. Their contact with, and accountability to, voters brings a valuable set of knowledge lacked by the technocrats, sometimes tragically.

FURTHER WATCHING AND READING

Mr. Trump is not the first to notice the value of experimentation. Trial and error, even in directions that seem contrary to "good reason," is a widely respected algorithm in the sciences. It is so respected that the "Optimization by Simulated Annealing" article describing it has become one of the most cited science articles of all time. Nobelprize. org hosts Guglielmo Marconi's December 11, 1909, Nobel lecture, which explains how experimentation ran ahead of theoretical understanding. See also Erik Larson's description in the 2006 book *Thunderstruck*. The Hawthorne effect is named after an Illinois factory (coincidentally my grandfather Donald Mulligan worked there; see also Chapter 11) credited for its discovery; Richard Gillespie's 1991 *Manufacturing Knowledge* book documents the intellectual history. (Every chapter has a bibliography at the end of this book; listing of social media citations are in a separate social media bibliography).

The *New York Times* hosts a short video showing candidate Trump's evolving position on the individual mandate. Donald J. Trump's *2019 Economic Report of the President* (prepared by CEA) provides technical analysis of the individual mandate, estimating that continuing it and similarly-motivated regulations from the previous administration would have cost consumers and taxpayers a net of almost $50 billion per year. The economic value of removing those regulations (estimated around 0.2 percent of national income), as President Trump has done, therefore rivals some of the most famous deregulations in U.S. history, such as the deregulation of trucking in the 1970s. Comments by Barack Obama on the individual mandate are reported in the memoir of Dan Pfeiffer, who served as communications director in the Obama Administration.

CEA's 2019 economic analysis shows that the ACA's individual mandate and its tax penalty are wasteful—beyond unnecessary—because the ACA subsidizes insurance so much. At the same time, the Federal Department of Justice (DOJ) has supported the legal position in *Texas v Azar* that the 111th Congress *viewed* the tax penalty as absolutely essential to the ACA (see also 1501(a)(2)(H) of the law passed by that Congress). The White House and DOJ had opposite incentives in this situation. We wanted to release quantitative results related to the President's deregulatory agenda. Moreover, Democrats in Congress would be trying to overturn these important health insurance deregulations, and their testifying experts should have to consider the amount of consumer harm documented in the CEA report. But the DOJ was concerned that a partisan judge in the case would ignore the distinction between what the 111th Congress believed and what the CEA found nearly ten years later and cite CEA's report as evidence against DOJ's position. The release of the report was blocked for more than three months until the White House Counsel's office (especially Steven Menashi, who had a deep understanding of both the economic and legal issues) helped tightened CEA's legal references enough for DOJ to concur.

Although several members of White House and Congressional expert staffs have long opposed the individual mandate, it was not until 2019 that they could decisively and quantitatively engage the seductive arguments for the ACA's individual mandate and team-Obama's prohibitions of nonconforming insurance plans. Those arguments treat consumer choice as a negative- or zero-sum game. A person who reduces his or her net premium spending by $1,000 when he or she forgoes an unwanted category of coverage, so the argument goes, only increases by $1,000 the premiums that must be collected from those who retain the full coverage. This assumption does not fit the reality of the ACA because of administrative costs, moral hazard (a consumer buying too much when he is spending other people's money), and especially that the ACA plans are heavily subsidized.

The story of the individual mandate continues. When we techno-crats finally were able to quantify the costs of the ACA's individual mandate, I began to look at other Federal programs that might be imposing similar costs. I found that the Federal "Medicare" program of health insurance for the elderly also has individual mandate pen-alties, albeit under different names ("late enrollment penalties" and automatic social security deductions). Within six months, President Trump issued an executive order directing the Secretary of Health and Human Services to find, no later than March 2020, ways to eliminate or ease Medicare's individual mandate penalties.

Joseph Rago's February 7, 2014, article in the *Wall Street Journal* described changes in ACA analysis by the Congressional Budget Office, as well as my role in that. The experience of Ben Winslett's family was described on his blog and retold in my 2015 book *Side Effects and Complications: The Economic Consequences of Health-Care Reform*. An article by the *Washington Post* "Fact Checker" on May 15, 2013, discusses estimates of the number of pages of Federal regulation issued pursuant to the ACA.

The Laffer curve is often credited to economist Arthur Laffer, who duly notes that the idea has a long history. President Trump honored Mr. Laffer on June 19, 2019, with the Presidential Medal of Freedom. John Maynard Keynes made one of the most impressive applications of the idea in his 1919 book *The Economic Consequences of the Peace*, where he warned that the taxes ("reparations") levied on the losers of World War I were beyond the capacity of the German economy. He predicted, cor-rectly, that attempts by the Allies to extract reparations from Germany would shrink its economy to such an extent that Germany would have too little capacity to pay and become politically unstable.

"I WISH THAT HE WOULD STAY OFF TWITTER"

POTUS SPEAKS DIRECTLY WITH VOTERS

"Dan, come in here. We've got to tweet this!"
PRESIDENT DONALD J. TRUMP, MOST DAYS

THE PRESIDENT OF THE UNITED STATES is presented with a staggering amount of information on a wide range of issues. With advisers in place to digest the technicalities, President Trump processes this information from a communications perspective. How is it best delivered to voters? For this he looks to television, news outlets, debates, speeches and, especially, Twitter. This Chapter and Chapter 3 tell the unknown story of the ways the President communicates with voters.

CUTTING OUT THE MIDDLEMAN WITH TWITTER
Referring to the immensely popular social media platform where users

broadcast messages ("tweets") in 280 characters or less, 72 percent of voters think that President Donald Trump uses Twitter too much. The respondents to that poll may have been thinking of @realdonaldtrump's peculiar tweet "I too have a Nuclear Button" or the quixotic "Trade wars are good, and easy to win" (@realdonaldtrump is Mr. Trump's Twitter handle). Or they were only tired of the dozens of tweets about the "Witch Hunt." Much of the White House staff thinks the same thing.

But this attitude neglects the President's experimental method, discussed in Chapter 1. More important, it ignores the critical question of how he gets so many Twitter followers (almost 70 million as of the end of 2019) and keeps their attention. A steady stream of bizarre, bombastic, and sometimes hilarious messages helps of course. Even more, the messages are rebroadcast on Twitter, on news programs, and word of mouth. A Gallup study found that three-quarters of U.S. adults see, hear, or read about @realdonaldtrump's tweets "a lot" or a "fair amount." That's 190 million people, far beyond the population of his Twitter followers. That's even more people than watch the annual Super Bowl, and more than double the number of people watching the typical Presidential debate. A top-rated television news program gets only 3 million viewers.

The President's gamble is that voters aware of his successes on substance will tolerate his eccentricities and improprieties in form. As explained throughout this book, the Trump Administration has significant accomplishments and failures that go unreported. Twitter is essential for @realdonaldtrump to communicate the successes. As his supporters say, follow @realdonaldtrump for "real news."

President Trump explained to us how having a large social media staff is a mistake. It is just him and Dan Scavino, he says. Dan is the Senior Advisor to the President for Digital Strategy, which especially means running the @realdonaldtrump Twitter account. Dan's office is barely a closet, but it is closer to the President's Oval Office than any other. Dan is also the rare person allowed to bring a laptop computer, or any personal electronic device, into the Oval Office.

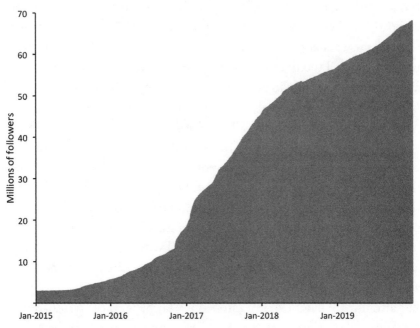

@realdonaldtrump's Twitter following over time. Many people receiving rebroadcasts are not included.

Take the day that CEA's leadership and I reviewed the highlights of the *2019 Economic Report of the President* with him in the Oval Office. The first exhibit showed how the U.S. economy had grown 3.1 percent during calendar year 2018. This had not happened since calendar year 2005. The President went into communication mode, noting first that this accomplishment "is not getting fair coverage." POTUS called for Dan who hustled into the Oval Office with his laptop. The two of them began composing a tweet, with POTUS dictating and Dan typing.

POTUS began with a now familiar strategy for getting the press to cover a new fact, which is to exaggerate it so that the press might enjoy correcting him and unwittingly disseminate the intended finding. POTUS asked whether the tweet should say that it was the fastest growth in 20 years. Or 50? What would be the sweet exaggeration spot that would get media attention? He asked Hassett, but Hassett sheepishly replied that he had only 3,000 Twitter followers, as compared to 70 million. POTUS quickly decided, as he did on many occasions, to initially report the result with 100 percent precision, exactly as provided by CEA. Later his communications team could gauge whether the coverage needed exaggeration.

Dan was handed the top page of our presentation, which had both a title and a chart related to the growth accomplishment. POTUS correctly determined that the chart would not convey the finding as well on Twitter as the title would. Dan then tweeted verbatim to POTUS's 70 million Twitter followers "GDP growth during the four quarters of 2018 was the fastest since 2005. This Administration is the first on record to have experienced economic growth that meets or exceeds its own forecasts in each of its first two years in office. GROWTH is beating MARKET EXPECTATIONS!" (Dan added the capitalization.)

This pattern is typical in the economic sphere if not in other policy areas. The raw material comes from the advisers. Sometimes this material is requested by POTUS, but most of the time the raw material is part of normal operations, as with the preparation of the *Economic Report of the President*. POTUS supplies the inspiration. Other times the material may go straight from the advisers to Dan Scavino who tweets it understanding the President's interest in the subject.

A single tweet sourced from advisers would typically be vetted among dozens of them. Chapter 9 of this book explains how the tweet about falling prescription drug prices originated in my office at around 5 p.m. on Thursday, January 10, followed by a spirited Friday conference call including officials ranging from White House communications to the Health Secretary's office. To that call I brought the results of months of CEA research on the subject, which included interviews with experts at the Bureau of Labor Statistics and the Food and Drug Administration. The call was augmented by a number of conversations in the halls of the Eisenhower Executive Office Building. Dan Scavino would have also conferred with various officials before he posted the tweet at the end of the day on Friday. (Even more people would have participated if the Federal government had not been shut down over a funding dispute with Congress.) Although it may support the authenticity of @realdonaldtrump, the image of POTUS alone tapping tweets from scratch on a cell phone is inaccurate.

COMMUNICATOR IN CHIEF

The following figure shows the typical layout of an Oval Office meeting without press. The Chief of Staff's office arranges chairs around the President's Resolute Desk for those requesting the meeting. Seating that day was assigned to the National Economic Council, the Health Department (HHS), the Domestic Policy Council, CEA, and the Office of Management and Budget, represented by Brian Blase, Secretary Azar, Joseph Grogan, me, and Russ Vought, respectively. Behind the chairs and in front of the fireplace are two parallel couches and an armchair for others who might give advice to the President.

From left to right: POTUS, Russ Vought, Joe Grogan, Alex Azar, Brian Blase, May Davis, Casey Mulligan, Kellyanne Conway, Mercedes Schlapp, Sarah Sanders. Official White House Photo by Shealah Craighead. Used with Permission.

The importance of politics is clear in the figure, especially on the desk and on the couch. In past meetings the President had heard the arguments for and against Secretary Azar's policy proposals and had been following the media's reaction. He wants the Secretary to answer for the two negative full-page ads, which POTUS had on his desk before any of us came into the office.

On the righthand couch are communications specialists: Kellyanne Conway, Mercedes Schlapp, and Sarah Huckabee Sanders. President Trump not only wants to anticipate the technical advantages and disadvantages of the policy choices, but also how voters will react to them. After the wonky advisers have said their part, POTUS elevates his head to look over the row of chairs at the communications couch: "Can we message this?"

The messaging question cannot be neglected. We learned that in many cases policy debates should be shared with the communications specialists before they are presented to President Trump. Otherwise, they must offer an impromptu answer to the President's inevitable messaging question. On the day shown in the figure, Secretary Azar had already learned that lesson and had previously met with them. While Kellyanne answered the President's question equivocally, Sarah and Mercedes were confident that it would be easy to educate the public about the Secretary's scheme to regulate business-to-business transactions in the prescription drug industry. Unpreparedness for the President's messaging question (by Russ, Joe, Brian, and me) allowed the scheme to make it to the next level of communication: a Presidential rally.

"But prescription drugs, look, it's a rigged system, okay, if I told you how crazy it is, the Web, it's the Web, you need 193 I.Q. to even understand. This web of geniuses, they put this thing to lower drug prices. It has 19 effects here and 27 …." A few weeks had passed, and President Trump was in Green Bay, Wisconsin in front of a 10,000-person capacity crowd. For some of the same reasons that Secretary Azar's regulatory scheme was bad economics, it was proving impossible to explain to voters. As discussed further in Chapter 10, President Trump would soon end the proposed regulation.

Earlier in the year we were in the Oval Office to discuss the various chapters of the *2019 Economic Report of the President*. President Trump, who needed hardly any explanation, treated the stack of exhibits as an exercise in communications triage. Everything CEA had done was under-publicized, and marketing enhancements were urgently needed. As discussed above, he directed Dan to push out the first exhibit (caption only—no chart) on Twitter. We (he) also had to call Commerce Secretary Ross and tell him to change his department's web page, although that task would wait 30 more minutes. Another exhibit needed to be sent over to Congress, he said. Yet another should go to *New York Post* columnist Michael Goodwin, adding that "Goodwin is doing a great job."

Lou Dobbs, the host of cable TV's most-watched business show, needed to receive the next exhibit. "Wait!" POTUS exclaimed, "Let's call Lou right now." "Kevin," he told CEA Chairman Hassett, "go back to the beginning so that Lou can hear about all of them." We used the speakerphone on the President's desk. That night *Lou Dobbs Tonight* told hundreds of thousands of viewers about CEA's findings, with a picture of D.J., Tom, Kevin, Rich, and I sitting around the Resolute Desk. That's at least one-thousand times CEA's normal audience.

Photo shown on Lou Dobbs Tonight. From left to right are D.J. Nordquist, Tom Philipson, President Trump, Kevin Hassett, Rich Burkhauser, and Casey Mulligan (foreground is Larry Kudlow and Mick Mulvaney). Official White House Photo by Shealah Craighead. Used with Permission.

After hanging up with Lou Dobbs, the President returned to the subject of the growth rate for calendar year 2018, which was 3.1 percent. Following convention, the Department of Commerce was also reporting a second "annual-average to annual-average" measure of economic growth that (for good statistical reasons) is not featured by CEA, the Federal Reserve Board, and other agencies as descriptions of what happened during the calendar year. The President thought that Commerce's convention was bad marketing and, over some meek protests from the economists in the Oval Office, got Commerce Secretary Wilbur Ross on the speakerphone. He instructed Secretary Ross to remove the second measure from its internet press release.

Often lacking information about what the President is really doing, the President's critics complain that his messaging on the economy is insufficient. Take the August 2018 jobs report, which was released on Friday, September 7 and full of good news about employment and wages. As soon as President Trump saw our memo summarizing the report, he called CEA Chairman Kevin Hassett. Hassett was unable to answer because he was on a flight to Ireland, but on landing received this voicemail: "Hello Kevin, this is your favorite president calling. That's a fabulous jobs report and we've got to get out there spreading the news."

Kevin emailed me at around 3:00 a.m. Washington time. My government phone was in another room while I was sleeping but somehow the email woke me up. I called him back immediately. We reviewed and expanded CEA's messaging about the jobs report. Later that day I saw the pundits falsely asserting that despite great economic news, POTUS is incapable of thinking about anything except the border wall.

MORON OR EVIL GENIUS?

In an Oval Office meeting about healthcare regulation, I was present as CEA's representative in case the President needed answers to technical economics questions. With so many political questions surrounding health policy, much of the conversation that day was about politicians, candidates, and elections.

President Trump insisted that it is not enough to be against Medicare for All, which is the ambitious but ill-advised proposal sponsored by the majority of Congressional Democrats (see Chapter 3). By refusing to put forward a real Republican plan, Republican Senate Majority leader Mitch McConnell was unwittingly setting up the 9-year-old Obamacare as the alternative to Medicare for All. Why should Americans be limited to two lousy choices? The President recalled, "I don't know how many fucking times on the campaign trail I said that we had to get rid of Obamacare, but it was a lot!" He recalled how five months earlier Montana Democrat Jon Tester and Michigan Democrat Debbie Stabenow had won Senate seats by emphasizing health policy. "Mitch McConnell will lose his ass" in the 2020 elections.

The President's colorful language was not only directed at Republican Senate Majority leader Mitch McConnell. The White House communications team itself thought supporting an affirmative health plan amounted to political suicide, and that the safest politics is talking about opponents' plans' weaknesses. Perhaps the political conclusion is correct, but that should have not stopped us from doing the demanding work of formulating a plan for internal review. We got the message.

His remarks about McConnell also showed the intensity of his interest in the 2020 election, almost two years away. "They say that I have a good sense for politics ... I don't know about that." Looking briefly around the Oval Office, he acknowledged, "Then again, look where I am! One for one and soon to be two for two." Referring to his political opponents, he laughed, "They cannot decide whether I'm a moron or an evil genius. One moment they'll say that someone like me wins only by luck, and the next moment announce that I've devised a way to become a three-term President."

His performance continued. How funny is it that (soon-to-be) 2020 Presidential candidate Joe Biden likes to smell women's hair in public? Why would Mr. Biden be kissing women on the lips in public (as he did, for example, with a California Little League usher)? POTUS concluded, "If Pence gets caught kissing women on the lips, I am quitting politics!"

"Socialism is difficult to beat ... just ask Joe Biden." Even with the election far away and Mr. Biden appearing to be the Democratic front runner, President Trump also imagines himself on the debate stage with a socialist. Knowing that Bernie Sanders' campaigns are also fueled by populism, he assesses a few ideas with his Oval Office audience. "Socialism is easy to campaign on but tough to govern on, because the country goes down the tubes." Can we find a way to cancel some of the student debt? Sitting furthest from the President, and growing uncomfortable with the policy direction of the debate hypotheticals, former Congressman Mick Mulvaney bellowed, "Mr. President, for a hundred years Republicans have won elections against socialists."

Okay, why don't we say that Democrats promise "a Rolls-Royce in everyone's pocket?" He laughed expecting the *Washington Post* would dedicate time to fact checking, and unwittingly publicizing the Rolls-Royce claim. (Months later he would publicly use this meme as a dual attack on the foolishness of Sanders' Medicare for All and the "mainstream media.")

We were in the Oval Office the day (in March 2019) when 2020 Presidential candidate Joe Biden became a subject of @realdonaldtrump Twitter messages. "Ed Kennedy said that Joe Biden was the dumbest in the Senate, so this morning on Twitter I tried out 'Low IQ Biden.'" Since that time, @realdonaldtrump has sent out messages about Joe Biden an average of every other day.

Candidate Bernie Sanders was in the news that weekend for a head injury that he suffered. Remembering 1988 candidate Michael Dukakis' legendary public-relations disaster on a tank, President Trump wondered, "Will Bernie Sanders' forehead band aid prove to be like Dukakis' tank picture?"

Presidential candidate and Senator Bernie Sanders in February 2019. Cropped AFGE photo licensed under the Creative Commons Attribution 2.0 license.

1988 Presidential candidate Michael Dukakis, shown in 1984. City of Boston Archives photo licensed under the Creative Commons Attribution 2.0 license.

Listening to the President's performance on political subjects reminded me that he is a populist president. As documented throughout this book, a small and insulated ruling class made, and continues to make, costly, unacknowledged policy mistakes. The angry 2016 voters paying for those mistakes wanted this to end. Discomfort for the ruling class is a feature rather than a bug. Should President Trump stay off Twitter to avoid irritating people? We might as well ask him to disrupt without being disruptive.

THE PERSON AND THE TWITTER PERSONA

The conventional wisdom is that @realdonaldtrump is a window into the "presidential id." In other words, the person and the Twitter persona are in essence the same. That's a nice theory, but how well does it fit the evidence? Let's compare personal interactions between two 2016 Presidential candidates and look at President Trump's use of nicknames for his staff.

Stanford's Hoover Institution got involved with the 2016 Presidential campaign. The senior economists there invited me to join a small roundtable to discuss economic policy ideas with the leading candidate at the time. Eagerly introducing me, they asked that I tell the candidate a bit about my findings related to President Obama's economic policies as reported in my 2012 and 2015 books. Explaining how the Obama Administration, with the intention of helping the poor and unemployed, had created and expanded more than a dozen programs that subsidized them, I said, "When you subsidize something, you get more of it."

The candidate had little to bring to the conversation, so he mocked me instead. Why would anyone write two books to say something so obvious? The candidate was wrong: the Obama Administration was full of smart people who had yet to realize these "obvious" points. More important, the candidate was bullying the youngest person in the room in front of more senior economists. (In my profession, gatherings like that have real money at stake because someday the senior economists would decide whether and how I could be affiliated with Hoover.)

If all we had were representations of the candidates provided by the major news outlets, we would conclude that this arrogant and egotistical candidate was named Trump. Instead, the July 2015 Hoover roundtable was for John Ellis "Jeb" Bush. It was said by the *New York Times*, and Jeb Bush himself, that he was suffering a regrettable campaign handicap. In contrast to a purported mean-spirited Mr. Trump, Mr. Bush was brought up to be polite and kind. Why then was I slinking down in my chair, desperately wishing for the roundtable to end? At the same time as Jeb's visit to Hoover, candidate Trump was beginning to surge past him in the polls, never looking back.

It is President Trump who often was polite and kind (not to mention interesting) in personal relations, in contrast with many of his Twitter performances. Take the Oval Office meeting when he had Secretary Ross on the phone. As that call was wrapping up, thirty more of the CEA staff were coming into the office for a large group photo. When the picture taking had finished, President Trump singled me out and said, "It's good to see you." As my colleagues watched intently, we shook hands and he continued, "Are you doing well? You're a good man." All I could manage was to blurt out the truth that "I love working here!"

President Trump does occasionally use nicknames with his staff, but for opposite purposes of his Twitter persona. At the conclusion of the health regulation meeting pictured earlier in the chapter, the President was taking Secretary Azar's position and letting the rule continue its path toward final publication. Speaking to those of us opposing the rule, he said, "I want you 'young geniuses' to put your heads down and move ahead with this." We understood that as an expression of appreciation for our skills and how they were distinct from Secretary Azar's. It was also a clear acknowledgment of our disappointment, even if he was not taking our recommendation on probably the most significant internal debate of the year.

As another example, the President wanted briefly to express his regrets that OMB veteran and longtime television personality Larry Kudlow had been absent from the meeting. So, he said to 38-year-old Brian Blase, who was there in Larry's place, "You are better looking than Larry." Sarah, Mercedes, and Kellyanne protested that they all loved Larry and found him to be quite handsome. POTUS shifted his head to look between the row of chairs at the communications couch: "Can we at least agree that Brian is stronger?" We all laughed.

FURTHER WATCHING AND READING

To easily browse historical tweets by Mr. Trump, use the URL http://www.trumptwitterarchive.com/archive. The site allows you to search tweets from @realdonaldtrump or show his tweets for a specified date range. Another measure of the President's communication success has been compiled by the GDELT Project, showing how television news mentions President Trump three times as often as it mentioned Barack Obama during his presidency. A similar discrepancy between Presidents Trump and Obama is found in Google searches.

Before the White House, Dan Scavino was social media director for the 2016 Trump campaign. He had also been general manager of one of Mr. Trump's golf clubs, where he became well acquainted with other members of the Trump family. CEA and other White House advisers also know Dan for his long work hours and remarkable dedication.

Twitter.com shows the March 18, 2019, GDP growth tweet as sent by @realdonaldtrump from "Twitter for iPhone" at noon Eastern time. But I was with the President at that time. He did not have any electronic device. Dan Scavino was typing the tweet information on a laptop computer. It is possible that Dan transferred the information to an iPhone before tweeting (does his laptop software allow it to appear on Twitter as an iPhone?). More than 98 percent of the Twitter messages sent by @realdonaldtrump show on Twitter.com as "Twitter for iPhone."

The "annual average to annual average" growth rate formula is one of the most misunderstood formulas among professional economists. The classic scientific article on the subject is "Note on the Correlation of First Differences of Averages in a Random Chain" by Holbrook Working. The March 18 speakerphone call between the President and Secretary Ross got awkward when the President avidly picked up the handset and began referring to the formula, which even professionals do not easily understand without pencil and paper or some other computational aid. None of the economists in the Oval Office had the courage to let the President know that not all his formula references were correct.

The Green Bay and North Carolina rally videos, and other social media cited in this book, have URLs listed in the social media bibliography at the end. In the Green Bay video, President Trump also discusses the trends for prescription drug prices (Chapter 9) and the foolishness of the individual mandate (Chapter 1). The Lou Dobbs Tonight segment about the 2019 Economic Report of the President is viewable at archive.org.

The President was onto something when he insisted in April 2019 that Obamacare should not be the default choice in the 2020 election. Later that year, Democrats began assessing the costs of their new health insurance proposals, such as "Medicare for All," compared to Obamacare. In doing so, they suddenly reached the conclusion that Obamacare is quite costly, so that switching to a new Democratic plan would not cost much extra.

This chapter and Chapter 3 emphasize the President's approach to communications. He is also a capable and eager consumer of policy analysis, skills discussed in Chapters 5 and following.

3

"AMERICA WILL NEVER BE A SOCIALIST COUNTRY"

WHITE HOUSE ANALYSIS AND MARKETING SHIFTS THE 2020 CAMPAIGN

"America will never be a socialist country."
DONALD J. TRUMP, 2019 STATE OF THE UNION ADDRESS

REFERRING TO THE AFFORDABLE CARE ACT (ACA), House Speaker Nancy Pelosi infamously said, "We have to pass the bill so that you can find out what is in it—away from the fog of controversy." As a scholar of government policy, my career has taught me the accuracy of Speaker Pelosi's statement. Lots of smart people pretend to know what's in important bills in Congress and regulations in the executive branch, without reading them. The *New York Times*, *Washington Post*, and other news outlets publish interviews and statements from so-called experts, often economics professors, whose only knowledge of the bill or regulation comes from what they read in the *New York Times*, *Washington Post*, and other news outlets. We end up with an echo chamber, or what I call a "perpetual circle of fake news": the news outlets recite the experts, who repeat the news outlets, who recite the experts.... Given this inertia, there is little incentive to explore what is actually in legislation.

I saw this perpetual circle of fake news early in my career with social security legislation. Again, I saw it in the ACA and the so-called "stimulus law" of 2009, which reportedly was going to "make work pay," even though any trained economist who read it knew that it had almost a dozen new ways of subsidizing layoffs and paying people for not working. We had to pass it to see that the economic recovery would fall miserably short of what was promised. Little did I know how the events of November 8, 2016, would allow me to join an enterprise successfully delivering good economic analysis directly to the American public, bypassing the perpetual circle.

EASY READING

By 2015, traditional TV watching had practically disappeared on college campuses, replaced by social media, especially YouTube. Regularly, I watched the *Young Turks*, which has been described as "the most-watched online news show in the world," with about 2 billion cumulative video views and over 2 million subscribers by that time. I also followed the 2016 Bernie Sanders campaign and by 2018 I was regularly watching the *Jimmy Dore Show*, a *Young Turks* spinoff with some foul language and *Rising* with Krystal Ball (later joined by Saagar Enjeti). All of this was part of my ongoing efforts to keep abreast of the evolving interests and attitudes of my customers: young adults circa age 22, close to the age of many Congressional staffers.

We can extend some grace to public intellectuals who do not read Federal bills and regulations, which can go on for more than a thousand pages, though the commentators should more readily acknowledge their lack of specific expertise. They should also recognize that neither Republicans, Democrats, nor civil servants are likely to generate an original thought on each of the pages they publish. A lot of cutting and pasting is going on in the authorship of "new" bills and regulations.

Having read earlier Federal publications as well as consuming the online news media helped me to think like a Democratic Congress of the 21st century: that big government is likely to achieve big progress, that incentives are of second-order importance, that the title of a bill need not reflect its contents, and that profits are glorified theft by private business from workers and consumers. By the time I arrived for my White House position, I had read the "Medicare for All" bills sponsored by Congressional Democrats. I was not surprised to see that the proposal was to end the existing Medicare program, ban all private health insurance, and prohibit health providers (doctors, hospitals, etc.) from earning a profit or charging any type of copayment at the time of service. The latest version of the bill in the U.S. House of Representatives is succinct (emphasis added):

"There is a moral imperative to correct the massive deficiencies in our current health system and to <u>eliminate profit</u> from the provision of health care."

Medicare For All bills, including prohibitions of private health insurance, have been in the House since at least 2003. Senator Bernie Sanders sponsored a Medicare for All bill in 2013. Prior to that he sponsored "American Health Security" Acts, which also prohibited private health insurance. (In 2007, Senator Edward Kennedy sponsored a "Medicare for All" bill S. 1218, but it allowed private health insurance and included copayments).

The chart that follows shows how the popularity among Democrats of Medicare for All has evolved over time, receiving significant support among Democrats since 2005. This chapter tells the story of how it belatedly became widely known that the bills end private health insurance and prohibit profits in the health sector.

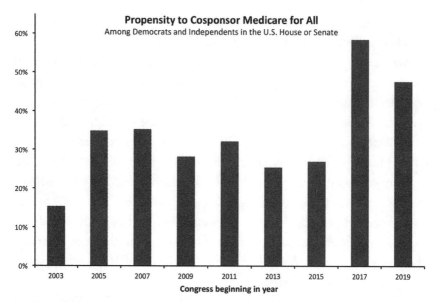

Calculations by the author from congress.gov, senate.gov, and house.gov.

Karl Marx inspired intellectuals around the world with his critiques of capitalism and arguments for socialism. His primary economic idea was that profit derives exclusively from exploitation and must be eliminated. The popularity of Marx's ideas waned when it became clear that the governments touted by Marxist intellectuals—USSR, China during Mao, Cuba after 1962, to name a few—were exploiting their people more than any "capitalist" economy did. But the equation of profits with exploitation and the virtues of state ownership are ideas making a comeback in the United States. Working in the Trump White House, I concluded, would be a unique opportunity to update, refine, and publicize the economics lessons from socialism.

On the first business day of July 2018, I started working in the White House. By the third business day, I had finished orientation, collected badges, equipment, etc., and met with the members of the Council of Economic Advisers—Kevin Hassett (our chairman), Richard Burkhauser, and Tomas Philipson—regarding my tasks. Earlier, I had provided them with a list of research ideas and areas where I thought my unique talents would be valuable to President Trump. The first of those was to update and extend my University of Chicago lectures on the economics of socialism.

Kevin Hassett was the only one among us with any political acumen. He knew that the economics and journalism professions were still unaware of where the Democratic party was headed. We would be ridiculed and then ostracized (especially, the CEA chairman) for using the word socialism, which they would understandably misinterpret as a vulgar slur word. CEA resources would be used up in defense. But he also understood the mission of the CEA, which is to bring economic research to the policy arena. Like it or not, state ownership and profit prohibitions are currently active policy proposals, and decades of economic research has been conducted on these topics. Moreover, Congress instructed the CEA in its founding statutes "to foster and promote free and competitive enterprise." Just as important, our boss President Trump would face competition from socialist policy proposals and find an accurate summary of what economics has to say about them advantageous. To his credit, Hassett turned away from a more comfortable life of ignoring the socialist proposals, which he could have easily justified on the grounds that earlier CEAs had little to say about socialism after the fall of the Berlin Wall.

Tom and I got working on the economics of socialism. Among other things, we considered the public schooling system, where the U.S. had considerable experience with state ownership. Reaching out to a good friend and schooling expert at the University of Chicago, he proceeded to tell me with great confidence that the Medicare for All bill did not outlaw private health insurance or prohibit profits. Reminded of the perpetual circle of fake news, I was hurt and a bit angry that he would question my lying eyes. But after cooling off, I realized that we needed to learn from this experience: if a smart scholar had trouble absorbing the truth about Medicare for All, we should be prepared to meet other less receptive skeptics. Printing Section 107 of the Senate bill, I kept it in my suit pocket, ready for presentation to the next doubter.

TOO MARXIST TO BE TRUE

The Navy Mess is the small restaurant in the West Wing of the White House on the floor below the President's Oval Office. It has a few small tables available for reservation plus a round table seating eight people, available first-come/first-served. CEA member Tomas Philipson and I went there about once a week during the lunch hour for impromptu meetings with non-CEA staff. In one of those first lunches we met Vince Haley and Ross Worthington, which began an ongoing and productive relationship between economic analysis and Presidential speechwriting.

The Common Table in the White House Navy Mess. Photo by Oliver English. Used with permission.

Ross and Vince taught Tom and me about the ingredients of a successful speech and the topics expected to get voter attention. Vince and Ross are deeply knowledgeable of the great speeches in history and avid consumers of scholarship, which is why they had worked closely with former House Speaker Newt Gingrich. They can predict the duration of the President's speeches within seconds, carefully accounting the time for cheering, laughs, chants, etc. The President's rallies serve as 10,000-person focus groups. Understanding crowd composition is also part of the science of presidential speech writing. They, and indirectly Tom and I, were being mentored by Pulitzer Prize winner Anthony Dolan, who was a Presidential speech writer during both Reagan terms, writing some of the legendary speeches that President Reagan delivered about the Soviet Union (see also Chapter 8).

Tom and I helped Vince and Ross digest significant economic policies and events that were happening but distorted or unreported in the news. They were incredulous when I told them about the contents of the Senate and House Medicare for All bills. Vince had run for office himself and knew that openly proposing to end private health insurance was no way to win an election. But having Section 107 in my pocket settled the matter.

Soon, a draft of a Presidential speech declared that Medicare for All would abolish private health insurance. As Stephen Miller, senior adviser and Director of Speechwriting, reviewed the draft speech in late September, I was in Vince and Ross' office two floors below mine where we were discussing what parts of the Soviet and Chinese government archives might include interesting material for a presidential speech. Then Vince's phone rang with Miller saying that the President could not falsely accuse Medicare for All of ending private health insurance. You too, Stephen?! I thought. Again, I pulled out Section 107 from my breast pocket to convince the incredulous.

Days later President Trump began telling the American public that Medicare for All would be "outlawing the ability of Americans to enroll in private and employer-based plans" and the CEA released its 72-page report on the "Opportunity Costs of Socialism."

POTUS BREAKS THE PERPETUAL CIRCLE OF FAKE NEWS

It didn't take long for journalists to declare that POTUS was lying. According to CNN's chief White House correspondent, the lie potentially surpassed all falsehoods in the history of the presidency. Both economics professors and journalists mocked the CEA for doing something as "bizarre" as looking at the economics of socialism. Former CEA chair and University of Chicago colleague Austan Goolsbee jettisoned all allegiances (and violated the ethics rules of the American Economic Association) by ridiculing CEA for "contemplating Karl Marx." CEA Chairman Kevin Hassett and Chief of Staff D.J. Nordquist were unenviably buried in substance-free criticisms from around the world. They took the rare step, which I fully endorsed, of telling the press that a significant part of the CEA report came from my University of Chicago lectures (normally the government is rigidly hierarchical, and the chairman does not state who in the CEA made what contributions).

Could we break the perpetual circle of fake news? Tom and I discussed with Ross and Vince in the Navy Mess whether POTUS should read directly from either Senate or House bill at one of his rallies.

President Trump sensed that this perpetual circle was fragile. Not even the Scandinavian countries, extolled by many progressive Democrats, prohibited private health insurance, or gave free health care. For fifteen years the Marxist contents of Medicare for All bills had remained widely unknown, and now to the frustration of establishment Democrats the truth was coming out less than a month before the midterm elections.

POTUS knew how to overcome the communication barrier in such an environment. He began saying that "the Democrat plan outlaws private health plans"—a 100 percent correct description of Section 107 in my pocket. Then he changed it to "Democrats want to outlaw private health plans," which is an accurate description of 141 members of the 115th Congress who sponsored or cosponsored Medicare for All bills, if we assume that they knew what they were sponsoring. Finally, he added "*the* Democrats want to outlaw private health plans," which many assumed included the 98 or so Democratic members of the 115th Congress who did not sponsor or cosponsor Medicare for All. Adding a definite article enraged Democratic Senate Minority Leader Chuck

Schumer (not a sponsor or cosponsor), who raised the debate volume. Years of frustrating attempts by me to convince experts to read the laws they touted appeared over.

CNN never apologized to President Trump but by January 2019 was acknowledging that Medicare for All prohibits private health insurance. To its credit, CNN began asking sponsors about the prohibition, especially those running for President in the 2020 cycle. When asked, candidate and Senate cosponsor Kamala Harris answered, "Let's eliminate all of that [private health insurance]." Within hours she came to understand the way Stephen Miller and many others thought about it: advertising such intentions is a quick way to get more than 100 million Americans mad at you. Senator Harris reversed course in a subsequent interview, and then wavered when she was reminded that a significant segment of her party really does believe that profits are akin to theft. Her Medicare-for-All confusion partly helped change her from the "Democratic frontrunner" (per CNN) to an early campaign dropout. Regular requests for candidates to explain their stance on the prohibition of private health insurance proved to be the enduring factor in the 2020 campaign.

The October socialism report became a chapter in the *2019 Economic Report of the President.* In preparing the report, we met with President Trump in March, who immediately got Fox Business Network host Lou Dobbs on the speakerphone to hear what we had to say about socialism, regulation, the labor market, and other economics matters (Chapter 2 of this book). Although it was six weeks after his state of the union address declared "America will never become a socialist country," the President was still thinking about alternative communication scenarios. "I'd like Bernie to be my opponent in the general election—he's the least presidential. We may be releasing the socialism findings too soon, giving the Democrats extra time to pivot away."

FURTHER WATCHING AND READING

The American Psychiatric Association's "Goldwater Rule" states that "it is unethical for a psychiatrist to offer a professional opinion unless he or she has conducted an examination...." Should there be an economic version of the Goldwater Rule, saying, "it is unethical for an economist to offer a professional opinion on a law unless he or she has read it?" Without it, we are getting the perpetual circle of fake news noted in this chapter. Another example of the perpetual circle can be found with the "stimulus law" opinions professed by the Chicago Booth IGM "Economic Experts Panel" that betray failures to read the law (although it is hosted by the University of Chicago's Booth School of Business, the panel has zero Chicago PhDs on it). I do not use the label "fake news" lightly and apply it only to significant discrepancies between my firsthand knowledge and unrepentant news reports, which are numerous (see especially chapter 9).

The Medicare for All bills in the (current) 116th Congress are S. 1129 and H.R. 1384. The CEA reports mentioned in this chapter refer to the bills in the 115th Congress (S. 1804 and H.R. 676). As an example of *The Young Turks* analysis of single-payer healthcare, see their YouTube video listed in the social media bibliography. The "new" U.S.-Mexico-Canada Agreement (USMCA) is another instance of cut-and-paste: from the Trans-Pacific Partnership (TPP) and from the North American Free Trade Agreement (NAFTA).

The idea that business owners, who are compensated with interest and profits, are akin to thieves was popularized by Karl Marx, especially in his book *Capital: A Critique of Political Economy*. Even though Marx was born over 200 years ago, and "Marxist" countries have tragically failed their citizens, his ideas still receive a significant following today in academic and intellectual circles. Marxism is sometimes called "communism" or "socialism," although occasionally there are non-Marxist versions of socialism. The survival of Marxist ideas is why we should not be surprised to see a major bill where Congress declares that "There is a moral imperative ... to <u>eliminate profit</u>" and direct that all capital investment in the U.S. health sector (a sector larger than most countries) be financed and approved by the Federal government (H.R. 1384, Section 614).

Even socialist scholars today acknowledge that government ownership and control has historically increased the profit share rather than decreased it, and put it in the hands of a government elite that lacked expertise on running the businesses (*Class Theory and History* by Stephen A. Resnick and Richard D. Wolff draw this lesson from the Soviet Union). The historical lessons of government ownership have not yet been learned by socialists in Congress.

The idea that the government must own the businesses (in socialist jargon, "own the means of production") is why the Medicare for All bills dating back to 2003 require the elimination of all private business from the health insurance industry. In *The Communist Manifesto*, Marx and coauthor Friedrich Engels mocked the "utopian" idea that participation in socialist institutions remain a matter of voluntary individual choice, like "moderate" Democrats today are ridiculed on the left for suggesting that individuals be permitted a choice to participate in a private health insurance plan.

Communism or socialism is mentioned in most editions of the *Economic Report of the President* up until the fall of the Berlin Wall in 1989. The *1992 Economic Report of the President* concluded that "The failure of economic socialism and central planning have brought about a fundamental rethinking by their proponents. In many respects the model of central planning is no longer even a hypothetical ideal." This historical assessment of socialism was like that in Chapter 8 of the *2019 Economic Report of the President*, although only the latter provides statistics and references to academic articles.

During the college summer break of 1990, I worked at Stanford's Hoover Institution, which is a center for Soviet studies and launched my ongoing interest in the economic performance of socialist economies. One night around midnight I met Yegor Gaidar when he was knocking on my office window on the south side of the Lou Henry Hoover building. At the time he was the leading economist in USSR's communist party advocating for privatization and price deregulation. He explained to me that Soviet economists had understood the problems with socialism as well as I did but lacked the freedom to say so. Not long after that, Mr. Gaidar followed Boris Yeltsin as acting Prime Minister of Russia. The United States had, and continues to have, economists who were less aware of socialism's problems than their Soviet counterparts.

During the same Hoover visit I also learned about a fascinating Stanford dissertation, *Collective Farms and Russian Peasant Society*. It used regional Communist Party archives to document fundamental flaws with socialism derived from central planning and lack of material incentives. The author of the dissertation was Nellie Hauke Ohr, who became somewhat famous while we were writing CEA's socialism report. President Trump repeatedly complained on Twitter about her role in what appears to be the relay of opposition research from the 2016 Clinton campaign to President Obama's Federal Bureau of Investigation (see pages 9 and following of Mr. Ohr's August 2018 testimony to Congress). Although her dissertation is included on the reading list for the University of Chicago's *Economics of Socialism* course, it was excluded from CEA's bibliography because the appearance of her name in the report would have helped the President's opponents pivot away from the real problems of socialism to imagined scandals involving Russia (for a genuine Russian scandal, see Chapter 11 of this book). Other studies have by now reached similar conclusions from similar data.

Paul Krugman's Twitter is another social media that I followed as Chief Economist. He is wrong about most economic subjects, which is why he is included in a computer science library of deductive reasoning (http://smtlib.economicreasoning.com; see also Chapter 10) that is easy for computers but difficult for people, who are susceptible to logical fallacies. Professor Krugman's Twitter proved helpful for predicting mistakes that would be made by the President's opponents. To his credit, Professor Krugman has a good understanding of the essentials of international trade (the basis for his Nobel Prize Award) and explains them well.

4

"NO ONE IN OHIO CARES ABOUT BURMA"

THE WASHINGTON BUBBLE AND THE OPIOID EPIDEMIC

"They desperately tried to prevent the truth about the Famine from reaching the ears of the higher ups."

HELEN RALEIGH IN *CONFUCIUS NEVER SAID*

TEENAGE BOYS NEED A FATHER, but Matt and "little Luke" would be carrying on without one. "At least big Luke is not in pain anymore," it was said that day at the suburban Chicago funeral home. Luke Sr. had been prescribed opioids when he suffered an injury at work. We were gathered because he overdosed on those addictive painkillers. Our group was one among 70,000 others that year doing the same in funeral homes across America.

By this time, employees throughout the Trump administration had heard loud and clearly that President Trump wanted all talents applied to ending the opioid epidemic that had been growing for nearly two decades. But I saw firsthand how the Federal government was, and is, often incapable of receiving critical information from the public, let alone acknowledging its own mistakes. President Trump faces a nearly impossible task of reversing the epidemic before it gets worse.

OBLIVIOUS

Less than 600 Federal employees are directly accountable to the voters: President, Vice President, 100 Senators, and 441 members of the House of Representatives. Close to a half million Federal employees live in the Washington DC metro area and are accountable to someone who also lives in the DC metro area. Naturally, Federal agencies are sensitive to media coverage, and journalists and think tanks covering Federal matters also disproportionately live in the DC metro area.

This results in groupthink, otherwise known as the Washington bubble. People in the bubble hold many common beliefs, which peer pressure discourages them from questioning. The practice of majority voting in the U.S. Congress worsens groupthink, as each political party expects its members to conform to the party line. The subjects garnering attention inside the bubble can be far different than the topics of concern elsewhere in the country.

President Obama understood broadly that his administration would sometimes fixate on topics of little interest to the general public, such as the politics of Burma (a southeast Asian country). Speaking to his adviser Ben Rhodes, Mr. Obama counseled, "Ben, no one in Ohio cares about Burma."

Washington bubble fixation is tragic when it comes at the expense of an ongoing emergency in Ohio and other states. Between the years 2000 and 2016, over 300,000 Americans died from drug overdoses involving opioids. Mr. Rhodes' White House memoir mentions Burma 34 times and climate change 21 times (and Trump 95 times), but never comments on opioids, heroin, fentanyl, or drug overdoses.

Mr. Rhodes might say his job was to focus on foreign policy. Yet such an objection would doubly prove my point. Why are we surprised by a surge of populism when President Obama's speechwriter puts so much emphasis on foreign affairs? Moreover, during much of the Obama Administration, many of the opioid abusers were obtaining illicitly manufactured fentanyl and heroin through international supply chains originating in Mexico and China. (Fentanyl is a particularly potent and deadly kind of opioid.)

Further supporting the conclusion that even the domestic segments of President Obama's White House paid little attention to the opioid epidemic, a memoir by its communications director, Dan Pfeiffer, mentions climate change nine times but never refers to opioids, heroin, fentanyl, or drug overdoses. The lack of attention is especially troubling given the fact that the death rate from opioid overdoses had been sharply elevated for several years before the Obama Administration.

The Federal Register, which is the daily publication of U.S. government agencies, shows a similar pattern throughout President Obama's administration. The chart that follows shows that every 10,000 pages published between 2009 and 2016 had only six documents mentioning "opioid" or "opioids" or "opiate." By contrast, the same 10,000 pages had nearly 40 documents mentioning "climate change."

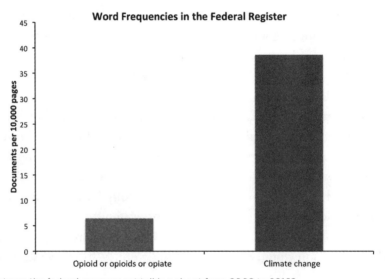

What was the federal government talking about from 2009 to 2016?

To be clear, I am not saying that climate change is unworthy of Federal attention. What I am saying is that the public views the opioid epidemic to be of comparable importance. The figure, memoirs, and further sources cited on the following pages show that the interests of the ruling class from 2009 to 2016, at least, were out of sync with most Americans. The considerable divergence between the priorities of the public and ruling class is why populism is a major factor in national politics today. Inattention to the opioid epidemic is also a source of Federal policy failures documented on the following pages.

The gulf between the ruling class and the rest of America is the accidental star of *The Final Year*. The film was intended to highlight the 2016 activities and achievements of "30 people [in the White House West Wing] setting the direction for the entire U.S. government and in that way the entire world," such as Ben Rhodes. Those officials display little interest in the everyday concerns of Americans during the film. Neither the opioid crisis nor the recession is mentioned. Creating jobs for international refugees gets more screen time than creating jobs for American workers. When the Obama team visits China, Mr. Rhodes lists what he sees as the important topics of the meetings and condemns the American public for not paying attention to any of them. Conspicuously absent from his list are the China-trade topics that do interest the public, such as intellectual property theft or illicit exports of fentanyl.

The film reveals how the populist uprising in America may be better understood by the people of Laos, living on the opposite side of the planet, than the 30 officials working in President Obama's White House. In a scene filmed four months before the 2016 election, viewers hear a conversation between a Laotian woman and Mr. Rhodes. Citing a recent surprise populist victory in the British "Brexit" election, the woman expects that candidate Trump will win. Mr. Rhodes confidently assures her that Mrs. Clinton will be the new president. But late on election night, the best that President Obama's team can discern is that the "retrenchment forces got their hands on the levers of power." Mr. Pfeiffer's memoir further characterizes those forces as "unrepentant racists wandering the halls of the White House doing dumb, mean shit...." Failures by the ruling class to see any substance in populism ironically add fuel to the populist fire that scorches it.

FEDERAL POLICY FAILURES

The Obama Administration's inattention to what was important to Americans was coincident with three significant Federal policy failures. One of those failures is a provision of the 2010 Affordable Care Act (ACA) that requires health plans to cover "benzos," which are prescription tranquilizers such as Valium and Xanax. This requirement dramatically reduced the out-of-pocket cost of those drugs and increased the quantities sold, especially when distributed through the federally-financed health insurance program Medicare, which had not previously covered the drugs (Medicaid had limited coverage of them).

Benzos are part of the opioid crisis because they are the other half of the opioid-benzo cocktail that is a favorite among opioid abusers. The tranquilizers "enhance" the feeling of opioid consumption. For the same reason, benzos carry serious risk of death when used in combination with opioids. Not until seven years into the ACA would the prescription tranquilizers carry a mandated warning about the risks of fatal interaction with opioids (opioids include prescription drugs such as oxycodone as well as illicitly-manufactured drugs such as heroin and fentanyl).

To paraphrase House Speaker Nancy Pelosi, America had to pass the ACA to see the results of the tranquilizer provision that was in it. The most recent data show that prescription tranquilizers are present in a large fraction of the drug-overdose fatalities involving opioids. When you subsidize something, you get more of it. It looks like the 2010 ACA spent taxpayer dollars to accidentally increase the number of fatalities from drug overdoses (the causal connection between subsidies for tranquilizers and opioid overdoses is primarily a question in the economics of "complements" rather than a medical determination). I am unaware of any effort in Congress or in the executive branch to study, let alone repeal, the tranquilizer provision of the ACA. (In 2017, Republicans did try to repeal the ACA in its entirety and the White House continues to watch a Federal court case that may fully overturn it.)

At the very least, President Obama's Health Secretary, Kathleen Sebelius, could have adhered to the guidance from her own department as well as the Office of Management and Budget as to the calculation of regulatory costs. Public commenters warned her that benzos are vulnerable to "misuse and abuse." The costs of that abuse, especially the fatal drug overdoses that would be part of the opioid epidemic, should have been reported on page 22,156 of the 2012 Federal Register where costs of this regulatory provision are cited. She did not do so, following a long tradition at the Health Department of ignoring significant regulatory costs (see also Chapter 7).

Most of the overdose fatalities were coming from prescription opioid abuse, which means that the opioid pills were taken for nonmedical use and often crushed so that they could be injected or snorted (contrary to the prescribed method). The Food and Drug Administration (FDA) in 2010 approved reformulated opioids that could not be abused as easily. Economics suggests, but does not prove, that high volume abusers might respond by switching to illicit heroin or fentanyl that is even more affordable in large quantities. In other words, the reformulation might increase the total number of abuse episodes and overdose deaths by shifting them from prescription opioids to illicitly manufactured opioids, unless the reformulation were combined with enough additional law enforcement effort.

The Department of Justice (DOJ), which is the Federal law enforcement agency, was about to do the opposite. Its leader, Attorney General Eric Holder, thought that it was time to end the war on drugs and in 2013 issued his infamous "Holder Memo" directing Federal lawyers to stop prosecuting nonviolent drug crimes. The Washington bubble nodded with approval. Meanwhile, as described in the book *Dreamland: The True Tale of America's Opiate Epidemic*, a new heroin business model involved dealers who were "never violent. They never carry guns. They work hard at blending in." Now the casualties would be among the customers.

On numerous occasions prior to the Holder memo, illicit fentanyl would appear in U.S. markets and law enforcement would successfully drive it out. Just months after, the fentanyl traffickers would be the successful ones. Illicitly manufactured opioids became cheaper and more common. Fatal overdoses involving illicitly manufactured opioids would thereafter grow at a much faster rate, yet the Holder Memo and the approving news media did not mention any risk of this type.

Early on, various medical professional organizations began to recommend more aggressive opioid prescription practices and downplay addiction risks because they wanted to help alleviate chronic pain and did not foresee that opioid addiction would become such a problem. The Federal government uncritically looked to incentivize hospitals to adhere to the new recommendations. As described by Physicians for Responsible Opioid Prescribing, hospitals were "financially incentivized by CMS [the Centers for Medicare and Medicaid Services] to obtain high scores on HCAHPS Survey questions. The questions on the Survey pertaining to treatment of pain have had the unintended consequence of encouraging aggressive opioid use…." In other words, physicians that prescribed extra, or more potent, painkillers would tend to produce higher HCAHPS scores, and therefore added funding, for their hospital. CMS, which is a division of the Health Department, began this practice in 2007. A 2016 article in the *American Journal of Public Health* further concluded that the financial incentive left "well-meaning professionals with the unsavory choice of prescribing opioids or facing dissatisfaction from disappointed patients on patient surveys." The CMS incentive remained for 12 years until the removal of pain treatment questions from the survey in October 2019.

ENABLING ADDICTION WITH FEDERAL DOLLARS

Between the years 2000 and 2010, the overdose death rate involving prescription opioids almost tripled, as did the morphine-equivalent per capita sales of those drugs. Although the Obama administration should have studied both supply and demand causes of the epidemic, it was not until 2017 that the Council of Economic Advisers looked at the two together. CEA estimated that, while deaths were increasing, the out-of-pocket prices (what consumers pay when they pick up prescriptions at the pharmacy) were falling dramatically at least through 2010. The same real income can now purchase five or ten times more opioids than it could 20 years ago. Nobody disputes these findings.

The reasons for the opioid-price drop are also clear. Some of the major opioids came off patent, so that manufacturers were charging less to compete with new generics. At least as important was the creation of a new government program that heavily subsidized prescription drugs, including prescription opioids. That program is known as Medicare Part D, which by itself reduced the annual cost of a program participant's 0.75-gram daily habit from $39,420 to $2,677. Most of the difference is paid by taxpayers. Between 2001 and 2010, three-fourths of growth of opioid prescriptions came from government programs.

Many people simply do not have enough money to spend $39,420 annually on a drug habit. The new Medicare program changed all that, making an opioid habit financially possible for just about anyone on the program. The program participants include the elderly and a rapidly growing group of nonelderly people on Federal disability programs. Medicare Part D even makes opioids cheaper for people not on the program because Medicare-financed pills are sometimes given away, resold, or fraudulently obtained. Statistical analysis has confirmed that young people who were not eligible for Medicare Part D were nonetheless at greater risk of opioid overdose if they lived in a region in which more Part D purchases were occurring.

Citing a family physician from Ohio, Sam Quinones' book *Dreamland* asserts that "seniors realized they could subsidize their retirement by selling their prescription Oxys [a potent opioid] to younger folks. Early Oxy dealers, in fact, were seniors who saw the value of the pills in their cabinets. 'It's like hitting the Lotto if your doctor will put you on OxyContin.... People don't even think twice about selling.'" None of the government data I saw quantified the share of supply in the secondary market for prescription opioids that originated with sales by senior citizens.

The law of demand says that when you subsidize something, you get more of it. For opioids that means more opioid sales and more opioid overdoses. CEA estimated that as much as "83 percent of the growth between 2001 and 2010 in the death rate involving prescription opioids" was due to reduced prices. The other side of the coin is that some, perhaps a lot, of the growth came from other factors that may include advertising, physician prescribing norms, and interactions with other drugs (the following pages describe more about this).

The Holder Memo came seven years after Medicare Part D's effect on the prices of prescription opioids. The 2013 memo, I suspect, reduced the prices of illicitly manufactured opioids such as heroin and fentanyl. Noting that data from illicit markets may be unreliable, CEA estimates that potency-adjusted prices of illicit opioids fell more than 50 percent immediately after 2013. The anecdotes in the Quinones book describe how nonviolent dealers were supplying cheaper heroin and delivering it more conveniently.

A low price of opioids can lead to overdose deaths through various channels. The extra supply may increase the number of people who try opioids and thereby become addicted. Even without any effect on the number of opioid abusers, each abuser might consume cheaper opioids more often, such as every day rather than twice per week. Those five extra consumption episodes reduce the likelihood that an opioid abuser survives the week. Low opioid prices may also reduce the willingness of patients to consider or continue rehabilitation. Academic studies have confirmed that opioid consumption, like any good or service, obeys the law of demand.

Although he refers to the smaller Medicaid health insurance program, Mr. Quinones reaches a similar conclusion as CEA, albeit with entirely different methods. Medicaid operates in tandem with the Supplemental Security Income program (SSI), he explains, but "[i]t wasn't the monthly SSI check people cared so much about; rather, they wanted the Medicaid card that came with it. ...For a three-dollar

Medicaid co-pay, therefore, an addict got pills priced at a thousand dollars, with the difference paid for by U.S. and state taxpayers. A user could turn around and sell those pills, obtained for that three-dollar co-pay, for as much as ten thousand dollars on the street. Combined with pill mills, the Medicaid card scam allowed prolific quantities of prescription medication to hit the streets." The anecdotes and academic studies are not gospel, but at least we should agree that, with such a high fatality rate, the roles of prices, Medicare, and Medicaid require urgent study.

AGENCIES DESPERATELY TRY TO BLOCK

In February 2018, CEA informed Federal agencies about the role of opioid prices. According to protocol, their approval was requested before the White House released any findings to the public. To the dismay of CEA and many others in the White House, at least two agencies refused to allow the findings to be released to the public or be shared with President Trump. Those agencies were the Department of Health and Human Services (hereafter, "Health Department") and allegedly the Department of Justice (DOJ).

DOJ did not relay any objections directly but was represented in the White House by Don McGahn's Office of White House Counsel (WHC). WHC told CEA that the Federal government was joining lawsuits against pharmaceutical companies for wrongdoing in connection with the opioid epidemic. It would not look good, they said, for a part of the Federal government to acknowledge that roles were also played by Federal policy and legal company actions, such as lowering prices to compete with generics. Although I suspect that WHC was exaggerating at the behest of the Health Department, it is pretty scary that WHC would be saying that defendants in government suits are not entitled to see all that the government had found in relation to their case. And it is disturbing that legal maneuvers might take priority over understanding and remedying the true causes of the epidemic.

The Health Department has been led by Cabinet Secretary Alex

M. Azar II since January 2018. His department has some impressive achievements, including enhancing incentives for kidney donation and allowing investigational drugs to be tried by patients suffering from life-threatening conditions. In cooperation with the Departments of Labor and Treasury, his department has also implemented health insurance rules that are among the most valuable deregulatory policies in American history (see Chapter 7 of this book). Mr. Azar impressed me as an articulate person with a good command of healthcare laws and bills pending in Congress. But with Matt and little Luke on my mind, I cannot stay silent about the approach to the opioid epidemic taken by him and the Health Departments past and present.

Medicare Part D, which is the primary Federal program subsidizing opioid prescriptions, features prominently in Mr. Azar's earlier experience in the Health Department. He was its Deputy Secretary when the program began in 2006. Mr. Azar was the Department's legal counsel when Part D's legal rules were prepared in 2004. By 2018, he and his Chief of Staff, who was also part of the team that created Medicare Part D, were understandably proud of the program. Indeed, it uses private insurance in clever ways to more cheaply supply prescription drugs to vulnerable senior citizens.

Secretary Azar refuses even to consider that the introduction of Medicare Part D might have helped fuel the opioid epidemic. CEA had a call with him intended to work out differences but, to put it charitably, the possible effects of Medicare Part D were not something that he would scrutinize or permit CEA to include in public reports.

Although Secretary Azar's department is heavily engaged with economic regulation, I saw no sign that he consulted the PhD economists in his department (see also Chapter 10 of this book). The lone exception was in this opioid episode, where his economists served as a fig leaf for his requirement that CEA's findings stay hidden from the public and the President. Those economists agreed that opioid prices had fallen sharply, but suspected that, unlike "normal consumers," the behavior of addicts has nothing to do with the price of the object of their addiction.

In other words, they were confident that opioid addiction is an exception to the law of demand.

Secretary Azar's Department has no moral obligation to accept CEA's findings blindly. The Department should engage vigorously in inter-agency deliberations. But, if reversing the opioid epidemic is a genuine priority, there is no excuse for not studying the facts rigorously, regardless where they might lead us. The Health Department could have convened its own meetings of economists and other experts to determine the role of falling opioid prices. It could have also issued a report explaining to the public why opioids are the rare exception to the maxim, "When you subsidize something, you get more of it." Yet two years and counting after the CEA told the Health Department what happened to prices, it has done no such research.

THE TRUTH NARROWLY ESCAPES

Shortly after Azar and WHC decreed the eternal secrecy of the findings, I arrived at CEA. A number of CEA staff had taken turns revising the report to address what proved to be fake criticisms. On this subject, their morale was low. Yet, honorably, they resisted the overwhelming urge to leak the findings.

Our leader, Kevin Hassett, tried to cheer everyone up, while at the same time keeping his eyes open for a political shift in the West Wing. He saw an opportunity in late 2018 when Don McGahn, as well as two WHC attorneys loyal to the Health Secretary, left the White House. We appealed to Steven Menashi, a new attorney in WHC, who readily digested economic arguments and was eager to help. He had already shown me how to edit other CEA reports so that they did not accidentally conflict with DOJ cases. Steve worked his magic again; DOJ approved when it saw the report's added discussion of pharmaceutical marketing efforts and changes in physicians' prescribing norms.

Honing the CEA's opioid-price analysis, I reengaged with the economists at the Health Department. Pushing back against their impression that addicts do not respond to price incentives, I asked had they ever seen the classic article by Chicago's Nobel Laureate Gary S. Becker showing how the law of demand works even in markets where none of the consumers are rational? Couldn't they see that, "rational" or not, many people simply do not have enough money to afford the $39,000 per year that an opioid habit had been costing without health insurance? To their credit, in April 2019 they let Secretary Azar know that they would no longer be his methodological fig leaf because they were concerned that suppressing the price findings could be consequential.

Thinking that all hurdles had been cleared, the Staff Secretary and CEA scheduled a public release of the findings. It would be Monday, April 29, more than a year after CEA had initially notified the various agencies. But two hidden obstacles were about to surface, potentially delaying the release long enough for opponents to conjure a scheme for delaying it indefinitely.

At 4 p.m. on Friday afternoon, we learned that a group in the White House was uncomfortable with the findings but had stayed quiet perhaps believing they could count on WHC and the Health Department to block the project. Now it was their turn to veto the public release. CEA's three Chicago graduates—Kevin Corinth, Don Kenkel, and I—went to the meeting organized by the exasperated Staff Secretary to hear the critiques.

Miraculously, my overwrought mind was still able to think, recall, and strategize while listening to the others talk. Briefly, I had worked with one of the women from the Office of Management and Budget (OMB) and remembered her to be sincere, reasonable, and highly proficient in her subject area. But could we communicate well enough to reach a solution in so little time?

Luckily, I had made a point of being versed in the President's budget, a 400-page tome published by the OMB that reflects the aspirations and priorities of the various parts of the administration. Trying to recall the part that she wrote, I wanted to determine how CEA's report might appear to conflict with it. Guessing that she contributed to what I considered the budget's most important proposal, reversing the massive distortion in the "catastrophic phase of Medicare Part D," I suggested that CEA's report be expanded to explain how implementing the budget proposal would help alleviate the opioid epidemic. The meeting adjourned at 5 p.m. with the understanding that I would draft the report's new part. I did so quickly, and she gave her approval via email by 8 p.m. Correct in my hunch that she was not a Trojan horse for the Health Secretary, a hurdle was cleared when her colleagues also deferred to her expertise!

But there were more hurdles. The Health Secretary sent a team of lawyers, led by his Chief of Staff Peter Urbanowicz less than three hours prior to the release, to deliver a bizarre warning to CEA about supposed legal ramifications of publicizing CEA's findings. If the CEA report were released and the public asked the Health Department about it, his team said, the Department would refuse to acknowledge anything. CEA and the Staff Secretary released the CEA report anyway.

Secretary Azar claims that "when it comes to this [opioid] crisis, failure is not an option," while in reality he and his department's leadership summarily disregard key findings. Publicly pledging "better research to combat the opioid crisis," the Department instead ignores the effects of falling prices on opioid addiction and overdoses.

From the beginning, Kellyanne Conway, who is Counselor to the President, supported good research into the role of opioid prices. If the Health Department had successfully blocked CEA's April 2019 release, its secretary might have been called to the Oval Office to explain to POTUS why the research should remain hidden. The Health Department presumably dreaded such an outcome and believed it likely because Kellyanne had the president's ear.

Most important, under President Trump's leadership many of us felt empowered to follow the facts where they took us, even if that were a critical assessment of a "Republican" Federal program such as Medicare Part D. It is a modest achievement that reports from the Federal government (authored by CEA and the President's Commission on Combating Drug Addiction and the Opioid Crisis) would be the first to seriously consider the possibility that Federal policies were fueling the opioid epidemic.

HEALTH POLICIES FURTHER DISAPPOINT

In addition to not accounting for opioid prices and Medicare fraud, and not reviewing its subsidies for prescription tranquilizers, the Health Department's actions have been unsatisfactory in three other opioid-related areas. Those areas are accounting for illicit markets, examining financial incentives for over-prescribing opioids, and the expectations it has set for the overdose-reversing drug naloxone.

The FDA's approach to illicit drug markets is harmful and illogical. The FDA asserts that it intends its policies to "*actually result* in a decrease in misuse and abuse, and their consequences, addiction, overdose and death, in the community" [emphasis added]. The actual result, however, involves illicit markets, yet the FDA refuses to recognize that any illicit activity is a result of its policies, even retrospectively. "As FDA we don't have much control over Mexican cartels and the availability of low-cost heroin.... Don't try to measure things you can't control." These statements and more are available online in the transcript of the FDA's July 11, 2017, meeting in Silver Spring, MD. They are contrary to sound logic and the recommendation of the National Academies of Sciences, Engineering, and Medicine that FDA "consider the potential effects of these interventions on illicit markets ... and take appropriate steps to mitigate those effects."

In 2017, the President's Commission on Combating Drug Addiction and the Opioid Crisis concluded that CMS was creating financial incentives for over-prescribing opioids. Specifically, CMS was evaluating and reimbursing hospitals based on the hospital-quality survey that included pain-communication questions. The Commission recommended the removal of those questions from the survey. Although CMS repeatedly denies that there is any "empirical evidence that the questions [were] influencing providers to prescribe opiates," removal of the pain-communication questions happened in October 2019.

As with FDA policy changes, the effects of changing the hospital-quality survey must be evaluated in the context of the currently active market in illicitly manufactured opioids. Such an evaluation should have been reported by CMS on page 59,176 of the 2018 Federal Register where costs of this regulatory provision are cited, but illicit markets are not even mentioned. Contrary to the directives of the Office of Management and Budget's Circular A-4 and its own internal guidelines, the Health Department has a longstanding tradition of evaluating regulations without considering the various markets that would be significantly affected. To be blunt, not only is the Health Department incapable of acknowledging past mistakes (actively concealing at least one), it is not changing the fundamental processes that created them.

By contrast, the financial incentives created by the hospital-quality measures were recognized earlier by an Indiana task force assembled in 2015 by then-Governor Mike Pence, which also recommended enhanced criminal penalties for drug dealers. The 2017 President's Commission further stressed the urgency of disrupting the illicit fentanyl supply. In 2018, President Trump threatened to leave the international organization of postal systems, which motivated it to (among other things; see also Chapter 8) upgrade monitoring of illicit fentanyl shipments. (Both the Pence task force and the Trump commission also recommended enhancements to state "Prescription Drug Monitoring Programs," which help prevent abusers from obtaining simultaneous opioid prescriptions from multiple physicians. It appears that the quantity of first-time opioid prescriptions has finally declined. President Trump has also reduced opioid supply by helping households return unused and expired opioid prescriptions.)

The hospital-quality measurement matter also illustrates how CMS does not recognize the effects of its financial incentives on health and business. CMS mistakenly assumes that its hospital-reimbursement policies have no effect on the employment contracts between hospitals and doctors, merely because CMS declares that it is not intending or endorsing any effects on those contracts (see especially pp. 59,141-59,143 of the 2018 Federal Register, which reiterate assertions from President Obama's CMS). To the contrary, basic economics tells us that a hospital profiting from high scores on HCAHPS surveys will encourage their doctors to help raise the scores. That encouragement would likely include financial incentives in their employment contract. Economics applies regardless of whether hospitals and their doctors are legally distinct entities, and regardless of any CMS rhetoric.

As described by the National Institutes of Health, "Naloxone is a medication designed to rapidly reverse opioid overdose." First responders, family members, and others can administer the naloxone when they see somebody overdosing. The problem is that the Health Department is promising the public that making naloxone more available will help reduce the death rate from overdoses (e.g., Secretary Azar in the video cited in the social media bibliography). Such policies may instead increase addiction, the number of overdoses, and the overall death rate even while they increase the likelihood of surviving a single overdose. As New Jersey Dr. Lewis Nelson puts it, "I'm 100% in favor of using naloxone and distributing it widely, but I don't think people should think it's all upside. We have to stay very open-minded about the implications of this. It wouldn't be the first time in medical history to introduce a product that turned out to have a terrible downside" (cited in the August 2018 *Annals of Emergency Medicine*).

Even worse, the Department's messaging about naloxone distribution to first responders may be giving addicts and members of their community a false confidence about the drug's effectiveness at preventing fatality by opioid overdose. Naloxone primarily reverses the short-term effects of opioid overdose, such as apnea (failure to breathe), which most first responders are traditionally trained to deal with using other means (basic and advanced life support). Therefore, it is unclear how much naloxone is adding to the first responders' toolkit. (Moreover, once a patient has stopped breathing, irreversible damage to organs can occur before first responders arrive). A false confidence about the increment to first responders' toolkit may cause addicts to take more risk because they misperceive that opioid abuse is safer than it used to be. It may also reduce the urgency with which family members and friends exhort an addict to seek treatment.

FURTHER WATCHING AND READING

The funeral described on the first page of this chapter happened as described, in 2017, although the names are fictional. Since the year 2000, over 400,000 Americans have died from drug overdoses involving opioids. The data in Figure 7-1 of the *2020 Economic Report of the President* shows that the upward trend in death rates stopped, finally, in 2017 and did not resume in 2018. Express Scripts' large database shows that the quantity of opioid prescriptions in 2018 fell more than 10 percent from what it was the previous year. However, the death and prescription rates stay high by historical and international standards. The prospects for further price reductions, and therefore further death-rate increases, are real, especially in the illicit market for methamphetamine ("meth" is another abused drug with frequent fatal overdoses). An October 2019 report from CEA estimates that costs in terms of lives lost (valued using the Federal "value of a statistical life"), additional healthcare and treatment costs, criminal justice costs, and reduced worker productivity, have been about a half trillion dollars per year recently.

Ben Rhodes and Dan Pfeiffer authored the two memoirs cited on this chapter's second page. A new memoir by President Obama's National Security Advisor, Susan Rice, proves to have similar word counts relating to opioids and climate change. More directly, she profoundly disapproves of President Trump's reference to "American carnage" in his inaugural address. She gives no sign that it refers to what he said just seconds earlier—"… drugs that have stolen too many lives and robbed our country of so much unrealized potential." Instead, the reference is misrepresented as more evidence of his unthinkable "cynicism and ugliness" and that our nation is saying "farewell to the moral universe."

J.D. Vance's *Hillbilly Elegy* offers a revealing contrast. His engaging memoir of life in Ohio cites the opioid epidemic ten times and climate change zero times. Helen Dale's 2016 review of the book aptly ties the memoir to populism in politics: "This high-handed [policy-making] process relieves us of the burden of thinking about what our rules will do to individuals on the receiving end. ...when people rebel at the ballot box, we are shocked."

Oxford Professor Timothy Garton Ash concluded from the 2016 elections that "[t]he biggest lesson for liberals [would be]: Beware groupthink." They were already aware—in August statistician Nate Silver noted that journalists were "constantly trying to browbeat 'outlier' polls into submission"—but groupthink flourished, nonetheless. Chapter 7 of this book further describes the homogeneity of thinking in the Washington Bubble with, for example, 2016 candidate Clinton receiving 19 times the political donations from Federal employees than candidate Trump did. The phenomenon of groupthink and its intellectual history is described in a 2013 *Review of Economic Studies* article by Roland Benabou.

That experts did not predict Donald Trump's victories is just a symptom of groupthink. The fundamental problem is that the ruling class is a tiny fraction of the population and does not fully appreciate the concerns of the rest of the country and is rarely accountable to them. The ruling class does not understand the costs of forcing people to buy health insurance. It struggles to remember that more people might see reversing the opioid epidemic as more urgent than reversing climate change. And, even while lacking many dimensions of wisdom, the ruling class will sometimes mock those that they rule. Some of those dimensions are described in *The Tyranny of Experts* by William Easterly and *Expert Political Judgment* by Philip E. Tetlock. *The Final Year* is available on Amazon Prime Video.

Washington's neglect of the opioid epidemic can be quantified in several other ways. As recently as 2013—the third consecutive year in which the death rate was almost triple normal levels—the Congressional Record includes "climate change" 27 times as often as "opioid" or "opioids." The annual *Economic Report of the President* dates to 1947, but never mentioned opioids or heroin until 2018, which was President Trump's first report.

Chapter 7 of the *2010 Economic Report of the President* declares that expanding insurance coverage would reduce preventable deaths, without mentioning how earlier and future expansions did and might do the opposite. The 2006 insurance expansion known as Medicare Part D made opioid addiction more affordable. The 2010 Affordable Care Act (Section 2502) further expanded that coverage to prescription tranquilizers with deadly (and unlabeled) opioid interactions. Insurance coverage may save lives in other ways, but the point here is how Washington's calculus perennially ignored the opioid epidemic.

Sam Quinones' book emphasizes the role of pharmaceutical marketing and doctor prescribing practices, as well as the growth of the market for illicitly manufactured opioids. The 2017 article by Eric Sun and coauthors studies the deadly interactions between opioids and prescription tranquilizers (benzodiazepines). The 2015 paper by Powell and coauthors links Medicare Part D to overdose fatalities among people not eligible for the program. Molly Schell's PhD dissertation measures and analyzes quantities and street prices of prescription opioids across cities. My 2020 working paper shows how a shift from prescription opioids to illicitly manufactured opioids may increase opioid consumption and thereby fatalities. It also explains why the highest fatality rates occurred during the period of lax drug law enforcement initiated in 2013 by Attorney General Holder and ended in 2017.

This chapter refers to volume 83 of the daily publication of the U.S. government agencies as "the 2018 Federal Register" to clarify which administration published the information. The traditional citation method refers to the Federal Register volume number instead of the calendar year.

The White House includes an Office of the Staff Secretary, which manages documents for POTUS and public releases by the White House. Its tasks include distributing draft reports to relevant agencies who return comments and concerns. Special Assistant to the President and Senior Associate Staff Secretary Nick Butterfield handled the CEA opioid-price report during 2019, not to mention around three million other words (the equivalent of fourteen 500-page textbooks) published by President Trump's CEA.

Normally, the agencies return valuable comments that result in significant enhancements to the report released to the public. Nick had the good judgment to recognize the ulterior motives of the Health Department on the opioid issue. Releasing CEA's opioid-price report also required his courage to risk an "I told you so" episode if the public discovered any kind of mistake in it.

Millions loved to hate sportscaster Howard Cosell but recognized that the glory days of "Monday Night Football" were over when he retired. If our generation has a Howard Cosell, it is polling expert Kellyanne Conway. She became manager of candidate Trump's 2016 campaign, which surprised the world by winning the election, and is still one of President Trump's most important and visible advisers. MSNBC perpetually banned her from its morning cable news show, claiming that she only pretends to be in "the key meetings" at the White House. The Kellyanne I know is smart, digesting a variety of complex policy issues and advising POTUS on how they might affect communications and politics (yes, MSNBC, those are key meetings). She makes her high-pressure White House job look easy. The job is easy, she insists, by comparison with readying the four Conway children and escorting them to school on time every morning!

The 2012 trailer for *Breaking the Taboo* cited in the social media bibliography conveys the Washington bubble's attitude at the time of the Holder memo. The film shows former Presidents Carter and Clinton, among others, criticizing the "attitude to narcotics" held by former Presidents Nixon, Reagan, and George H.W. Bush. Urging Eric Holder and then President Obama to end the war on drugs, and evoking sympathy for residents of Latin America, the film does not mention that an opioid epidemic is escalating in the U.S. or that it would escalate further when illegal drugs became cheaper. A lengthy *Washington Post* article from March 13, 2019, features the unintended consequences of the Holder Memo for the opioid epidemic. Former Attorney General Eric Holder was asked to comment for the article but declined. Also expect the Health Department to decline comment on this chapter. They have not seriously considered the possibility that Federal policies have been part of the problem, rather than part of the solution.

On multiple occasions, Secretary Azar tried to eradicate disagreement among White House staff sitting lower in the Federal hierarchy. He would demand that the Cabinet-level manager of the disagreeing party end his employment. No White House employee has ever been fired at the Secretary's direction that I am aware of (firing a Federal employee is in fact a monumental task, but that is another story). However, as a compromise over a "process foul" (a violation of etiquette and procedure) by Tom Philipson, CEA Chairman Hassett agreed that Tom would be banned from any meeting where Secretary Azar was present (Tom's ban was overturned almost a year later when Mick Mulvaney became acting Chief of Staff). These episodes quickly taught White House staff that Secretary Azar is, to say the least, loathe to hear information challenging his positions.

Secretary Azar's "fire him" approach to disagreement produced an interesting life lesson. Two of his targets, Tomas Philipson and Joseph Grogan, were instead promoted to the highest level in the federal hierarchy. Banning Tom from meetings left an empty chair filled by a polite and obedient military-school graduate (me) and helped make this book possible.

"WE HAVE A LOT OF LOVE IN THE ADMINISTRATION"

SOME EVIDENCE ON THE CHAOS QUESTION

"The day-to-day management of the executive branch was falling apart before our eyes."
ANONYMOUS IN *A WARNING*, 2019

"The White House is truly, as you would say, a well-oiled machine."
PRESIDENT DONALD J. TRUMP, SEPTEMBER 6, 2018

CONVENTIONAL WISDOM HOLDS that the Trump White House is in perpetual chaos, directly attributable to the President, that saps everyone's productivity and encourages back-stabbing as the primary way for colleagues to engage each other. Many voices warned me against joining a Trump Administration because of such perils. This chapter supplies instead real data on the collegiality, predictability, and productivity in the Trump White House while I was there. Admittedly, my observations center on the economic sphere. However, to those who assert that other spheres show something entirely different, I say, go beyond anecdotes and prove it with evidence.

COLLEAGUES

The National Economic Council (NEC) was grossly mismanaged. The NEC Director, the CEA Chairman, and the Treasury Secretary fought like animals. The working atmosphere was unbearable, and change was urgently needed. The President, ever concerned with the superficial, added that the NEC Director needed to work on his personal appearance.

The paragraph above was not about the Trump administration but the second year of the George W. Bush administration, as reported in 2002 by the *Washington Post* and the *Los Angeles Times*. The President fired the NEC Director and the Treasury Secretary, and the CEA chairman resigned less than three months later.

Although we came to the Trump White House through different channels, NEC Director Larry Kudlow and I are old friends. I asked him for advice and prayed for his health. We met frequently, often impromptu at the west entrance to the West Wing. A CEO or Cabinet Secretary with him at any moment had to listen to Larry brag about my accomplishments. It is the kind of thing that my grandfather did in the 1980s when bringing me to lunch with his friends.

The staff of the Council of Economic Advisers with President Trump, Ivanka Trump, and Larry Kudlow. Official White House Photo by Shealah Craighead. Used with Permission.

Larry disagreed with me once. It took him less than ten minutes to (properly) convince me of my error. The NEC and CEA staffs enjoy working together (the rare deviation from this pattern is reported in Chapter 10 of this book). Larry, and another friend of CEA, Ivanka Trump, photobombed the annual CEA-POTUS photo. We can ask ourselves, do the people in the figure look unhappy with their boss and colleagues?

Our interactions with Kudlow's staff reveal a lot about the social life in the Economic Office of the President (EOP, which is in the two office buildings in the White House security complex: the West Wing and the Eisenhower building). Unlike the CEA, the joint NSC-NEC team frequently dealt with top secret information and were therefore prohibited from having personal electronic devices (iPhones, etc.) in their offices (NSC refers to the National Security Council, which was led by John Bolton at the time). The hallways of the Eisenhower building have a number of cabinets with several individually keyed compartments where the occupants of those offices, and their visitors, store their personal devices. This made the hallway an especially likely place for meeting the staff who were taking a break to check with spouse, children, etc., using their personal devices. Such meetings were even more common with Kudlow's team who had offices across the hall from me with the common interests of economics and trade policy. The bonds were even stronger when we had the common adversary of Peter Navarro (Chapter 11).

We also enjoyed working with the Office of Management and Budget (OMB), which occurred often on matters of health and economic forecasting for the budget. They had good technical knowledge, and we all liked working with numbers. Although the budget results do not show it, the OMB staff fights back vigorously on every penny that agencies try to add to their spending (see also Chapter 10). Joe Grogan and his teams were typical. The *Washington Post* accurately described Joe as "a good-government type," adding (with a little exaggeration) that Grogan had "the power to nix or give the nod to hundreds of regulations." CEA's strong working relationship with Joe continued when he left OMB to become Director of another White House component, the Domestic Policy Council (see also Chapter 9).

Goodwill was also felt between CEA and the offices of Legislative Affairs, National Drug Control Policy, Science and Technology Policy, the Staff Secretary, the U.S. Trade Representative, the Vice President, and the Press Secretary. I remember Treasury Secretary Mnuchin being especially welcoming to me soon after arriving in Washington; I joined him and others for lunch in the Ward Room of the White House Navy Mess. Acting Assistant Treasury Secretary Diana Furchtgott-Roth was also exceedingly kind.

The Office of Information and Regulatory Affairs (OIRA) is an important part of the OMB that reviews new Federal regulations. They are implementing the regulatory budgeting system (Chapter 7). While CEA acknowledges OIRA's historic accomplishments since 2017, I regularly complained that OIRA did not require agencies to follow the longstanding OMB guidelines designed to prevent unnecessarily costly regulations. Parts of the OMB resisted this criticism, and in one heated (an unusual) moment a career OIRA economist called me "the carpetbagger of regulatory impact analysis," or something to that effect. Eventually, they not only acknowledged a need for improvement but began taking real steps to change. This is atypical as Federal agencies go.

There is not a lot of love surrounding HHS Secretary Azar. Some of that is described in Chapter 4 and Chapter 10. For example, it is unpleasant to serve as Mr. Azar's Commissioner of the Food and Drug Administration (FDA) or as his Administrator of the Centers for Medicare and Medicaid Services (CMS). Indeed, the CMS Administrator is so perturbed with Azar's leadership that POTUS and VPOTUS occasionally intervene on her behalf. Nevertheless, I enjoyed working with Jim Parker (a senior adviser), FDA commissioner Scott Gottlieb (see Chapter 9), and others from HHS, even when disagreeing with them.

As further evidence of a productive relationship during the Trump Administration, HHS was prompt in sending comments on CEA's reports, including the opioid-price report. Former CEA member William Niskanen had a vastly different experience during the Reagan Administration, where many CEA reports fell into the "black hole" of political review. Niskanen described a number of Reagan Administration reviewers as nothing more than "horseholders."

Although an alarm clock was purchased for my DC apartment, I never used it. Enthusiasm for the people and the work usually woke me up before 5 a.m. Flying home to Chicago every other weekend (including Friday), I voluntarily worked in the White House during my DC weekends (almost always alone). It also helped that my CEA office was luxurious by comparison with the small basement apartment. Admittedly, I got a bit cranky a few times at the 18 days of consecutive work in the White House (a few times there were two consecutive DC weekends). CEA colleagues forgave that occasional crankiness, I hope.

Most other White House staff enjoy their jobs too, with a few notable exceptions. Although I never had an intimate conversation with Chief of Staff General Kelly, I saw and heard him enough to discern that by the second half of 2018 he was annoyed and frustrated. I got a similar impression from Don McGahn, though I base it on only two cursory observations. Their successors, Mick Mulvaney, Emmet Flood, and Pat Cipollone, showed different attitudes.

PREDICTABLE

The opposite of chaos is predictability. Evidence easily shows how, from my perspective at CEA, the Trump White House was and is exceptionally predictable. Unless similar evidence can be garnered from other administrations, the more rigorous assessment would be that the Trump White House is among the least chaotic.

Take the administration's stance on prescription-drug pricing. In the spring of 2018, it was saying how much prescription drug prices were rising, requiring a new regulatory "drug-pricing blueprint." At CEA, we expected that emerging evidence would convince the President to take a second look at how deregulation could reduce drug prices as

Secretary Azar was already looking at more regulation. Tom Philipson and his team had started digging into the details and discovered that long overdue policy changes at FDA were allowing generic drugs to enter the market with greater ease. As early as the summer of 2018, we could already see results in terms of greater entry. It was only a matter of time until the competition started reducing prescription drug prices.

CEA therefore assembled a lengthy report, finished in October 2018, that went through the details of generic drug entry and the measurement of the rate of inflation for prescription drugs. Sure enough, in January 2019, the data started coming in showing how prescription drug prices were falling after decades of increases (see also Chapter 9). President Trump soon adjusted his approach and various parts of the "blueprint" were discontinued. The evidence shows how, despite being situated in an allegedly chaotic White House, CEA was nine months ahead on this issue. CEA also expected that prescription drug prices would stop falling further below trend after a couple of years, which is why it always assumed that the consumer savings from generic deregulation would continue but not increase beyond mid 2019.

Chapter 3 features another example where CEA anticipated the administration's approach to health policy debates and the 2020 campaign. Before President Trump and NEC Director Kudlow began "putting socialism on trial and convicting it," CEA had already authored a 72-page report on the economics of socialism.

In January 2019, I began looking at the Obama Administration's rules for vehicle emissions standards for the model years 2021 and after. It was soon clear that those rules would function as a hidden tariff on European automobile imports (see also Chapter 10) allowing automobile companies to overcharge American consumers. The Trump Administration had, in the consumers' interest, proposed eliminating those rules. Because Michigan is both an electoral swing state and the headquarters of American automobile companies, I was skeptical that even President Trump could end such a special interest favor. Predictably, in August 2019 the President took to Twitter to test the waters. By October 2019, the Administration had decided to compromise with the car companies and allow part of the Obama rule to go into effect (close to half in terms of emissions and one fourth in terms of consumer cost).

From my very first week in the White House, it was clear that OIRA and the entire White House staff up to the President himself would want a detailed analysis of deregulation. It would have to include a comprehensive measure of the net costs and benefits, as well as specific down-to-earth examples of consumer savings. We would treat OIRA, which had already published wildly inaccurate numbers, delicately. Ample work like this might not even be possible in a one-year period.

In a truly chaotic White House, only a fool would self-embark on such a labor-intensive long-term task. In the Trump White House, the task was begun immediately. When OIRA eventually came asking for such a report, we were able to tell them that nine months of the work was already complete. Six hours from the end of the last day of my sabbatical, the report was released to the press and the "unpredictable" President began publicizing it.

PRODUCTIVE

It is difficult to work in a chaotic environment. As the anonymous author of *A Warning* alleges, aides get "so worn down by the roller coaster of presidential whims" that there is little capacity left to do "the day jobs we'd been hired for." Conspicuously absent from anyone's allegations of chaos are metrics of the productivity of White House components.

On the following pages you will read how President Trump's NEC and Domestic Policy Counsel have been historically productive. President Trump's OMB has also enlarged its responsibilities, for example, by reviewing Treasury regulations and budgeting agency regulations for the first time in history.

CEA was often months ahead on requests from POTUS and his staff. President Trump's CEA published roughly three million words (the equivalent of fourteen 500-page textbooks) during its first two years. That CEA published, for example, seventeen supply and demand analyses (and counting) in its first three *Economic Reports of the President*, as compared to one by the Obama Administration and only eight for all other Presidents combined.

As another measure of how little economics the Obama Administration was doing by comparison, consider the elementary economics concept of "marginal." That word is found dozens of times in a typical *Economic Report of the President* issued by, say, the Reagan Administration. But the 2011 *Economic Report of the President* does not use it once. Indeed, a regular task in the Trump Administration is to clean up problems that began with the Obama Administration's ignoring the "marginal way of thinking" from economics.

President Trump's CEA was the first CEA to publish anything on the economics of the ongoing opioid epidemic or coming flu pandemics, let alone full analyses of causes and costs. It was first to include the neoclassical growth model, or a supply and demand analysis of homelessness, in any *Economic Report of the President*. As explained further in Chapter 10, President Trump's CEA rigorously proved dozens of economic theorems as part of confirming and extending its conclusions. Dozens more were taken directly from the graduate-level textbook *Chicago Price Theory*. While I cannot prove it, I believe that President Trump's CEA did more of this type of work than did the CEAs of all other presidents combined.

About 10 percent of my time was spent preparing "regulatory impact analyses" (RIAs) for CEA. RIAs are supposed to be quantitative estimates of the costs and benefits of a regulation. The twenty-three I prepared were. The Congressional Budget Office (CBO) estimated that the average RIA costs the Federal government about $826,000, converted to 2018 dollars, in terms of salary, benefits, and overhead for the employees doing the work. (The economics analysis is of greater quality in my 23 RIAs than RIAs in CBO's sample, although the latter are subject to more legal scrutiny.) In other words, the work I did in ten percent of one year would normally have cost the Federal government roughly $19 million. Regardless of whether the cost estimate was $19 million or just $19,000, I do not understand how to reconcile results like this with the assertion that President Trump inhibits his aides from doing their "day jobs."

Using hundreds of articles published in economics journals also enhanced our productivity, because we could build on years of work done by others. Kevin Hassett's January 2019 address to the *American Economic Association* described this process as it played out in CEA's tax analysis.

Relying on the academic community was no free lunch, however. Authors would publicly contradict their own academic publications and some of the best-known results in economics when they saw the Trump Administration relying on them. Obama adviser, Harvard professor, and former Harvard University President Larry Summers is a prime example. He taught generations of students, including me, how taxation is not a zero-sum game. The economic damage from any tax exceeds the revenue received by the Treasury, he taught. In economic theory it is the well-known concept of "deadweight cost." But the November 8, 2016, election changed his teaching apparently. Summers wrote in the *Washington Post* how President Trump's CEA was "dishonest, incompetent, and absurd" for concluding that the dollar amount of the economic damage from corporate taxes exceeds the revenue received by the Treasury. Another Obama adviser, and now teacher of the largest economics course at Harvard, Jason Furman, shared Summers' novel conclusions.

Neither Summers nor Furman informed their readers that it was they who were contradicting textbook economics (Furman was later convinced by Harvard Professor Robert Barro to conduct a joint study of the Trump tax cut using a model that, like CEA's, has corporate taxes with deadweight costs). Summers and Furman have the full support of major news outlets, which perpetuate the myth that "the resistance" is grounded firmly on principle while President Trump's staff reverses long-held beliefs and practices in order to serve its evil master.

Early on, Tom Philipson and I responded with an op-ed in the *Wall Street Journal* entitled "A Turnabout on Corporate Taxes." But Hassett found a way to prevent the needless public back and forth with authors of studies. Before CEA relied on a published article, staff would contact the author to confirm that he or she still stood by the conclusions, or at least the arithmetic, in it. It also helped to have the economics robot (Chapter 10) and years of teaching experience to predict the logical errors that come naturally from "resistance" passions. Some of the errors would be noted in CEA's initial publication. I also compiled internal FAQ (Frequently Asked Questions) documents from which any CEA staff could quickly cut and paste when a reporter contacted us with the expected "critique," as they inevitably did. We never had the Summers-Furman problem thereafter.

Were Kevin Hassett, Rich Burkhauser, Tom Philipson, and I rare geniuses that were able to achieve historic output despite a fundamentally unproductive environment? That's an interesting hypothesis given what former Obama advisers call us. *The Washington Post* pronounced that we were an "unusually shallow bench of economic talent," and drove home its point by further lamenting how President Trump had to "settle for second-rate talent" (the same article predicted a recession in 2019 due to the trade war). The simpler and far more probable explanation is that the news media is wrong about the operation of President Trump's White House. President Trump creates a productive environment for doing quality economic analysis, which is why I was eager to join his team over any other.

Part of that environment is a relaxation of political correctness. CEA's August 2018 report on measuring poverty, entitled "Expanding Work Requirements in Non-Cash Welfare Programs," is a good example, benefiting from having Chicago PhD's Richard Burkhauser and Kevin Corinth on staff (and drawing on the publications of University of Chicago professor Bruce Meyer). We were free to use supply and demand and the marginal way of thinking on *any* aspect of human behavior (yes, even tariffs).

To be clear, political correctness is relaxed but not absent in the Trump Administration. Although scholars of socialism were urging me to raise publicly the serious question of whether socialism might be incompatible with democracy, a CEA discussion of this matter was viewed as unfair to progressive Democrats. (Vince and Ross heard me complain about this constraint on CEA's publications; probably not coincidentally President Trump told the United Nations, "Socialism's thirst for power leads to expansion, incursion, and oppression.") As another example, we were not allowed to challenge succinctly the conventional wisdom that health insurance improves health. But a byproduct of our opioid-price report (Chapter 4) is a challenge to that wisdom, albeit in many more words. A third example is the political correctness of immigration policy, which is a topic of Chapter 6.

Many of President Trump's opponents spent too much time in futile attacks on him, such as the infamous "Russia collusion investigation." (Even the *New York Times* acknowledged being caught "a little tiny bit flat-footed.") Those same opponents have had less left-over bandwidth to look at his aides' policy work. I suspect that the press distraction created by POTUS helped CEA stay well ahead of policy critiques. Sometimes it felt like the economic news was moving in slow motion.

Ironically, productivity can be reflected in higher, not lower, staff turnover. Other administrations had lower turnover in part because the presidents' advisers took so long to achieve their objectives. Take Ben Rhodes, who was President Obama's Deputy National Security Advisor. His tenure was 96 months. Chapter 23 of Rhodes' memoirs explains that by 2014 (around 70 months in), he understood that his policy goals were still unfinished. Normalizing relations with Cuba did not begin until the 71st month; the President's trip to Cuba was in the 86th month. The Iran deal completion was not until the 78th month.

Brian Blase's tenure as Special Assistant to President Trump for Healthcare Policy lasted only 29 months because that's how long it took to complete the health-insurance policy goals set out in President Trump's Executive Orders. Mr. Blase led three Federal agencies in three transformative Federal deregulatory actions that were celebrated in the White House Rose Garden in his final month. These actions allowed more small businesses to form Association Health Plans (17th month; creating an annual net benefit of $13 billion for some of the reasons discussed in Chapter 1). They further expanded Short-Term Limited Duration Health Insurance plans (19th month, creating an annual net benefit of $12 billion). And they created individual-coverage Health Reimbursement Accounts (29th month; CEA has not yet quantified a net benefit). Brian also contributed to the Administration's effort to set the Affordable Care Act's individual mandate penalty to zero (11th month; creating an annual net benefit of $20 billion). He also fixed the Affordable Care Act's formula for the Premium Adjustment Percentage. Indeed, the three health insurance deregulations achieved in Brian's 29 months have, as a share of national income, net benefits that are more than half of the legendary deregulation of airlines that began during the Carter Administration. Airline deregulation took more than twice the time that health insurance deregulation did.

Another example is Andrew Bremberg, who served 24 months as President Trump's Director of the Domestic Policy Council. With many accomplishments during that time, his most legendary was working with the 115th Congress to deregulate with the Congressional Review Act, which allowed Congress to overturn Obama administration regulations. Measured in terms of economic impact, this work was prolific, encompassing 16 separate parts. Together, they are expected to increase annual real incomes by more than $40 billion. Miraculously, it took only 16 months to achieve this.

In my own case, 12 months was just enough to complete the 8 or 10 projects for which my skills were especially applicable. Those same projects could easily have been dragged out over three or four years, but that would have been wasteful and prevented other economists from benefiting from the historic opportunities to serve in President Trump's CEA.

President Trump's Chief of Staff General Kelly (17 months) is another example. He came early in the Administration when more efficient operating procedures were needed and, as in most Administrations, leaks needed to be lessened or stopped. Like Doug Collins did for the Jordan-era Chicago Bulls, General Kelly improved the organization. With Kelly's accomplishments in place, it was time for a separate set of talents.

Because I did not arrive at the White House until July 2018, I cannot rule out the possibility that the working atmosphere changed over time. As the President's son-in-law, Jared Kushner, describes, the Trump Administration began with "a whole new crop of people. Maybe they didn't have the traditional résumés for doing their jobs, but many of them shared his vision. It took a little bit of time to figure out who were the right people and who were the wrong people." But descriptions, such as those recorded in 2017 by Britain's former ambassador in Washington of "vicious infighting and chaos" were the opposite of what was occurring when leaked to the press (two years later). Forced to resign in 2019, Sir Kim Darroch was further proven wrong in his assertion that the 2016 Trump campaign colluded with Russia.

There are Trump Administration officials with both short tenures and short accomplishments. But the evidence shows how turnover statistics are misleading.

A WARNING OR A PROJECTION?

In *A Warning*, an anonymous author claims to have seen firsthand how Mr. Trump is the most dangerous president ever. The book proves to be a long-winded exercise in psychological projection. Readers are asked to believe that President Trump makes decisions without reading or considering the facts, while the book itself is ironically devoid of facts. It says that the Trump White House can barely function, but the book cannot manage to supply even crude measures of how productivity compares between presidential administrations. If asked, I would gladly have provided him or her with data. The author may have seen me in the lower level of the West Wing, or had an office near mine, or both. He or she probably worked in the National Security Council (or an executive agency working in coordination with NSC), and therefore two of my former students working there could have made the introductions.

Mr. or Ms. Anonymous cannot grasp the fact that Americans are sick of excuses for why our troops are not brought home from the Middle East. Like the unelected Obama staff cited in Chapter 4 ("No one in Ohio Cares About Burma"), the anonymous author shows more concern that our Federal government should help foreigners rather than address real problems at home. Tellingly, a book full of foreign-policy discussion never mentions President Trump's policies toward Israel. Mr. or Ms. Anonymous fails to mention any mistakes committed by the ruling class, prior to the Trump Administration. Referring to the Trump era, the book manages to criticize about everyone in our country, except Democrats.

The author of *A Warning* reveals a sincere interest in history, but betrays no training in the methods of scholarship, either quantitative or qualitative. The only primary sources I noticed (there is no bibliography) were either a century old (or more), Twitter, or his/her anonymous self. Perhaps because its author is unaccustomed to being challenged or asked for evidence, the book does not seriously engage opposing views. It asserts that President Trump's policies have failed Americans, but the book does not address even one of the dozens of contrary conclusions provided in the *Economic Reports of the President*. It seems that Mr. or Ms. Anonymous, rather than the President, is the one who does not read.

FURTHER WATCHING AND READING

The President's quote that begins this chapter is from the September 7 video cited in the social media bibliography. Reagan CEA member William A. Niskanen's memoir was written primarily in 1986 and published in 1988 as *Reaganomics: An Insider's Account of the Policies and the People*. A July 9, 2019, interview of Mick Mulvaney, reported in Doug Wead's 2019 book, reveals how Mick thinks analytically about economic matters.

While General Kelly's tenure as Chief of Staff served an important purpose, he went overboard with stopping leaks. While he kept meetings small to prevent staff from knowing sensitive information, he unwittingly prevented staff from knowing what other components of the White House needed (Mick Mulvaney relaxed this policy when he became Acting Chief of Staff). As explained in this chapter, I helped make my group productive (that is, valuable to the rest of the White House) by predicting the needs of the other components. Most of that was done without speaking a word, but merely sitting in the back of the room and hearing what the various participants said and found interesting.

Ivanka Trump's workforce project is an example. She has a lot of interest in what Chicago economists would call "human capital," which was also on the CEA project list that I brought with me on my first day. But during the Kelly era I missed all the meetings where CEA and Ivanka were both present, and too much about her interests was lost in summaries provided to me of those meetings. I was completely unaware of any White House demand for my human capital project until it was too late. With nine weeks left in my sabbatical, I heard Ivanka speak for the first time and realized that a valuable opportunity had been missed.

Moreover, Mick Mulvaney's less strict approach to meetings did not produce the leaks that General Kelly feared. At multiple meetings I attended, the content would have been incredibly valuable to currency traders. These subjects never leaked to the press. Or more telling, currency markets did not react.

On April 12, 2019, the British embassy in Washington hosted a large reception in connection with the spring meetings of the World Bank Group and the International Monetary Fund. The reception was hosted by Ambassador Sir Kim Darroch, with the guest of honor being the British Chancellor of the Exchequer (i.e., Treasury Secretary) Philip Hammond. Sir Kim and Mr. Hammond were unable to see any substance behind populism (I met other diplomats, such as those from Ireland, who genuinely appreciated populist concerns). They showed no respect for the voting public in the U.K. and the U.S., which had voted for Brexit and President Trump. Mr. Hammond was delighted that "In the past year, we did not exit, and you did not build the wall!" Another pleasure was that "We don't know what will be the royal-baby name, except that it will not be Donald!" To this day, I wonder why they had no concern that the remarks would show up in the British press or would offend the dozen or so of President Trump's staff attending their reception. The populists got the last laughs, because Sir Kim was forced to resigned when his opposition to President Trump became widely known, and Mr. Hammond quit politics when Britain's leading populist, Boris Johnson, became Prime Minister.

6

"OUR COMPANIES NEED HELP"

POTUS BEGINS IMMIGRATION REFORM

"American citizenship is the most precious gift our nation has to offer."
PRESIDENT DONALD J. TRUMP, MAY 16, 2019

DEPENDING ON WHOM YOU ASK, President Trump is either heroic, or ignorant and racist, on immigration policy. In fact, the economic tradeoffs are obvious to the President. The challenge, which has perplexed earlier Administrations, is solely political.

Not a politician, I write this chapter to highlight the economic elements. The Samaritan's Dilemma features prominently. When you subsidize something, you get more of it. That's true whether the subsidies go to immigrants or to U.S. citizens who are poor or unemployed. Failure to acknowledge the Samaritan's Dilemma also helps explain why experts perennially overestimated economic growth during the Obama

Administration and then underestimated economic growth during the Trump Administration.

THE ECONOMIC APPROACH TO BORDER CONTROL

Workers' wages have grown significantly ahead of inflation during the Trump Administration. CEA Chairman Kevin Hassett showed the results to President Trump, who asked, "Isn't too much wage growth bad for companies?" Rich Burkhauser spoke up, saying that employers would have no problem with wage growth if productivity were growing commensurately. "That's a great answer," he told Rich. "We should be aware if something is needed for our companies. A merit-based immigration system would help them."

This was in March 2019. POTUS was about to task son-in-law Jared Kushner with drafting an immigration reform plan with his senior adviser Stephen Miller and CEA Chairman Kevin Hassett. Although both President Trump and Mr. Miller have been pigeon-holed as people who "build walls," formulation of the plan was a pretty standard exercise in economics. It was heavily reliant on economic data and understanding that an immigration system is a tradeoff between economic costs and benefits, with a further distinction between legal and illegal immigration.

The benefits from immigration are numerous. One of them is a source of labor for businesses, as President Trump mentioned to Rich. Immigrants contribute to innovation and can bring skills that are especially needed in our country. Immigration has costs too, some of which are disproportionately borne by a fraction of our population that lives in certain neighborhoods or is employed in particular occupations. As Nobel Laureate and my late colleague Gary S. Becker put it in his *The Challenge of Immigration—A Radical Solution*, "Immigration may also bring some negative features," noting that some immigrants "may take advantage of welfare benefits and other economic goods provided by a government."

In early April 2019, CEA's immigration team (including Hassett, Jeff Larrimore, and Andrew Baxter) met a couple of times with POTUS, Miller, Kushner, and others, both in the Oval Office and in the

Roosevelt Room. CEA brought a stack of prepared materials that POTUS quickly digested and, as usual, offered specific instructions on how to revise the materials so that they might be communicated better. On policy, he was aware of the various costs and benefits, and has talked publicly about them. He commented again on how our companies were having trouble finding certain types of workers. He explained to the CEA team that citizenship is the most precious thing our nation has to offer. If there were no political considerations, he said at multiple meetings, "we would sell citizenship." Of course, he is a politician; yet when POTUS had his economist hat on, he independently derived the same "radical" market-based solution that the late Nobel Laureate Gary S. Becker had a few years earlier. That says something about the way President Trump thinks about problems.

Gary S. Becker thought that the right immigration fee would be approximately $50,000. On one hand, the fee revenue would help cover the costs that immigration opponents are justly worried about. On the other hand, a fee system would create opportunities for foreigners who haven't been able to get through our bureaucracy to get American citizenship. When our country was in its early growth phases—especially in the 19th century—the right fee was close to zero. So lax immigration restrictions in those days did not do such a bad job in terms of getting the number of immigrants that was good for both the country and immigrants themselves. But then our welfare state grew substantially. In terms of cost, a lax immigration system was no longer the right policy.

CEA brought a lot of statistical analysis to the table. We looked at the immigration system in several other countries. We compared the parameters of those systems to attributes of the U.S. population in terms of education, occupation, age, etc. Ultimately, POTUS decided on an immigration points system (a.k.a., merit-based) of immigration like what Australia and Canada already have. Because each applicant would receive points according to proxies for contributions to the U.S. labor market, such a system might approximate the results of Becker's immigration-fee system.

The economic approach to border control also recognizes the Samaritan's Dilemma, a reference to the parable of the Good Samaritan in Luke's Gospel. As the Foundation for Economic Education explains, "a dilemma arises for the Samaritan who attempts to do good… if the donor's action leads to an increase in the amount of need." The well-intentioned policy of giving unaccompanied children at the border special access to the United States results in an increase in the number of unaccompanied children at the border. Referring to well-intentioned policies in his own state, New Jersey State Senator Steven Oroho explained, "[o]ur state is sending the message that if you come to our country illegally, New Jersey will make you eligible for virtually all of the benefits of citizenship…. New Jersey is enticing people with greater and greater promises to make an extremely dangerous journey that many will not survive." Due diligence in the search for solutions must consider policy reforms that reduce the leniency that children receive in the immigration process.

The number of unaccompanied children met by U.S. Customs and Border Protection more than tripled between 2011 and 2014. At the time, the Obama Administration received intense criticism merely for acknowledging the Samaritan's Dilemma. *The Washington Post* came to its defense, insisting that "there is nothing humanitarian in tacitly encouraging tens of thousands of children to risk their lives, often at the hands of cutthroat smugglers, to enter this country illegally." The number of children at the border stays high today. Trump Administration officials would like to say, as the Obama Administration did, that "They will be sent back." But officials have also learned that acknowledging the Samaritan's Dilemma on the border threatens their political survival because what was once common sense is now denounced widely by critics as cruel and inhumane.

GROWING THE ECONOMY

There was supposed to be a rapid recovery after the 2008-2009 recession. President Obama's CEA predicted 3 percent real GDP growth nearly every year through 2016, while the Federal Reserve and the Congressional Budget Office (CBO) offered similar predictions. Actual growth never exceeded the White House forecasts and usually fell far short of them: 1.5 percentage points short in each of 2011 and 2012 and 1.0 percentage points short in 2015. This all reversed in 2017, 2018, and 2019, when actual growth beat the Federal Reserve's forecasts each year.

As explained in my 2012 and 2015 books, the forecasters underestimate the economic costs of the Obama Administration's taxes and regulations and therefore underestimate the boost that results from ending many of those policies. I particularly singled out the Federal Reserve for not speaking up. They don't have to disapprove of President Obama's policies, yet should be blunt about the tradeoffs involved. When you subsidize unemployment and poverty, as the Obama Administration did to a historically high degree, do not be surprised when you have more unemployment and more poverty (the Samaritan's Dilemma again). But the Fed was perennially surprised, and Republicans were irritated at the unforced errors.

How many consecutive overpredictions have to occur during the Obama years before we suspect political bias among the forecasters? With every single year during the Trump Administration so far being *underpredicted*, Republicans, especially President Trump, begin to wonder whether something needs to be disrupted over at the Fed (Chairman Powell told me that the forecasts are prepared by the Federal Reserve technical staff, not by him or the Board of Governors). Why such optimism when Obama was in office yet pessimism when Trump is in the same office? The disruption began in March 2019, when President Trump started naming Fed Chairman Jay Powell in angry messages on his Twitter account. The *Wall Street Journal* accurately reported that President Trump also had a phone conversation where he told Mr. Powell, "I guess I'm stuck with you."

After underestimating economic growth two years in a row, the forecasts being offered in early 2019 were still pessimistic. *The Washington Post* had run a headline proclaiming that "A Recession is Coming." One survey of economists showed 42 percent predicting a recession soon. "I'm pretty surprised by that sort of assessment," I told reporters after a speech at the Capital Hilton in DC. "Growth has been in the 2-3 percent range over the past year. What is it that is going to bump us off 2 points to get into the negative territory?" The question to reporters was rhetorical yet I knew that they had nothing in mind except that "Orange Man" is bad.

We discussed the 2019 economic forecast with President Trump early in the year. Although he disagreed with the news media's "the recession is coming" predictions, POTUS told us that actual growth would most likely come in below CEA's forecasts. He turned out to be correct, with the actual growth coming in slightly below CEA's tariff-inclusive forecast and above the Federal Reserve's forecast.

I do agree with the forecasters that population growth, which is the combination of net births and net immigration, is an important determinant of economic growth. Although the U.S. population continues to grow, it is growing at the slowest rate of our lifetime. A normal population growth rate would significantly ease the Federal budget because there would be more people paying taxes that would fund various programs and finance the national debt. It is therefore significant that President Trump's immigration plan does not reduce the number of immigrants. To the contrary, it increases the economic contribution from immigration through the merit-based system.

POTUS AS IMPROMPTU ECONOMIST

Much of what President Trump says about the economy comes from CEA or Larry Kudlow's National Economic Council (NEC). That is our job, after all. But there are examples where, in private at least, he offered assessments without CEA or NEC preparation. A couple of them relate to the labor market (noted above), where he understood the relationship between wages and productivity, and how immigration might be better managed with a monetary fee. Coming from the real estate industry, he is also well versed in interest rates, loans, and other banking topics. Despite Mr. Navarro's attempts to confuse him, President Trump readily understood how predictions of a devaluation of the U.S. dollar would raise U.S. interest rates and thereby add to the Federal government's interest expenses.

In thinking about policies related to student debt, President Trump also concluded that college tuition increases over time because of increasing Federal assistance. In other words, Federal aid increases the demand for college and thereby allows colleges to charge higher tuition. This conclusion is known as the Bennett hypothesis (discussed below), which is controversial but I believe correct.

President Trump is provided with many economic charts, which he often digests before we offer any further explanation. It is easy for us to gauge his understanding because he is frequently advising us on how to improve the presentation or distribution of the results. This advice usually revealed that he understood the fundamental importance of what he was shown. An exception occurred with the complicated "annual average to annual average" growth rate formula cited in Chapter 2. He also finds and probes genuine weak spots in the charts, as he did with the prescription drug pricing chart (Chapter 9). Having prescription-drug prices ten percent below trend is better than nothing, he said, but more was needed.

President Trump speaks on economic matters a great many times in prepared settings, with an exceptionally low error rate. He is deliberate with numbers, usually citing them exactly the first time and later exaggerating if the "fake news" failed to adequately feature them or if they declared the exact number to itself be a "lie." One of his favorites is the comparison of economic activity between rural New York (where fracking is prohibited) and Pennsylvania (where it is allowed, see especially Chapter 8). "Difference in differences" is the term of art in economics, which routinely engages in comparisons of this type. President Trump is also careful with economic terminology, such as the distinction between "jobs" and "people employed" (one person can be employed in more than one job).

My observations are the direct opposite of what is anonymously asserted in *A Warning* claiming that Mr. Trump is the most dangerous president ever. It further claims that Trump "stumbles, slurs, gets confused, is easily irritated, and has trouble synthesizing information, not occasionally but with regularity." Mr. or Ms. Anonymous concludes that "Trump genuinely doesn't remember important facts." By this account, necessity would have diverted most CEA efforts to cleaning up POTUS mistakes on economic matters. To the contrary, I saw quite a low error rate. Arguably, President Trump's CEA is the most productive CEA ever (Chapter 5). Either the author of *A Warning* has massively distorted the truth or has no familiarity with the economic sphere of White House operations, or both.

FURTHER WATCHING AND READING

The Freakonomics blog hosts an interesting podcast about immigration. The 2015 podcast, whose link is cited in this book's social media bibliography, included an interview with me about Gary S. Becker's *The Challenge of Immigration—A Radical Solution*. The idea of charging a fee for immigration did indeed seem radical in 2015, but I predicted that "[m]aybe some of these immigrant crises that we have now around the world will motivate some of that thinking, and a country will try it, and we can see how it works." What happened in 2019 is that an immigrant crisis in the U.S. motivated its president to put forward a reform proposal that in important ways resembles the immigration fee system.

Many other economic reforms like this quickly move from radical to mainstream ideas. The all-volunteer (as opposed to conscripted) military, enacted by the U.S. in 1973, is an example that Mr. Becker often cited. Milton Friedman's classic book, *Capitalism and Freedom*, is full of such radical ideas that became mainstream. Allowing private companies to make deliveries in competition with the post office is another idea that was radical when Friedman wrote about it but unquestioned today.

The parallels between the immigration policies of the Obama and Trump administrations is the subject of a November 2019 *Wall Street Journal* article by Holman Jenkins. Volume 1 of Karl Marx's book *Capital* famously asserted that public policy ("acts of parliament" as he called it) "forces down wages," to the benefit of business owners. Marx is correct in that "our companies need help" is a factor in today's policy calculus. But I don't find that a merit-based immigration system would force down wages.

A 2019 *New York Times* article by Jim Tankersley shows the White House and Federal Reserve economic forecasts going back to 2010, and how they compare with the actual growth. Make sure that you view the online version, where an important data error was corrected in the chart (be aware that no prose was corrected either online or in print, even though it discusses the original mistaken chart). Another widely cited forecaster, Mark Zandi of Moody's Analytics, predicted that candidate Trump's economic policies would result in a long recession from which, contrary to the other recessions during our lifetimes, the recovery would take decades. Here in reality, however, the average household now has $6,000 more annual income than Mr. Zandi predicted.

After it became plain that experts were too pessimistic with their 2017 and 2018 forecasts, they switched to saying that economic growth was "merely continuing the trend of the Obama economy." If following an earlier trend is such an easy accomplishment, why wasn't it predicted then? Sadly, they still have their facts wrong. The *2019 Economic Report of the President* shows how economic indicators such as wages for low-skill workers or investment have been rising *above* the earlier trend. Something special happened in early 2017 that continues to surprise the experts.

The Bennett Hypothesis is said to originate in a 1987 *New York Times* article where Secretary of Education William J. Bennett asserts "increases in financial aid in recent years have enabled colleges and universities blithely to raise their tuitions, confident that Federal loan subsidies would help cushion the increase." A 2017 survey by Jenna Robinson concluded that Bennett was largely correct. Others, such as the 2010 book by McPherson and Schapiro, dispute the hypothesis. The textbook by Angrist and Pischke offers a good explanation of "difference in differences."

RUNNING THE GOVERNMENT LIKE A BUSINESS

PERSPECTIVES ON THE UKRAINE CALL
AND OTHER MATTERS OF STATE

"How much are we giving them? What are we getting in return?"
PRESIDENT DONALD J. TRUMP, ALMOST EVERY WEEK

CITIZEN DONALD J. TRUMP had been the head of a major business, as well as an entertainer playing the head of a major business. But would business experience help with running the government? With so many businesspeople in America, not to mention aspiring business-people graduated from business schools, wouldn't the public sector have adopted relevant best business practices years ago? The answer has been no, yet I saw two important, and disruptive, changes from POTUS that make government run more like a business: scrutinizing international aid and regulatory budgeting.

NO FREE LUNCH

Private businesses do not give things away for free. We can listen to broadcast radio stations "for free," but there are commercials. We can browse social media "for free," but the platform sponsor is using our personal data and showing us advertisements. The nothing-is-free way of thinking led President Trump to scrutinize international aid, with an unintended consequence that would disturb, if not debilitate, his presidency for many months.

The President speaks with world leaders, either in person or by phone. As President Trump prepared for such meetings, the conversation with his staff always began the same way. "How much are we giving them?" The answer was always that the U.S. is paying that country rather than the other way around. Although CEA does not specialize in international affairs—career employees in the Department of State usually fill this role—CEA Chairman Kevin Hassett was often present for the preparations in case there were questions about the economic activity of that nation. Kevin noticed how, after they supplied the dollar amount of the international aid, the administration specialists were often unprepared for the President's next question. "What are we getting in return?"

By the time I had arrived at the White House, the two-question routine had been repeated for many countries and was expected by all involved with the preparations. In August 2018, the same two questions preceded the visit of the President and First Lady of Kenya. When the Administration's Kenya specialists told POTUS that Kenya was perennially using U.S. aid to fight HIV/AIDS, they were unprepared for his third question: "Are they getting results?" A scramble followed to dig up data on trends for HIV/AIDS prevalence in that country.

Although I did not work in other Administrations and am not an international affairs expert, I formed the distinct impression that it had been many years since a President had asked about the purposes of international aid, let alone whether the recipient of the aid was delivering on its promises. As explained in Chapter 1, President Trump is results oriented rather than accepting ideological recommendations or protestations on faith. His questions undoubtedly made the State Department nervous, not to mention the various special interests around Washington that find Federal international aid programs beneficial to them. The odds are high that at least a couple of countries were not delivering, or at least would appear to be not delivering. Budget cuts might then follow. Indeed, when POTUS proposed to cut a couple of billion out of the $50 billion spent on international aid each year, there was an uproar from the Department of State and both houses of Congress.

The moods in Washington are relevant for what followed. A populist White House was looking for ways to cut government spending, and the rest of Washington knew this. White House staff repeated the two-question routine so many times that it became familiar and they took it for granted. Meanwhile, to the extent that people outside the White House with an interest in foreign policy were nervous, they would become defensive of their favorite international aid program. Several viewed POTUS as an adversary (see also the following pages), even while he was signing their paychecks.

In July 2019, President Trump said to the President of Ukraine, "I will say that we do a lot for Ukraine. We spend a lot of effort and a lot of time. Much more than the European countries are doing and they should be helping you more than they are." To State Department employees, this had to sound like a possible and unwelcome budget cut, with U.S. taxpayers paying less and European taxpayers paying more. When I read that the President followed with, "I would like you to do us a favor…," as a former White House staff I saw this as literally the hundredth time that POTUS would be insisting that the U.S. get something in return for our checks cashed by foreign countries.

It is easy for White House staff to forget that, as of July 2019, the American public had not been aware of the two-question routine. This had to be Acting Chief of Staff Mick Mulvaney's frame of mind when he infamously addressed the controversy around the Ukraine call with "We do that all the time, get over it." For half of America, no free lunch was a novel but common-sense approach to foreign aid. For the other half, it was novel and nefarious because they thought a personal benefit for the President was involved.

IS THERE A DEEP STATE?

To borrow words from a February 2017 *New York Times* article, the "deep state" refers to "an entrenched culture of conflict between the president and his own bureaucracy." As I explain on the following pages, the typical relationship in a Republican administration is a lack of sympathy rather than outright conflict. Yet it can be said that mischief from only a couple of federal employees actively resisting, out of hundreds of thousands just doing their jobs, can be politically destructive.

During the 2016 campaign, 95 percent of the presidential-campaign donations made by civilian Federal employees went to the Democratic nominee. Among employees at the State Department (the Federal agency in charge of foreign policy and international relations), the statistic was 99 percent. It is not controversial to point out the Clinton-Trump donation ratio among Federal employees, 19 to 1, is not representative of the 1.7 to 1 ratio among their fellow citizens. Candidate Romney collected far more Federal-employee donations in his 2012 bid for the presidency than candidate Trump did in 2016. Hundreds of thousands of Federal employees live in the Washington bubble (Chapter 4), where it is nearly impossible to hear why anybody would vote for candidate Trump. Most are not interested in Mr. Trump's brand of populism. Special interests are likely to command more sympathy in the Federal workforce than President Trump does.

The Democratic leanings of the civilian employees of Federal agencies were obvious to me in their analysis of regulations. Their economic-impact analyses overlook most of the costs of Federal regulations, with the exception of the amount of time it takes for households and businesses to read the regulation that upends their lives (the following pages explain further). Although Federal fuel-efficiency standards have existed for close to 50 years, none of the career macroeconomists I met knew how those standards affect value-added in the automotive industry or GDP for the country as a whole.

I did not see this as willful negligence despite their presidential preferences. As employees in a large organization, they have little incentive to deviate from their agency norms. Moreover, the organization known as the Federal government has no competitor that might show a better way of doing things. A small amount of willful negligence, however, (see Chapter 4) was promoted by agency leaders to protect their turf, more likely in support of special interests than opposing President Trump. Observing the regulatory work of the Departments of Labor, Treasury, and Health and Human Services especially closely, I was favorably impressed by the diligence with which they read and synthesized the thousands of comments submitted by the public.

I also saw how extraordinarily difficult it is to fire Federal employees, even when they obviously break the rules. In the high-profile cases of Federal employees making serious and obvious errors (former FBI director James Comey), a dismissed Federal employee by President Trump would receive a metaphorical badge of honor while POTUS received extra harassment from his political opponents. Career staff at the Consumer Financial Protection Bureau (CFPB) even sued to prevent President Trump from replacing the head of that agency. There are plenty of cases with no public notoriety but nonetheless high hurdles to dismiss a Federal employee for serious wrongdoing. Under these conditions, to what extent is the President in charge of a Federal agency? If not him, then who?

Talk of conspiracies is best left to others. Yet the deep state phenomenon from my experience exists because POTUS or VPOTUS can only monitor the activities of a small fraction of the Federal workforce at any time. Consider my own activities at the CEA. Little of what I did at CEA was literally directed by the President. The most time-consuming task was his instruction for CEA to investigate the costs and benefits of the rebate rule (Chapter 10), which took about five percent of my time. Close to 90 percent of my tasks were autonomously started by me or senior White House staff. President Trump did not specifically tell me, or tell chairman Hassett, to look at the economics of opioids, or socialism, or wage growth, or the costs and benefits of the individual mandate, or measures of drug-price inflation, or quantitative estimates of his deregulatory portfolio. Nevertheless, he found them valuable, judging by how often he uses the results of that work. Although reward structures for senior staff and aspiring senior staff are relevant factors in loyalty, so too is affinity for the President and his agenda, which is not universal in the federal workforce.

REGULATORY BUDGETING IS COMMONSENSE MANAGEMENT

In the corporate sector, the chief executive appoints managers whom she trusts to deliver results for the company. Nevertheless, no manager receives a blank check for pursuing those results. Each manager must also work within a budget. If a manager's budget proves to constrain the company's success, he must go to the chief executive and make his case that the company would find adding to his budget beneficial. Remarkably, none of the first forty-four presidents of the United States managed regulation this way. The heads of Federal agencies were allowed to create as many regulations as they wished. Here I explain how President Trump is one of the first chief government executives in the world to put regulation into a budget. Doing so uncovered three myths about Federal regulation.

Federal regulations originate in all three branches of government. The Congress can draft and pass bills, which are signed into law by the President or enacted over his veto. In writing the law, Congress can delegate enforcement authority to the executive branch, which includes executive agencies whose heads sit in the President's Cabinet as well as independent agencies such as the Federal Reserve System. The delegation can be explicit, as with the House Medicare for All bill directing that "the Secretary [of Health and Human Services] shall pay, from amounts made available for capital expenditures ... such sums determined appropriate by the Secretary to providers...." Congress can delegate implicitly by writing its bills with vague terms that the executive branch agencies or Federal courts must further interpret to make operational. Take the 1963 Clean Air Act, later amended by Congress, which requires the EPA to establish standards "applicable to the emission of any air pollutant..." from motor vehicles. The Act itself does not say whether the greenhouse gases (such as carbon dioxide) causing climate change are an "air pollutant." The EPA eventually decided that they are. The Supreme Court affirmed the EPA decision when it concluded that "greenhouse gases fit well within the Clean Air Act's capacious definition of 'air pollutant.'" The regulations issued by Federal agencies are called "rules" (but also see the following pages regarding "guidance"). Federal courts create legal precedents called "judicial decisions."

A set of administrative procedures have long guided the rulemaking process. Agencies must seek public comment on their proposed rules. President Reagan also got his Office of Information and Regulatory Affairs closely involved with overseeing the process. President Reagan also required major new rules to include a cost-benefit analysis, which is supposed to be a rigorous quantitative analysis of the costs and benefits of imposing a new rule. Unless Congress requires it, a rule should not go into effect if its costs exceed its benefits. Since 2003, OMB Circular A-4 gives guidelines for conducting the cost-benefit analysis.

However, this oversight is on a rule-by-rule basis. Neither the agencies nor OIRA made much attempt to determine the totality of the costs and benefits of rules (beyond paperwork burdens: see the following pages). President Trump's Executive Order 13771 changed all of that by giving each executive agency a budget for its regulation. Its most famous provision is that two new deregulatory actions be issued for each new regulatory action. More important, it also put a cap on the dollar costs of each agency's new regulations, with caps set at zero or negative. In other words, every agency's portfolio of regulations and deregulations for the fiscal year must result in a net reduction of regulatory costs for households and businesses of having those regulations. (Examples of negative cost deregulations are the 2018 and 2019 rules relaxing restrictions on small employers to form association health or retirement plans. The participating businesses had lower costs because of the rule.)

As shown in Chapters 8 and 9, President Trump has reduced regulatory costs by amounts that rival, if not exceed, the most significant Federal deregulations in modern history. The regulatory budget is more likely than not responsible for it. But a new culture of deregulation or ending an earlier culture of overregulation, must also be a factor. For example, the Federal Communications Commission and other independent agencies that do not have regulatory budgets have nonetheless made impressive reductions in regulatory costs since 2017.

THREE MYTHS ABOUT FEDERAL REGULATION

President Trump's regulatory budget helped me to recognize three regulatory myths. The first myth is that most regulation is environmental. This commonly repeated myth inaccurately equates deregulation with polluted air and water. The regulatory budget shows instead how most deregulation is economic deregulation. Letting Mr. Winslet keep his "junk" insurance plan is an economic deregulation and does not pollute air or water. No pollution is created by ending a foreign drug company's monopoly on the sales of generic prescription drugs. The air is not dirtier because university students are considered customers of the university, rather than employees. Removing regulatory barriers from the franchise way of doing business did not pollute air or water. More systematically, only 14 percent of all economically significant Federal rules issued by executive agencies between 2000 and 2017 came from the two environmental agencies (the Environmental Protection Agency and the Department of Interior, EPA and DOI, respectively). Among the significant independent agencies, only one has a primarily environmental mission (the Nuclear Regulatory Commission).

The fiscal year 2018 regulatory budget had over 200 rules from the executive agencies. Among the ten rules with at least 100 comments, only one was environmental. The quantity of comments received on that one rule, known as the "Waste Prevention Rule" or "Venting and

Flaring Rule," was wildly disproportionate to its costs and benefits. Because the regulation applies only to oil and gas operations on Federal and tribal lands, whereas at least 90 percent of oil and gas operations are on private lands, the annualized cost savings from the deregulation was only about $300 million as compared to an average of $4 billion for the nine nonenvironmental rules. In other words, less than one percent of the cost savings from deregulation in that year's budget came from environmental deregulation.

The vehicle-emissions rule will result in a large environmental share for fiscal year 2020, although Chapter 10 shows why that is the exception that proves the rule. The Trump and Obama Administrations are in comparatively close agreement on the environmental costs of vehicle emissions. The overwhelming difference between them is about the nonenvironmental economic costs.

The second myth, publicized in the *2012 Economic Report of the President* and elsewhere, is that Federal regulation is smart and evidence based. Just look at the various regulations related to prescription opioids (Chapter 4) or protecting the maritime industry (Chapter 11). No serious cost-benefit analysis is offered for these rules, which are likely to have large net costs. Most of the agencies perennially defy OMB Circular A-4 by documenting just a tiny fraction of the costs that their regulations create, as with the obviously costly Food and Drug Administration's (FDA) regulation of generic prescription drugs (the topic of Chapter 9). When the FDA put those procedures in place, which have now been reformed, no cost was assessed because they were issued as a "guidance" document exempt from the cost-assessment requirement. The "guidance" designation was in essence a regulatory loophole with no requirement to estimate costs. A second example is the prescription drug "rebate" rule proposed (although now withdrawn) by the Trump Administration. As a rule intended to "blow up the way the industry does business," it was intentionally creating large costs for parts of the industry in order to change the structure of drug prices. Nevertheless, the published proposed rule claimed that costs would be a mere 0.03

percent of the revenue of the industry segment being regulated. There is nothing "smart" or "evidence-based" about that estimate.

A third example was mentioned in Chapter 1 of this book: President Obama's prohibition of Mr. Winslett's "junk" insurance plan. No cost was assessed for that rule because it was labeled "not economically significant," which made it exempt from requirements to estimate costs. But this designation is only to be used if there are no material adverse effects on a sector of the economy, which is a ridiculous assessment of a product that two million people would be purchasing (as estimated by the nonpartisan Congressional Budget Office).

Not knowing the intentions of the rule makers, I cannot say whether the insignificance designation was a technical error or a strategic decision to obtain the exemption. If it is a technical error, it is curious that this underestimation error is common whereas the opposite technical error– overestimating annual costs by billions of dollars—is something I have never seen, despite having carefully examined dozens of Federal rules. Either way, the process has been systematically biased toward underestimating regulatory costs. As OMB told me when I provided it with improved cost estimates, revising an underestimate by billions of dollars is too disruptive. I appreciate that perspective because I found that most of the significant regulations (in the true economic sense) have their costs underestimated, so that taking a typical one and improving its cost estimate makes that regulation appear as an outlier, which it is not.

Errors/strategic decisions with the "economically significant" designation occur in the Trump Administration too. In April 2019, I was sent to a SCIF meeting about a Department of Commerce (DOC) regulation for countervailing duties. SCIF stands for "sensitive compartmented information facility," which is a meeting room for discussions confidential enough that electronic devices are prohibited. When I expressed displeasure at leaving my devices behind, I was told that the discussions in the meeting would potentially disrupt the world's multi-trillion-dollar currency markets. Meanwhile, DOC was labeling the rule as not economically significant. "DOC, take your pick," I insisted. "Either this rule is economically significant, or currency markets are uninterested, and we can have these meetings outside the SCIF!" The compromise was the less absurd "Other Significant" designation, although DOC still refused to consider it a major rule. Responsibility for writing a rule ultimately belongs to the regulatory agency, and the White House staff cannot command them to change without getting POTUS or VPOTUS personally involved. Understanding this, the White House staff reluctantly accepted their revised "Other Significant" label.

These are not cherry-picked examples: a study of the 53,838 Federal rules finalized between 2001 and 2014 found that only 246 of them (less than one percent) quantified regulatory costs; even fewer, only 160, quantified benefits.

Environmental regulations are more likely prepared according to the sound economic principles of Circular A-4 because they have been the subject of lawsuits. The first myth, that most regulation is environmental, thereby helps contribute to the second myth of smart regulation. The nonenvironmental regulations quantify hardly any of their costs. Even when they do, they get less attention from the administration because they are less likely to end up in court.

The second regulatory myth is the basis for the standard objection to regulatory budgeting: imposing a budget unnecessarily constrains the executive agencies. As President Obama's first OIRA Administrator, Cass Sunstein, puts it, "From the standpoint of the cost-benefit revolution, Trump's [regulatory budget is] hard to defend.... What matters is not whether the agency has added to the total amount of costs, or whether it has added more regulations than it has taken away, but whether it has produced benefits on balance." Mr. Sunstein does not explain why corporate chief executives limit their managers with budgets, yet a Federal chief executive would have no good reason to ask his regulatory managers to stay within a budget. If Federal agencies are allowed to commonly ignore most of the costs of their regulations, then regulation-by-regulation cost-benefit analyses will never be enough for the White House to properly constrain regulations. A regulatory budget helps fill the management gap.

The second regulatory myth has naturally led to paternalism among the ruling class, which further increases populist pressures in the rest of the country. The Oxford definition of paternalism is "the policy or practice on the part of people in positions of authority of restricting the freedom and responsibilities of those subordinate to them in the subordinates' supposed best interest." Grown adults do not like to be told, under the threat of Federal punishment, that they have to purchase insurance; that they must drive a fuel-efficient car; that their internet services must be of a particular type (of course, the more expensive type); or that their insurance must be comprehensive (and more expensive). As explained further in Chapter 10, the primary disagreement between the Obama and Trump Administrations about automobile regulations has little to do with the environment. Both agree that the consumer cost of a vehicle should reflect the environmental costs of the vehicle's pollution. But the Obama Administration was remarkably paternalistic, asserting that consumers are unable to understand their fuel budgets and how they are affected by vehicle choice. Paternalism was its justification for pushing consumers to fuel-efficient cars even beyond the environmental value they might have.

The third regulatory myth, reinforced by the other two, is that the main burden of regulation is paperwork. Encouraged by the Paperwork Reduction Act of 1980, Federal agencies are comparatively diligent at estimating the paperwork created or saved by their regulations. The paperwork costs seem large in an absolute sense: in 2016 OIRA estimated that the public spends about 10 billion hours per year filling out Federal forms. But this refers to all Federal rules, not just the new ones. Having looked at many of the Federal rules introduced since 2009, I clearly see that paperwork burdens are just the tip of the iceberg in terms of overall costs but the nonenvironmental regulations rarely include any estimate of the rest of the iceberg. (The 162-page 2016 "Overtime Rule" from the Department of Labor is an unusual but interesting case with billions of dollars of paperwork costs, mainly due to a requirement to track work hours for millions of employees who would have otherwise been salaried.)

Chapter 10's rebate rule is a typical example of the analysis from the Health Department, which is the single largest promulgator of economically significant regulations in the 21st century, outpacing EPA by more than 3-to-1. The Health Department only quantified the time it would take for businesspeople to read the rebate rule, to read their own contracts to check for compliance, and to fill out a form. Workers and consumers doing the reading and clerical work were disaggregated into four categories, with average hourly wages calculated down to the penny. The cost of the rule was calculated as the product of reading and clerical times hourly wage rate. Despite the fact the rule was intended to "blow up the way the industry does business," no cost was calculated for this economic "demolition" (the terms of art specified in Circular A-4 are "resource costs" and "opportunity costs").

Or take the case of the Seaman's Act's protectionism on behalf of the maritime industry (Chapter 11), which contributed to the drowning death of 844 people in Chicago. If the Health Department were to conduct a cost-benefit analysis of the Seamen's Act using its usual techniques, it would estimate a cost for reading the law's 22 pages and estimate no cost for the 844 fatalities! If Federal rules do not quantify resource and opportunity costs, there has been no "Triumph of the Technocrats," which is Cass Sunstein's way of asserting that Americans are now ruled over by nonpartisan career professionals who carefully balance costs and benefits.

FURTHER WATCHING AND READING

The February 2017 *New York Times* article cited above was authored by Amanda Taub and Max Fisher. The percentages of Federal employees donating to candidates Clinton and Trump were reported by Jonathan Swan, using data from the Federal Election Commission. *Massachusetts v. EPA* is the Supreme Court case cited.

The study of 53,838 Federal rules was reported by Clyde Wayne Crews. As described in his 2016 paper, Jerry Ellig has assembled a report card for the quality of regulatory impact analysis of rules issued during the years 2008-2013. Consistent with my experience for more recent years, he finds that the quality of Health Department rules is one of the lowest of all Federal agencies, e.g., by failing to articulate the market failure requiring Federal rulemaking or failing to quantify costs or benefits. A 2013 paper by Ellig, McLaughlin, and Morrall report, consistent with my experience, that regulatory analysis tends to be of lesser quality when the regulation relates to administration priorities (e.g., homeland security regulations from the Bush Administration and healthcare regulations from the Obama Administration).

The 2019 and 2020 *Economic Reports of the President* each have a chapter supplying overviews of regulatory trends and how they have changed since 2017. The *2019 Economic Report of the President* and CEA's February 2019 report on health-insurance deregulation each have sections on so-called "junk" insurance plans, which are more accurately described as short-term limited-duration health insurance (STLDI) plans. The STLDI plans are inexpensive because consumers can sign up for a short time and opt out of categories of coverage they do not want.

In agency-specific tallies of economically significant regulations, I use "Reg data" from the George Washington University Regulatory Studies Center. Patrick McLaughlin and I are preparing a data-intensive report on the "Three Myths about Federal Regulation" that will be released while this book is in press. The three myths have been repeated so often in the news media that, despite my meek protests, President Trump's senior staff repeat some of them too, as recounted in Chapter 13 of Doug Wead's 2019 book.

A handful of countries have elements of regulatory budgeting, which they launched anywhere from one to seven years prior to our Executive Order 13771. Those countries include Australia, Canada, France, Germany, Netherlands, South Korea, and the United Kingdom. Further details are available in the *Journal of Benefit Cost Analysis* article by Andrea Renda and the OECD working paper by Trnka and Thuerer, both listed in the bibliography. "Triumph of the Technocrats" is a quote from Professor Cass Sunstein's book, describing a technically capable Federal regulatory machine that purportedly considers relevant costs and benefits and thereby should not be subject to a regulatory budget. Professor Sunstein also makes a cameo appearance in *The Final Year* film described in Chapter 4.

8

"I AM A TARIFF MAN"

COMPARING PRESIDENTS REAGAN AND TRUMP

"I am a Tariff Man."
PRESIDENT DONALD J. TRUMP, DECEMBER 4, 2018

"We should beware of the demagogues who are ready to declare a trade war against our friends—weakening our economy, our national security, and the entire free world—all while cynically waving the American flag."
PRESIDENT RONALD REAGAN, NOVEMBER 26, 1988

ALTHOUGH DESPISED BY MANY ON THE LEFT, Ronald Reagan was overall a popular president whose administration coincided with the beginning of an economic boom reflected in everything from the stock market and interest rates to unemployment and women's wages. President Reagan is also famous for his eloquent defenses of free international trade and deregulation of domestic markets.

Some key members of the Reagan Administration are now working in the Trump Administration. President Reagan's first Deputy Trade Representative Robert Lighthizer is now serving one position higher as President Trump's Trade Representative, administering tariffs, and negotiating trade agreements with Mexico, China, and other countries. President Reagan's Associate Director for Economics and Planning at the Office of Management and Budget (OMB) was Larry Kudlow. Larry is now President Trump's Director of the National Economic Council (NEC), a cabinet-level position. Anthony Dolan served eight years as a speechwriter for President Reagan, reaching the position of Deputy Assistant to the President and Director of Speechwriting. Tony is working in the Trump White House too, now as a Special Assistant to the President and Advisor for Planning, especially mentoring President Trump's speechwriters. Elaine Chao was Chairwoman of the Federal Maritime Commission at the end of the Reagan Administration and is now Secretary of Transportation. The purpose of this chapter is to compare the two presidents in terms of two policy areas important to both: international trade and the deregulation of domestic markets.

Presidents Reagan and Trump. Public domain photos from the Executive Office of the President and the White House, respectively.

WHAT IS THE OPPOSITE OF A TRADE WAR?

One of the best ways to appreciate the virtues of free international trade is to listen to one of Ronald Reagan's speeches. In addition to his eloquent warning cited in the beginning of this chapter, Ronald Reagan also described "open trade policy" as "one of the key factors behind our nation's prosperity." He said that free international trade has "proven itself in the real world where we have seen free trading nations prosper while protectionist countries fall behind."

We all agree that Mr. Trump does not talk this way about international trade. But we should also agree to put aside any love or hate for these men while we look at their policy records. Both Reagan and Trump were television entertainers before they were politicians, so their rhetoric may not necessarily reflect actual policies.

Let's consider a domestic producer, such as a steel manufacturer in Pennsylvania, which competes with foreign companies for sales to American consumers. If an obstacle could be put in the way of foreign competitors, then the domestic producers could sell more, charge more, or do both. Either way, the trade obstacle should increase domestic producers' profits and workers' employment and wages. If domestic producers were running the government, most would certainly erect such obstacles, known as "protectionism."

Protectionism comes in three principle types: import prohibitions, tariffs, and import quotas. An outright prohibition of foreign products ("import prohibition") places American consumers captive to domestic producers, who would have the power to overcharge significantly for their products. For a century, prohibition and overcharging by factors of five to eight has occurred, for example, in the U.S. coastal shipping services market (Chapter 11 of this book).

An outright import prohibition is particularly harmful to consumers. Consumers themselves may be businesses and go bankrupt due to import prohibitions on products they use in production (again, see Chapter 11). Foreign producers, also upset by our import prohibition, might urge their own governments to retaliate by prohibiting American products.

Wanting their customers to stay solvent, even domestic producers might prefer milder forms of protectionism over import prohibitions.

Two potentially milder forms are import quotas and tariffs. A tariff is simply a tax on imports, with the revenue going to the U.S. Treasury. It raises the prices and profits of domestic producers, while reducing the U.S. profits and sales of foreign producers. Among other tariffs, the Trump Administration placed a 25 percent tariff on steel imported from most countries.

Naturally, foreign producers do not like it when the U.S. collects tariffs. They ask their own governments to put tariffs on American products. Although in 2018, Peter Navarro (President Trump's Director of Trade and Manufacturing Policy) confidently told the President that no country would dare retaliate against U.S. tariffs, tariff retaliation is exactly what happened in response to the Trump Administration's tariffs. The Trump Administration started a trade war.

In contrast to tariffs, import quotas can (and did) offer protectionism without a trade war. An import quota is an upper limit on the number of imports allowed (an import prohibition is the special case when the quota is set to zero). To circumvent international law, import quotas are sometimes euphemistically named "voluntary export restraints," referring to how foreign governments were "helping" us by limiting the amount of their U.S. exports. Instead of implementing a steel tariff, President Reagan used a steel import quota, limiting steel imports to 20 percent of the U.S. market. While better for consumers than an outright import prohibition, Reagan's import quotas did hike steel prices because at the lower prices consumers wanted to import more than the quota allowed (prices were driven up by customer competition for a limited supply of imports). Through higher prices, Reagan's various import quotas therefore harmed Americans buying autos, sugar, semiconductors, textiles, machine tools, and clothespins. While foreign producers of these products sell fewer units, they often have greater profits because Americans are paying them higher prices on lower supply. And as the Reagan Administration acknowledged, American consumers may not understand that they pay more through quotas as they would with an announced tariff, which has obvious political advantages.

Enriching foreign and domestic producers by restricting supply and driving up prices, Reagan's import quotas avoided a trade war that might have resulted if tariffs were used instead. Unlike tariffs that, as taxes, require foreign producers to share part of their revenue with the U.S. Treasury, import quotas do not bring any revenue to our government. The quotas allow the foreign producers to keep the extra profits they obtain from charging higher prices. From an economic perspective, the Reagan Administration used U.S. taxpayer money to bribe in effect foreign countries to stay out of a trade war. Perhaps Japan could have "retaliated" against Reagan's quotas by setting quotas on their U.S. imports, but that would have been a funny kind of war in which Japan took money from their own consumers and sent it to our companies.

To put it yet another way, if we had a trade war in the 1980s and used all of our tariff revenue to bribe foreigners to stop retaliating, the end result would be Reagan's international trade policy (Milton Friedman articulated this conclusion in an April 1987 *Wall Street Journal* article). As protectionism goes, import quotas are the ugly alternative to a trade war. Tariffs instead are the "America first" type of protectionism.

The reality is somewhat more complex. Table 1 (below) shows that the Trump Administration has relaxed an important quota and reduced a tariff, which the Reagan Administration did not do. Also note that, as part of the "rules of origin" provisions of the United States Mexico Canada Agreement (USMCA), the Trump Administration expanded the economic boundaries of existing tariffs. The Reagan Administration increased some tariffs too, such as raising the tariff rate for Japanese motorcycles by 45 percentage points; imposing a 100 percent tariff on imports of Japanese computers, televisions, and power tools; and putting a 15 percent tariff on Canadian lumber. But unlike President Reagan, the Trump Administration uses import quotas sparingly (limited to steel and aluminum from three countries). As discussed in Chapter 10, the

Trump Administration relaxed a significant quota on high-emissions/low-MPG vehicles, which is not specific to imports but disproportionately constrains European manufacturers.

Although ignored by experts, the Trump Administration uses a hybrid of tariffs and quotas, known as "tariff quotas." Like an import quota, the hybrids allow the foreign companies to make tariff-free sales (at an elevated price) to American consumers, but they also allow the U.S. Treasury to receive tariff revenue.

TABLE 1. TRADE POLICY ACTIONS DURING THE REAGAN AND TRUMP ADMINISTRATIONS *as of December, 2019*

TYPE OF ACTION	REAGAN	TRUMP
Quotas tightened	Autos, Textiles, Steel, Machine tools, Sugar, Clothespins, Semiconductors	*Steel from Korea, Brazil, Argentina* *Aluminum from Brazil, Argentina*
Quotas relaxed		*High-emissions vehicles, which are disproportionately imported.*
Tariff increases (including tariff quotas)	Motorcycles, Canadian lumber, Various Japanese imports	*Steel, Solar panels, Aluminum, Washing machines, Various Chinese imports*
Tariff decreases		*Reduced distortions in international postal terminal dues.*

Despite the additional complexity, the overall conclusions remain. President Trump is the tariff man that he says he is, while President Reagan was a quota man. President Reagan did not always practice the free trade that he preached. As Reagan CEA member, William Niskanen, put it, the Reagan administration "was on both sides of [trade issues], articulating a policy of free trade and implementing an extensive set of new import quotas." Another Reagan CEA economist Steve Hanke added "the share of American imports covered by some sort of trade restriction soared under 'free-trader' Reagan, moving from only 8% in 1975 to 21% by 1984." The Trump Administration also has key elements of protectionism, but unlike Reagan has so far mostly avoided protecting domestic producers in ways that profit foreign companies.

CHICKEN?

The United States does not have, and has never had, the free international trade described in Reagan's speeches. This is not to say that more tariffs are good (the following pages explain further). But it does say two things: (i) that protectionist pressures are effective and ever-present in Washington and (ii) that the most valuable progress on international trade comes from cutting back the most damaging protectionist measures. Looking at these in more detail reveals surprises.

The pioneer of economics, Adam Smith, described the ubiquity of protectionist special interests in 1776, which "like an overgrown standing army, [are] formidable to the government, and, upon many occasions, intimidate the legislature." William Niskanen explained how in modern times a "candidate has a strong temptation to make commitments to some groups of swing voters, whether or not these commitments are consistent with his or her general economic agenda.... Speaking at a Chrysler plant in Detroit, [1980 candidate] Reagan suggested that he would ask Japan to reduce its auto exports to the United States. In a speech to the national Maritime Union, he promised support of the maritime industry." Niskanen added that "in response to domestic political pressure... the [Reagan] administration imposed more new restraints on trade than any administration since Hoover." As described above, in Chapter 10, and in Chapter 11, 39 years later the very same groups are still applying the fiercest protectionist pressures.

The most damaging protectionist measures are the import prohibitions and their functional equivalents, tariffs that are so high that imports stop altogether. Unfortunately, for the past several decades, no president has succeeded in eliminating significant import prohibitions and their equivalents (as explained further on the following pages, President Clinton did exempt Mexico from one of these; in 2015, a repeal of a significant *export* ban was attached to a spending bill by Republicans in Congress, which President Obama signed). One of these is the century-long ban on imports of crew or vessels for the purpose of coastal shipping, whose discussion I defer until Chapter 11. So far, President Trump is the first president since Carter who has *not* spoken out in *support* of that import prohibition.

Another prohibition equivalent is one of the best-kept and worst-named secrets in international trade: the 56-year old "chicken tax." The tariff has been buried in the tariff schedules of every administration since Lyndon Johnson, when tariffs were placed on foreign pickup trucks in retaliation for tariffs on U.S. chickens. These government schedules contain more than 10,000 products but sorting by tariff rate reveals a group of products referenced as "Heading 8704 Motor vehicles for transport of goods" tariffed at 25 percent (imports from Mexico are exempted per the North American Free Trade Agreement). This is a fancy name for pickup trucks. The chicken tax is not top of the list for repeal because the pickup is not the preferred vehicle of the Washington bubble. Yet pickup trucks are the top three selling vehicles nationwide. There are about 50 million pickup trucks in operation in the U.S., which suggests that roughly one-third of households own one and thereby are effectively paying a "chicken tax."

The tariff is so high that no pickup trucks are made outside of the U.S., except for a few made in Mexico, where the chicken tax has not applied since NAFTA went in effect. The tariff is one of the rare and obvious examples of the Laffer curve in action (Chapter 1), where the government could obtain more revenue by cutting one of its tax (tariff) rates. Auto manufacturers have even deliberately destroyed part of their new vehicles in order to align what the chicken tax allows them to produce abroad without tariff and what consumers want to buy at home. If the revenue-free chicken tax is to be retained, it is not so crazy to put a tariff on the remaining vehicles. (For the record, CEA did not suggest or support extending the chicken tax or any other tariff. Kevin Hassett decided that CEA would never waver from a free trade position. Treasury and OMB agree with CEA on this subject, as they did during the Reagan years. NEC also agrees, but NEC was not created until 1993.)

Tariff analysis was not my area, although I did insist that the model (featured in the *Economic Reports of the President*), that the CEA uses for domestic taxes and regulations, be the same model used for tariffs. More specifically, my view is that tariffs are taxes on top of all of the other taxes and regulations in our economy and therefore have a particularly costly substitution effect, reducing employment, real incomes, and GDP. In other words, even while a tariff may create jobs in the protected industry, it reduces employment nationwide because any nation subjected to higher taxes has less incentive to work. (Some of the international trade textbooks, such as Douglas Irwin's, only go as far to say that losses in export employment "tend to cancel" employment gains in the protected industry). As CEA explained to the President (over Navarro's objections), this also means that a significant amount of the tariff revenue will be illusory because the tariffs reduce revenue from income and payroll taxes in industries not protected.

My tariff-as-tax approach also permits a succinct, albeit approximate, demonstration of why the new 2018-19 tariffs are not enough to offset (in terms of effects on real household incomes) the 2017 Tax Cut and Jobs Act (TCJA), let alone the deregulation agenda. TCJA had an annual static revenue foregone (that is, tax rate change times the amount of taxable income before the tax rate change) of $150 billion or more. The static revenue received from the 2018-19 tariffs (including those scheduled for December 2019) is about $100 billion per year. In other words, the net of TCJA and tariffs is a tax cut. The net is even greater if, consistent with the administration's intentions (and the joint U.S.-China announcement in December 2019), the tariffs are counted with shorter duration than TCJA. Those who conclude that the economic-growth effects of deregulation and TCJA are fully offset merely by collecting $100 billion in tariffs for a brief period need to explain how to reconcile their conclusion with basic arithmetic.

On the rare occasions that I worked on tariffs, another analytical tool I used was the Lerner Symmetry Theorem. As Professor Douglas Irwin explains, "The Lerner symmetry theorem holds that a tax on imports is functionally equivalent to a tax on exports" even without tariff retaliation by the other country. As a result, "governments that undertake policies to reduce imports will find themselves also reducing exports." To understand the Lerner Symmetry Theorem, consider the analogy of raising Manhattan bridge and tunnel tolls on inbound vehicles, with no change in outbound tolls. The inbound tolls are a tariff on vehicles brought onto the island of Manhattan, just as the Federal government's tariffs are levied on goods brought into the U.S. To the extent that they are successful at reducing the number of inbound vehicles, the tolls will also reduce the number of outbound vehicles. Vehicles cannot leave Manhattan that never arrive in the first place! So too will the Federal government's tariffs eventually reduce goods shipped out of the U.S. Foreign buyers of our goods need to have purchasing power here, which in the long run they cannot acquire without selling us something.

GETTING TO KNOW MR. NAVARRO

Protectionist parallels between the Reagan and Trump administrations end with Mr. Peter Navarro, who is a unique "China expert" and President Trump's Director of the Office of Trade and Manufacturing Policy. Before ever encountering him in a meeting, I had seen Mr. Navarro many times around the White House complex; he has a habit of loitering at the west entrance to the West Wing (perhaps keeping tabulations of who was entering). Mr. Navarro's reputation preceded him; even the President was annoyed with Mr. Navarro's boorishness and double dealing and barred him from running meetings. To the amusement of the rest of the White House staff, Mr. Navarro also flunked marketing in 2018 when he was promoting a "Fair And Reciprocal Tariff Act." So named, the "FART Act" had no chance of passing.

The relationship between imports and exports was the topic of my first meeting that included him and me, run by Kudlow's trade adviser Clete Willems. Following my usual habit, I arrived early to the White House Situation Room (WHSR) to meet people and compare notes on other topics of common interest. We were startled when Mr. Navarro stormed in bellowing, "It looks like we're having another meeting where I am the only one supporting the President!" Although not authorized to cause trouble, I mentally scrolled through a list of bully-incapacitation tricks learned in military school. Mr. Navarro and the others talked for about thirty minutes, at which point Clete turned to me to offer CEA's opinion. I gave the standard exposition of how exports equal imports in the long run, although for periods of time a nation can run a trade deficit while its investment exceeds its savings.

Perhaps knowing that CEA had the only other economists in the room, Mr. Navarro proclaimed, "CEA's opinion was disproven years ago!" Referring to the nineteenth-century economist David Ricardo, he continued that "If CEA would bother to familiarize itself with the Ricardian model of international trade, it might finally understand that trade deficits are usually the result of currency manipulation." Stunned, I realized why this meeting was in the WHSR, where even government-issued electronic devices are prohibited. Currency markets might panic if they realized that White House currency-policy discussions were so misinformed.

An internet search would have settled the matter, but we were in the WHSR without computer or cell phone. Pausing for a few seconds, I reviewed in my mind the components of the famous Ricardian model of "comparative advantage" in international trade. "Peter," I replied, "could you spare a few moments after the meeting to show us how currency manipulation works in the Ricardian model? The last that CEA checked that model lacked anything about currencies." Mr. Navarro mumbled something about "I meant Hume rather than Ricardo" while the others in the room bit their lips to prevent laughing out loud.

Mr. Navarro deserves credit for leading a real accomplishment that eluded the Reagan and Clinton administrations (others did not even try). For decades, the U.S. postal service has subsidized shipments originating in foreign (especially developing) countries, per the rules of the Universal Postal Union (UPU), which is the international organization of postal systems. As Alfredo Ortiz, president and CEO of the Jobs Creators Network, explained, "it costs around $20 to mail a small parcel weighing 4.4 pounds from one U.S. state to another, yet mailing the same package from China only costs about $5." To the distress of the Washington establishment, President Trump threatened to withdraw the U.S. from the UPU unless less distortionary rates were set. The UPU relented at the last minute, allowing the U.S. to end a source of rate discrepancies between, among other things, Chinese and U.S. shipments. CEA's Joe Sullivan also supported this effort, which may also help reverse the opioid epidemic and illicit drug shipments from China (Chapter 4).

TARIFF THREATS WITH A PURPOSE

Both the Reagan and Trump administrations used tariffs, or threats of tariffs, to induce foreign countries to remove barriers to American-made products. As the Reagan Administration described in its *1989 Economic Report of the President*, the foreign "nontariff" barriers include "deny[ing] American residents the protection of intellectual property rights." These include denial of copyrights, trademarks, patents as well as state-sponsored economic espionage against American companies. During the Reagan Administration the offending countries included Japan, South Korea, Taiwan, and Indonesia. The Trump Administration cites China as the main offender, which even the President's most vocal opponents acknowledge.

Today, it is often said that tariffs are not the proper way to address the real problem of international violations of IP rights. President Reagan's second-term CEA also warned that foreign leaders may not react favorably to tariffs and instead "may resist a mutually beneficial agreement to preserve national pride." If so, what is the proper way to protect American IP? Economists today have no respect for using tariffs, as President Trump does. But in 1990, respected M.I.T. international economist and Chicago PhD Rudiger Dornbusch articulated a "trade strategy" echoed by the Trump Administration, but with "China" replacing "Japan." Professor Dornbusch advised, "maximize the disruptive effects for Japan and minimize the costs to U.S. consumers. This objective could be served by developing a list of commodities for which substitute producers could easily and rapidly replace Japanese shipments. Or use across-the-board tariff surcharges on Japanese imports...." The change in economists' sentiment seems to be political rather than based on new research completed between 1990 and today.

It is worth remembering that the Reagan Administration eventually obtained IP reforms in Japan, South Korea, Taiwan, and Indonesia by threatening tariffs. Specifically, the Reagan Administration's tariff threats resulted in "beef and citrus," tobacco, and footwear agreements with Japan and "sweeping modifications of Korea's laws and regulations concerning intellectual property." Taiwan also "improved its intellectual property rights protection," while Indonesia enhanced its copyright protections. However, Reagan's successes did not occur until his second term. The Trump Administration used tariffs against China to reach a trade agreement that would protect U.S. intellectual property rights. By the end of the third year of his first term, President Trump signed a partial agreement with China that includes IP reforms.

REAGAN CONTINUES CARTER DEREGULATION

"Don't just stand there, undo something" was a favorite saying of Murray Weidenbaum, Ronald Reagan's first CEA Chairman, and a common sentiment in the Trump White House. Mr. Weidenbaum was referring to government regulations, which amount to restrictions on trades between Americans. Regulations may restrict trades between employer and employee (labor regulation), between borrower and lender (bank regulation), between internet provider and household (telecommunications regulation), etc. The opposite, deregulation, allows for freer *intranational* trade. Free intranational trade may be more valuable than free international trade given that more than 80 percent of private-sector purchases are *within* the United States.

There is wide agreement that some of the most significant deregulation in U.S. history (prior to 2017) occurred in airlines, trucking, petroleum, and natural gas. Each of those industries had Federal rules protecting the ability of companies to overcharge consumers. The results included higher consumer prices, lower wages and productivity, and less purchasing power. Air travel, for example, is something that most Americans today have experienced, while prior to deregulation, air travel was so expensive as to be confined to business travelers and higher income vacationers.

With the tone set by Mr. Weidenbaum, nearly all of Ronald Reagan's *Economic Reports of the President* reported favorable results from deregulations. Often lost in history is that most of these changes were due to laws passed earlier by a Democratic Congress and signed by a Democratic President, Jimmy Carter. They include the Airline Deregulation Act of 1978, the 1978 Natural Gas Policy Act, and the Motor Carrier Reform Act of 1980.

President Carter's natural gas deregulation left in place a number of price controls at the wellhead (the top of a natural gas well where the gas is removed for transport and sale) and along the pipelines that transport the gas. Further legislation was needed, but this did not come until President George H.W. Bush. President Reagan does deserve credit for appointing commissioners to the Federal Energy Regulatory Commission (FERC) who advocated for more deregulation and remained in their positions even beyond President Reagan's term. FERC finished the needed deregulation in 1992.

President Ford signed the 1975 Energy Policy and Conservation Act, which regulated energy industries in several ways. President Reagan never succeeded in stopping the law's fuel economy regulations, although in his second term he did reduce the standards from 27.5 miles per gallon to 26.0. He also did not remove the 1975 law's ban on crude oil exports. The 1975 law also included petroleum price controls, whose end President Reagan accelerated by eight months.

The Reagan Administration does deserve credit for the little-noticed Bus Regulatory Reform Act of 1982. It also created a market for landing slots at the nation's four largest airports.

"In order to reduce the burdens of existing and future regulations," President Reagan issued Executive Order (EO) 12291 requiring cost-benefit analysis of major new Federal rules. (Cost-benefit analysis is supposed to be a rigorous quantitative assessment of the strengths and weaknesses of a proposed course of action, such as implementing a new regulation.) EO 12291 also got the President's Office of Information and Regulatory Affairs (OIRA) seriously involved in reviewing new regulations. However, thirty-eight years later I can see that the effect of EO 12291 is limited because hardly any agency (EPA and DOT are exceptions) adheres to the principles of cost-benefit analysis.

The Reagan Administration was often more rhetorical and less active on deregulation. Part of the reason was that the GOP did not have a House majority to support Reagan for eight years. Yet as CEA member William Niskanen described the missed opportunity in 1986, "The failure to achieve a substantial reduction in or reform of federal regulations, building on the considerable momentum established during the Carter administration, was the major missed opportunity of the initial Reagan program." He added that special interests impeded intranational trade as much as they blocked international trade: "…all too often the administration ruled against a change in regulation that would benefit consumers at the expense of some *concentrated business group*" [emphasis added].

A VAST DEREGULATORY LANDSCAPE

Arizona's Grand Canyon is immense and beautiful. You pull up on the first day of a visit and at once you are in awe at the majestic colors and vast distances. It is difficult to wrap your mind around it or remember it properly. Then you go back to your hotel, tent, or camper, and come back the next morning and it seems all new. Was it that immense and beautiful yesterday? Yes, it was, but the human brain (my brain, at least) cannot remember it all.

The Trump Administration's deregulatory agenda has so many impressive components that administration officials struggle to remember its scope, let alone individual actions. One of the biggest challenges in my career was to prepare a summary of the agenda, beyond a mere count of "pages of regulation," that would still do some justice to the individual components. A key part of the summary is that industry after industry has seen special interest protections removed, thereby reducing prices for consumers and enhancing our nation's productivity.

The special interests are not faring as well under President Trump as they did under President Reagan (recall Niskanen's description). Hundreds of regulations have been removed, some of which had been put in place at the behest of large banks, trial lawyers, major health insurance companies, big tech companies, labor unions, and foreign drug manufacturers. Other special interests, such as automobile manufacturers (Chapter 10) and the maritime industry (Chapter 11) have so far prevented the administration from removing rules that allow them to overcharge consumers.

CEA estimates that President Trump's approach to regulation will increase annual household real incomes by almost $4,000 per year (including automobiles), as compared to what they would be with regulations continuing their trend under the Obama and Bush Administrations. The added income accrues to all types of households, but especially those with below-average income. Lower-income households have a disproportionate amount of their spending going toward telecommunications, health insurance, prescription drugs, and other goods and services that became less expensive due to deregulation. The net benefits of deregulation since 2017 compare favorably with the most significant deregulatory episodes in American history.

Health insurance (Chapter 1), prescription drugs (Chapter 9), and internet service are three areas where the consumer benefits are especially large. Internet service is a $200 billion per year industry, with households commonly having three receivers of internet service: a cable modem and two smartphones. President Trump's Federal Communications Commission (FCC) removed price controls from the wired and wireless internet service industries with its "Restoring Internet Freedom" rule. President Trump and the 115th Congress also sharply reduced internet service prices by nullifying an Obama-era FCC regulation on the types of internet services that are sold to consumers.

CEA estimated that these two actions alone have net benefits of more than $50 billion per year (about 0.3 percent of national income, which is a lot for the net benefit of deregulatory actions for just one industry). For example, when the FCC regulation was nullified by Congress (one of the two major FCC deregulations), the price of internet subscriptions immediately fell five percent, which is an easy way to see why the annual net benefits of FCC deregulation would be in the tens of billions of dollars. By contrast, former CEA member Niskanen cites a mixed record by the Reagan FCC in terms of promoting competition in telecommunications.

Banking is another important industry undergoing deregulation. As the CEA describes, the "2018 Economic Growth, Regulatory Relief, and Consumer Protection Act... removes the restrictions from smaller banks that were misapplied to them as part of prior efforts to alleviate the 'too big to fail' banking problem. The CEA posits that this act 'recognizes the vital importance of small and midsized banks, as well as the high costs and negligible benefits of subjecting them to regulatory requirements better suited for the largest financial institutions. [It] is expected to reduce regulatory burdens and help to expand the credit made available to small businesses....'"

President Trump and the 115th Congress also nullified Obama-era (and trial-lawyer approved) rules prohibiting arbitration agreements in financial contracts. His administration stopped the Consumer Financial Protection Bureau's (CFPB) rule "to largely eliminate the payday lending industry.... The CFPB expected that its rule would reduce activity in the payday loan industry by 91 percent, even while acknowledging that consumers found the loans helpful for paying 'rent, childcare, food, vacation, school supplies, car payments, power/utility bills, cell phone bills, credit card bills, groceries, medical bills, insurance premiums, student educational costs, daily living costs,' and other pressing expenses" (quoted from CEA).

Deregulation has a lot to do with populism, by which I mean conflict between everyday Americans and a small, unelected, and insulated ruling class. Special interests want regulations that force consumers to pay more. An effective lobbying tactic has been for them to convince the ruling class that consumers cannot be trusted to buy goods and services of "sufficient quality." Paternalistic regulations that prohibit cheaper health insurance, internet service, automobiles, financial products, etc., give consumers no choice but to purchase the more expensive versions at the same time that the ruling class can tell themselves that their regulations are for consumers' own good. It is no accident that one of the famous books related to modern populism, J.D. Vance's *Hillbilly Elegy*, includes an explanation of why payday loans really are the cheaper alternative for poor people. Special interests have been the losers as the Trump Administration has rejected many, although not all, regulations that were justified based on paternalism. Mick Mulvaney has particularly clear vision on this topic, not hesitating to support even unglamorous deregulations as long as they benefit consumers.

Earlier versions of the Federal Reserve's "Regulation Q" prohibited banks to pay interest to many of their depositors. This price control was relaxed by a law passed before Reagan was inaugurated, although the Reagan Administration helped extend the deregulation to savings banks. Niskanen concluded that the Reagan "Administration was less successful in changing other types of bank regulation."

The Trump Administration has removed or is removing (at times aided by Federal judges' rulings) a number of costly employment regulations from the Obama years. Probably, the costliest of these is the Federal rule, nullified by President Trump and the 115th Congress, giving states permission to mandate employers to enroll workers in state-administered retirement accounts.

Other Obama-era rules imposed large costs on employers and employees for the purpose of giving labor unions a small advantage in recruiting members from new industries. (How democratic is it to have unions setting labor policy, when less than 10 percent of private-sector workers are union members?) As a university professor, I was particularly bothered by the Obama National Labor Relations Board's (NLRB) assertion that university graduate students are employees of their university rather than customers, and thereby should have the terms of the university-student relationship set by labor unions. With President Trump's appointments to the NLRB, this approach was stopped at the University of Chicago just days before it was to go into effect. CEA estimates that employment deregulations by the Trump Administration have net benefits of more than $40 billion per year as compared to the prior trend for labor regulation.

The Department of Health and Human Services (HHS) has some other impressive deregulatory achievements, including enhancing incentives for kidney donation and allowing investigational drugs to be tried by patients suffering from life-threatening conditions. As former Reagan economist Steve Hanke put it in July 2019, "every president since Reagan could have pushed the deregulatory envelope to save lives, but they didn't. Well, Trump did …."

At the same time, over the objections of CEA and other White House components, HHS has proposed a number of prescription drug regulations, such as the rebate rule controlling pricing between businesses (Chapter 10), a rule prohibiting pharmacy "gag clauses," a rule linking prices to an international index, and a rule requiring advertisers to show the "list price" of a drug. The president withdrew the rebate rule, a court struck down the advertising requirement, and (as of December 2019) the status of the international index is still to be determined.

Although it is not included in the estimates above, we should not ignore regulation of energy production. Impressive technological change has occurred with shale production, which refers to new "fracking" and related techniques for extracting oil and gas from underground. The state of New York, controlled by Democrats, prohibits shale production. Many Democrats on the national scene are also calling for a nationwide prohibition. As the President explained at his August 13, 2019, rally in Pennsylvania, "To see the destructive results of the far-left's energy nightmare, just compare the enormous success here in Pennsylvania with the tremendous folly happening … in New York. Both states have vast energy reserves, but New York prohibits development while Pennsylvania welcomes it. From 2010 to 2017, natural gas production plummeted close to 70 percent in New York, but it soared almost 1,000 percent in Pennsylvania."

A nationwide prohibition of shale production would have cost consumers more than $200 billion annually (a CEA estimate). For the lowest one-fifth of households in terms of income, this would be a seven percent loss in their purchasing power. Moreover, contrary to intentions, such a prohibition would add to climate change by increasing annual energy-related greenhouse gas emissions by hundreds of millions of metric tons. The prohibition has this unintended consequence because it increases prices of natural gas compared to coal, which is a dirtier source of energy. The prohibition would also make it more difficult to use wind power, which needs an alternative source such as natural gas that can provide power during lulls.

Using different methods from above, Patrick McLaughlin and former OIRA administrator Susan Dudley also concluded that President Trump's deregulation is extraordinary even when using President Reagan as a benchmark. Dudley's chart, reproduced as the following figure, shows how President Trump's "executive agencies completed 33 final economically-significant regulations, in contrast to 89 during the same period in the Obama administration and 63 in the Reagan administration."

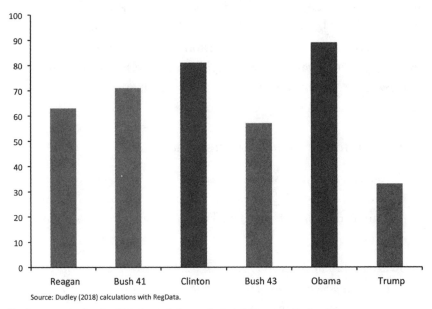

Source: Dudley (2018) calculations with RegData.

Final economically-significant regulations—first eighteen months in office.

With the approval of the U.S. Senate, POTUS appoints Federal judges. In addition to passing laws, appointing agency heads, and approving agency regulations, the appointment of judges is the fourth method by which our elected officials can affect Federal regulation. As of the end of 2019, President Trump had nominated over 200 judges. This puts him on pace to someday surpass the number of appointments by Ronald Reagan, which is the most by any president. The White House estimates that "judges appointed by President Trump are expected to give the Nation more than 2,600 years of combined judicial service." The appointments have a potentially important effect on the amount of regulation because the judges may interpret regulations when they are challenged in court. However, I have not yet been able to quantify this effect on national income, but its potential is significant.

As President Reagan did, President Trump favors the regulation of illegal drugs. Neither was swayed by political opponents gaining some fanfare by promising to deregulate ("legalize") marijuana. Reagan increased sentences for drug offenders, while President Trump's Department of Justice rescinded the 2013 Holder memo (Chapter 4) that had ended Federal prosecution of low-level drug offenders. President Trump has also used regulation, international agreements, and law enforcement to combat trafficking in fentanyl, which is a particularly potent and deadly kind of opioid.

FURTHER WATCHING AND READING

A compelling Reagan speech on free trade is the 1988 video cited in the social media bibliography. This is the source of the quote beginning this chapter. President Trump's quote is from his Twitter account.

Reagan CEA member William A. Niskanen wrote a memoir entitled *Reaganomics: An Insider's Account of the Policies and the People*. Regulation and international trade policy are the subjects of that book's fourth chapter; page 14 discusses the influence of auto companies and the national Maritime Union. He also describes on pages 126 and following how an imperfect interface between the EPA Administrator (Anne Gorsuch, who is the mother of the recently appointed Neil Gorsuch) and the EPA staff stymied possibilities for reforming environmental regulation. The Reagan Administration's *Economic Reports of the President* are also useful sources on these subjects, especially the 1987 and 1989 reports, although I could not find any mention of the chicken tax there. The quotes on IP theft are from pages 135 and 177 of those reports, respectively. I discuss and link these sources on one of my blogs: http://reaganvstrump.com. See also this book's bibliography for various Reagan-era newspaper articles citing trade agreements.

For further explanation of how today's trade patterns with China resemble Reagan-era trade patterns with Japan, see the 2019 Hanke and Li article cited in the bibliography. Steve Hanke, who was an economist in the Reagan administration, writes in a 2018 article that President Trump's Treasury Department wavers on free trade more than Reagan's did. A 2014 law review article by Keith E. Diggs explains how presidents have historically supported the coastal-shipping import prohibition. My sources on pickup trucks include Matthew Dolan's September 2009 *Wall Street Journal* article and aftermarketnews.com.

Professor Douglas A. Irwin published several books on international trade policy and drafted parts of the *1987 Economic Report of the President.* My quotes of him come from pages 81-83 of the 2009 edition of *Free Trade Under Fire,* which discusses the origins of the chicken tax but not that it still exists and acts as an import prohibition. His 1994 book, *Managed Trade: The Case Against Import Targets,* explains how much Japanese companies profited from Reagan-era import quotas, which Irwin prefers to call "voluntary export restraints" in order to emphasize the fact that foreigners have a lot to say as to how they are administered. Indeed, foreign governments were asking the Reagan Administration for these policies.

A University of Chicago dissertation, published in 1969, was the first to show how "rules of origin" provisions, which would later be included in NAFTA and the USMCA, expand the economic boundaries of existing tariffs. A book chapter by Arik Levinson also interprets vehicle-emissions regulations as restrictions on imports. John Frittelli's reports give estimates of the price effects of prohibiting imports of coastal shipping.

The neoclassical growth model, a dynamic version of supply and demand that offers a good representation of "supply-side" factors, is a workhorse at President Trump's CEA. Although the model has been a staple of economic analysis for the past couple of generations (see Robert E. Lucas' 1990 article, Chapter 2 of the *Economic Growth* book by Robert J. Barro and Xavier Sala-i-Martin, Chapter 17 of *Chicago Price Theory*, or videos.chicagopricetheory.com), President Trump is the first president to ever mention it in *Economic Reports of the President*. As explained in the 2019 report, for the purposes of regulatory analysis I used a version of the model that adds a labor market, taxes, and multiple sectors. I did the same for tariff analysis, as I had done seven years earlier for examining the 2008-2009 recession.

The FART act is mocked in a 2018 article by Kate Lyons in *The Guardian*. The UPU tariffs are discussed in a report by CEA, as well as articles by Shawn Donnan, Alfredo Ortiz, and Nick Cumming-Bruce. I also relied on articles about international IP reforms by Fabiola M. Suwanto, Y. Kurt Chang, and Michael L. Doane. An article acknowledging the importance of Chinese IP theft was published by Paul Krugman in the April 5, 2018, *New York Times*.

CEA issued three standalone reports on Trump-era deregulation. In preparing the June 2019 report, I found OMB estimates of regulatory cost to have little relation to the true costs (see also Chapter 7). Therefore, I used "populist" metrics to initially select potentially costly regulations: attention from Congress or from the public as measured by the number of comments on the rulemaking. Much of the deregulation reports is also covered in the 2019 and 2020 *Economic Reports of the President*, which also show how low-income households disproportionately benefit from deregulation. Here I have also included my estimate of the effects of rolling back vehicle emissions standards, which has not yet been included in a CEA report. CEA also issued a report on the benefits of the shale revolution, including a comparative analysis of Pennsylvania and New York. President Trump's speech on this subject is the August 13 video cited in the social media bibliography. My statistics on numbers of judges are from Wikipedia.

A pair of articles, in the *Washington Post* and *Globe Asia*, describe Ronald Reagan's advocacy of privatizing Federal lands, which is a form of deregulation. No privatization occurred during his presidency, but his influence on public discourse may have pushed real changes later.

In an apt example of the perpetual circle of fake news, the 2019 *Washington Post* "fact checked" one of CEA's deregulation reports. Not knowing (among other things) that the most significant deregulations in the 20th century were acts of Congress, its author asserted that CEA exaggerates the effects of deregulation by including acts of Congress in the total. Despite CEA's objections, the *Post* relied entirely on "experts" that privately acknowledged that they had not read CEA's reports on the subject, let alone the actual statutes and regulations that are the subject of CEA's reports. Tellingly, neither the *Washington Post* nor the experts had their own estimate of the effects of Trump-era deregulation even though an initial estimate could have been obtained with some simple arithmetic (see the FCC arithmetic above, the FDA arithmetic in Chapter 9, or the auto arithmetic in Chapter 10). But they are confident that the Orange Man is bad and that anyone working for him has a "thumb on the scale."

9

"FAKE NEWS SHOULD BE TALKING ABOUT THIS"

HOW DEREGULATION REVERSED THE TREND
FOR PRESCRIPTION DRUG PRICES

"Prescription drug prices have been like a rocket ship until I got here."
PRESIDENT DONALD J. TRUMP, JANUARY 23, 2019

OF THE HUNDREDS OF DEREGULATORY ACTIONS taken by the Trump Administration, one is especially revealing about the economics of regulation, national politics, and internal government politics. That deregulation occurred at President Trump's Food and Drug Administration (FDA) when Scott Gottlieb served as its Commissioner beginning in May 2017. A historic reduction in prescription drug prices was the result. Because this partially fulfilled a major promise from his 2016 campaign, President Trump also faced the challenge of convincing the news media to acknowledge what was happening. The "fake news" about drug prices fit a general pattern of news reporting that had emerged after the 2016 election.

TO REDUCE PRICES: DEREGULATE

Economic history has repeatedly shown deregulation to reduce consumer prices by promoting competition among the producers. Deregulation of airlines circa 1980 sharply reduced airfares. About the same time, deregulation of trucking reduced significantly what businesses had to pay to ship their goods by ground. It makes sense that removing prescription-drug regulations at the FDA would reduce what consumers paid for prescription drugs.

FDA deregulation is not to be taken casually. Charged with "protecting the public health," FDA has many rules to prevent unsafe drugs from reaching the marketplace even though it costs the drug companies, and consumers, to comply with those rules. However, other FDA rules were doing more to protect companies' profits and little to protect public health, as Commissioner Gottlieb knew from his days at FDA during the George W. Bush Administration.

When a drug is invented, patented and approved by FDA, the inventor has the exclusive "monopoly" right to sell the drug for several years until the patent expires. After the expiration, other companies can produce and sell the same drug, usually as a generic, which in principle should make the drug a lot cheaper as there would be many more sellers but still the same pool of potential buyers. However, generic drugs must also be approved by the FDA even though such drugs have little need for elaborate testing because patients, health professionals, and manufacturers already have years of experience from when the drugs were sold under patent. The FDA had such a burdensome approval process for generic manufacturers that as few as one company was making a generic. A handful of lucky, or well connected, companies were able to sell a drug they did not invent at a price about as high as when the inventor had the monopoly. Commissioner Gottlieb's FDA changed that.

Take Teva Pharmaceutical, an Israeli company known as the world's foremost producer of generic drugs, with many of them destined for U.S. consumers. Teva's stock crashed in the summer of 2017. Industry analysts said that Teva would henceforth be less profitable due to "greater competition as a result of an increase in generic drug approvals by the U.S. FDA."

From CEA's perspective, it looked like the U.S. generic drug market, which is almost 90 percent of all prescriptions, would be repeating the familiar pattern: regulation removed, more producers enter the market, and consumer prices fall. Lower generic prices might pressure brand names to have lower prices too. By mid-2018, the data clearly showed more producers in the market.

Confident that data showing lower prices would soon be available, Tom Philipson led a CEA team to gather everything we knew about how generic drug approvals work at FDA and how prescription drug prices are measured. The result was a lengthy public report released in October 2018 to little fanfare but serving as a reservoir of industry facts that would repeatedly prove useful in the year ahead.

MOMENT OF TRUTH

As economic advisers to the President, CEA receives new government data the afternoon before the public receives it. January 10 would be CEA's first look at the Department of Labor (DOL)'s Consumer Price Index (CPI) report for December 2018. Because December is the last month of the year, the report would tell us what happened to various consumer prices over the full calendar year of 2018. The drug-price inflation rate reported by DOL would be a progress report on one of the President's signature campaign promises and would help shift the debate between the White House and the Health Department as to whether drug prices should be reduced by deregulation, or by regulation.

I was anxious. Although experience has repeatedly shown me that deregulation reduces prices, new conclusions are best grounded in real-world data. With the Federal government shut down over a funding dispute with Congress, I also worried that there would be no CPI report because the DOL was shut down too. However, the DOL statisticians calculating the CPI were still at work, although it might arrive a bit later than usual.

As it was getting dark, Hershil Shah provided me with the confidential new 70-plus-page report filled with tiny numbers showing inflation rates for everything from "olives, pickles, relishes" to "intercity bus fare." It seemed like an eternity for me to fumble to page 13 where the prescription drug price index appears. And there it was: from the end of 2017 to the end of 2018 prescription drug prices had fallen close to 1% in nominal terms and nearly 3% below general inflation. It had been 46 calendar years since prescription drug prices did that.

Normally, CEA would be working that evening on related economic materials to share the next morning when the data was released to the public and the rest of the White House, but CEA was running on a skeleton crew of about a half-dozen "essential" employees. President Trump was visiting the Mexican border, working on another campaign promise. Kevin, Tom, Rich, and DJ were all out of the office and therefore not allowed to receive communications from me about the findings. I did have CEA's October report on FDA deregulation, whose contents and calculations I committed to memory that evening due to the fact that Tom would not return to CEA for a couple of more days. Hershil and I also drafted tweets for @realdonaldtrump.

During the only restless night of the year, I got an idea. Commissioner Gottlieb was a close friend to three of us at CEA, and I had joined them for dinner in the past. As soon as the public could see the data in the morning, I would send Scott an email with the CPI result. He was already familiar with CEA's October report predicting that his deregulatory efforts would be lowering drug prices. Likely, he would have the entire FDA bragging about it; internally, at least. This might help promote a cooperative spirit the next morning between the White House and the Health Department (the FDA is one of its agencies).

COMBAT WITH FAKE NEWS

Friday, January 11, was the busiest of the year. Email traffic in my inbox tripled. Although excited by the news, CEA and the rest of the White House staff felt pressure that comes with making real progress toward one of the President's signature campaign promises. Filled with people who have an especially low opinion of Mr. Trump, the press and academia would issue mistaken (if not deliberately false) proclamations in attempts to discredit a success for the President.

Secretary Azar's office, the FDA, Kudlow's National Economic Council, the White House Domestic Policy Council, White House Communications, the Office of Management and Budget, to name only six, all had probing questions about how the CPI is calculated by the Labor Department (DOL). What is DOL's prices sample size? Does it reflect list prices? How are the various pharmaceutical products weighted in the overall average? Normally, technical questions like these would require days for a definitive answer, but they were all addressed in the earlier CEA October report. The report allowed me to supply immediate answers and, just as important, assure everyone that the answers themselves had already been given a thorough vetting in October as part of the report's public release.

Based on the day's discussions and edits, CEA sent this tweet language to Dan Scavino: "Drug prices declined in 2018 the first time in nearly half a century. During the first 19 months of my Administration Americans saved $26 Billion on prescription drugs. Our policies to get cheaper generic drugs to market are working!" A new battle with the fake news thus began when it was tweeted by the president.

Within minutes, the Associated Press (AP) had a story that was picked up everywhere from the *New York Times* to the small-town newspaper where I grew up. The headline was: "Trump hails drug price decline not supported by the evidence." We had reached the point where the CPI is no longer evidence, even though the CPI is trusted to set the Federal poverty line, social security benefits, and index thousands of private-sector contracts. CEA contacted AP to remind them of these facts, but of course no apology, retraction, edit, or update was forthcoming. (Repeated experience showed me that, although news outlets never apologize to President Trump and rarely edit a mistake, contacting them is still worthwhile because it slows down the pace at which they repeat a falsehood.) The major news outlets continue to assert that the President's nickname for them, "fake news," has no basis in fact.

As noted in Chapter 3 of this book, failure to read original sources is essential fuel for the perpetual circle of fake news. Matthew Fiedler, an expert with a Harvard PhD who had worked at President Obama's CEA, told the *Washington Post* that drug price inflation was low during the Obama Administration too, except that the CPI inflation rate was skewed up during that time by the entry of some high-price drugs such as new cures for hepatitis C. If he had read CEA's report, or the DOL's methodologies for calculating CPI, he would have known that the hepatitis drugs were skewing the results in the opposite direction (at various times DOL has used "geometric" and "Laspeyres" formulas, whose biases should be familiar to any economics PhD although not laypeople). In other words, the 2018 inflation rate for prescription drugs was even further below the rate from the Obama years than the DOL data show.

To the credit of the *Washington Post*, after much back and forth with CEA, it did lightly edit Mr. Fielder's nonsense about the effect of hepatitis C drugs on the CPI. It even acknowledged that two of the three sentences in @realdonaldtrump's tweet were indeed facts, while the third was a reasonable opinion. But @realdonaldtrump was dishonest nonetheless, says the *Washington Post*, because he dared to include all three sentences in the same tweet without further context. Never mind that tweets are limited to 280 characters and that the White House had already been hosting a detailed public report supplying "context" and containing 30 references to related academic studies.

Later the *New York Times* editorial board would ignore the CPI data, and all data on generic drugs. It asserted, "despite years in the spotlight, [prescription-drug inflation] is no closer to being resolved: Prescription drug prices rose four times faster than inflation in the past six months alone." The website Politifact would assert that @realdonaldtrump was "mostly false" to say that prescription drug prices fell.

Conspicuously absent from all the "fact checks" was any graph of the CPI data. The following figure reproduces the chart from the most recent CEA report. It shows the 12-month inflation rate for prescription drugs back to the year 1970. The months during the Trump Administration are shaded more lightly. The inflation rate ranged from about negative 2 percent in 2019, which means that prescription drug prices fell by an average of 2 percent over the 12 months, to about 13 percent in 1982. The chart shows quite obviously that price changes for prescription drugs are unusually low—negative, in fact—in 2018 and 2019 to a degree that is unmatched since the early 1970s. The President's political opponents do not want you to see this figure.

CPI for Prescription Drugs, Jan. 1970 to Sept. 2019. Source: CEA October 2019.

To be charitable to news organizations, perhaps they have a sixth sense that something is wrong with the CPI data used in the figure and are yearning for a different formula, lacking the technical training to articulate their concerns. If so, then an excellent opportunity to measure progress toward the President's campaign promise was missed less than a month later when Express Scripts released its *2018 Drug Trend Report*. Not only does Express Scripts have one of the world's largest databases on consumer costs for prescription drugs, but it measures drug-price inflation using "unit cost," which is a formula that is significantly different from those used in the CPI. But the fact is that the major news outlets were silent about the report's findings. Might their silence be explained by the fact that unit costs were less in 2018 than they were the year before, closely in line with the results coming out of the CPI formula? Or that the report highlighted "the lowest commercial drug trend in 25 years"?

The American public knows what is going on. As President Obama's communication director put it, "the voting public ... has a great bullshit detector." He advised "objective news sources" to "abandon normal political spin to ensure that our statements, positions, and analyses of the other sides are factually bulletproof. The smallest error will allow Republicans to call the truth 'fake news,' but we have the power to deny them that opportunity." The news organizations have shown how often they disagree with Mr. Pfeiffer.

CABINET MEETINGS WITH POTUS

At first, I was a bit disappointed to see my place card on the President's side of the table, where it would be difficult to make eye contact with him. But I would soon learn about the four phases of a Cabinet meeting.

The Cabinet Room is on the same colonnade, along the Rose Garden, as the Oval Office. It has fifteen or more chairs, with a slightly larger chair in the middle for POTUS with its back to the Rose Garden. The first phase of the meeting occurs without the President. We all stand when he enters the Cabinet Room, often from the colonnade, for the second phase of the meeting. The third press phase begins when President Trump says, "Let's bring in fake news." The two hallway doors, which are on the opposite side of the room from the Rose Garden, open and the press rushes in with microphones, camera booms, and lights. Phase three is torture for those sitting across from the President. The press is packed into that side of the room, pressing against the backs of the chairs at the table. Microphones and cameras are shoved in between the heads of those on that side of the table. The fourth and final phase consists of press questions. At some point, Press Secretary Sarah Huckabee Sanders would tell the press, "The meeting is over! It is time for you to leave!" and begins to herd the press back into the hallway. As she directs them, they yell last minute questions to POTUS, pausing their retreat whenever he teases them with a bit of an answer. But the retreat continues.

When the President meets with a smaller number of Cabinet officials, the same four phases play out in the Roosevelt Room across the hall. One of these smaller meetings occurred on the afternoon of January 23. The agenda included various deregulatory efforts by DOL and the Health Department related to health insurance, as well as the problem of "surprise medical billing." But, twelve days after the new CPI data, POTUS was frustrated that the press was not talking about it. In the 17 minutes of the press phase, the President talked about the CPI data four times. By now, "first time in nearly half a century" had turned into "first time in over fifty years."

An hour later, POTUS was across the hall in the Cabinet Room in a meeting related to immigration. Again, the CPI data became a topic. Now, it was "prescription drugs, for the first time in the history of our country, have gone down in 2018. So, for last year—just got the numbers—for the first time in the history of our country, prescription drug prices have gone down. They've been like a rocket ship until I got here." He added that "you guys [the press] don't want to report it, but that's a big thing, because drug pricing has been very important to me...."

Two weeks later, as part of the 2019 State of the Union Address, it was back to "in 2018, drug prices experienced their single largest decline in 46 years." He continues to cite one of these variations, so many times that I have lost count.

NO JOY IN MEDIAVILLE

Working on the Affordable Care Act (ACA) for several years, I saw news reporting about the law unrelated to what was actually in it and what was actually happening with its programs. Wondering about the accuracy of news outside my area of expertise, on arriving at the White House I aspired to compile a "fake news" file. Not taking the label lightly, my file would collect only news articles with reporting that contradicts my firsthand experience. Soon, I realized that the sheer volume would overwhelm me.

Take the July 30, 2018, *New York Times* article by Robert Pear. For context, please note that, prior to the Trump Administration, I found Mr. Pear to be far more dependable about the ACA (the subject I knew firsthand) than other reporters. His 2018 article characterized an internal Trump Administration debate over expanding Medicaid (the Federal health insurance program for the poor) as "furious." The opposite happened. Unlike a typical debate among, say, university professors, this debate was mostly through exchanges of polite memos and responses to memos. Ultimately, when we met in person, a voice was raised only once (Secretary Azar took some offense at the memos, perceiving them to insinuate that he is a "lefty secretary"), which was immediately followed by sincere apologies from Mick Mulvaney and others of the senior staff. Again, by comparison university faculty meetings are the furious ones.

The article went on to say that "some senior officials" supported expanding Medicaid, while in fact it was only Secretary Azar and, temporarily, Andrew Bremberg. Mr. Pear made the supporting list look longer by citing the Administrator of CMS, who works for Azar but did not attend the meetings or author the memos. Of course, no other sub-Cabinet personnel were listed because that would show how outnumbered the Secretary was. Instead, Mr. Pear gives the impression that the opponents of expansion were fringe players in the debate, "hard-liners," who just got lucky that POTUS did not go ahead with the expansion.

Mr. Pear acknowledges that his source was a "confidential memorandum written to help inform the White House decision." One of the memos, I wrote, while the others I had read carefully, so Mr. Pear would have known that there were other memos expressing opposition to Medicaid expansion. Mr. Pear's article does not acknowledge the existence of those memos or cite their conclusions. Instead, Secretary Azar's "confidential memorandum" was repeatedly quoted as if it were the entire story. In light of these half-truths, President Trump's decision would appear arbitrary, at best.

An enormous number of other "fake news" articles were written about the White House and I have documented some of them in this book. With the amount of time needed, I decided that it would be far easier to collect articles with reporting that matched completely my firsthand experience. Over an entire year, only two were found (not counting *Wall Street Journal* articles, which contributed many correct stories). Curiously, one of them was published by the website buzzfeed-news.com. Entitled "Inside the Trump Administration's Secret War on Weed," it described new internal deliberations about the harms of producing, trafficking, or using marijuana. The article accurately omitted CEA as one of the components that was assembling information about these harms. The second article was published in June 2019 by politico.com, describing the ideological divide between the Health Department and health experts in the White House. Although I disagree with much of the commentary in both articles (e.g., anyone disagreeing with Secretary Azar is "hard-line"), the various statements they represented as facts agree with my firsthand experience other than the occasional exaggeration. The politico.com article is particularly unusual in the sheer number of its accurate statements. When I expressed my amazement to White House staff, I heard third hand that the politico article used more than a dozen sources, which if true would help explain how it achieved what no other article did.

Another veteran of the Reagan Administration (and conservative television personality), Mark R. Levin, has recently published a book entitled *Unfreedom of the Press*. The book's purpose is to "jump-start a long overdue and hopefully productive dialogue among the American citizenry on how best to deal with the complicated and complex issue of the media's collapsing role as a bulwark of liberty, the civil society, and republicanism." Although he wrote it before the events of this chapter took place, they fit the same pattern. Levin identified the core problem by citing journalist Jim Rutenberg: "If you're a working journalist and you believe that Donald J. Trump is a demagogue playing to the nation's worst racist and nationalistic tendencies, that he cozies up to anti-American dictators and that he would be dangerous with control of the United States nuclear codes, how the heck are you supposed to cover him? . . . [I]f you believe all of those things, you have to throw out the textbook American journalism has been using for the better part of the past half-century ...." To me, that's the best lens through which we should understand reporting about prescription drug prices, deregulation, tax cuts, and about every other aspect of today's economy. My experiences have shown that any fact that is favorable to President Trump, other than the obvious or unavoidable, will go unreported by the "fact checkers." Citizens are left on their own to confirm or deny the validity of what he says.

Standing with my family on the White House North Lawn on the evening of Sunday March 24, 2019, anyone could see the sky's glorious color behind the majestic slate roof of the Eisenhower Executive Office Building. We were near the end of a West Wing tour. The next and final exhibit was the Press Briefing Room, which is a small auditorium with its own external door so that credentialled members of the press can come and go as they wish. We ran into several glum faces. One reporter was sitting in a chair with his tired chin propped up by the palm of his hand. Another drooping journalist sighed and stepped out the door. In close to ten tours, not to mention dozens of walks past the press room during business hours, never had I seen anything like this. What happened to ruin their day? Did a beloved celebrity unexpectedly pass away?

It turns out that Attorney General Barr had just released a summary of the key findings of the famous "Mueller Investigation." The investigation, which had been confidential up to that point, had long been hyped by major news organizations as driving toward, to use U.S. Congressman Nadler's words, "very substantial evidence that the President is guilty of high crimes and misdemeanors...." Such a finding would have been a sad moment in our nation's long history. In saying the opposite, the Mueller report and Mr. Barr's summary should have been celebrated. That the White House correspondents found no joy that evening speaks volumes.

FURTHER WATCHING AND READING

CEA's 2018 report on FDA deregulation of prescription drugs is called "The Administration's FDA Reforms and Reduced Biopharmaceutical Drug Prices." CEA also expected that the inflation rates shown in the figure would eventually become positive again, perhaps in mid 2019, which means that the consumer savings from generic deregulation continue indefinitely but stop growing in amount. This assumption is reflected in a June 2019 report from CEA that put the FDA deregulation in the context of some of the legendary deregulations in U.S. history, such as airlines and trucking. In October 2019, CEA released a report supplying a glossary of terminology around drug prices, a comparison of methodologies of eight price indexes, and specifically addressing several false statements in the press. Brett Matsumoto, who is normally one of the DOL experts preparing the prescription-drug CPI, wrote most of the October 2019 report while he was on detail at CEA.

The figure supplies a rough indicator of the consumer benefit from reduced prescription drug prices. If those prices would have continued to increase at 4 percent per year after 2016, that would put them 8 percent higher after two years. In fact, they fell about 2 percent over two years, and therefore were around 10 percent below the earlier trend. With the average household spending about $2,700 annually on prescriptions (including what they pay in taxes to support government programs buying prescription drugs), that is an annual savings of $270. While a full calculation would also account for additional gains and losses as the price changes ripple through the U.S. economy, the $270 from one market's deregulation shows why the cumulative effect of deregulating more than one hundred markets would easily be in the thousands of dollars per household per year.

President Trump's State of the Union address is online as a transcript as well as on YouTube. Three cabinet meetings where he discusses the decline in prescription-drug prices are also cited in the social media bibliography. In his December 17, 2019, letter to House Speaker Nancy Pelosi, President Trump cited the decline in prescription-drug prices as well as policy achievements described elsewhere in this book.

INDUSTRY LOBBYISTS EXPOSED BY A ROBOT

THE "YOUNG GENIUSES" TAKE ON THE
REBATE AND CAR RULES

"Henry Ford would be very disappointed if he saw his modern-day descendants wanting to build a much more expensive car that is far less safe and doesn't work as well...."
PRESIDENT DONALD J. TRUMP, AUGUST 21, 2019

"...this rule is corporate welfare...."
VICE PRESIDENT MIKE PENCE, APRIL 3, 2019

FROM MY FIRST REGULATORY MEETING TO MY LAST, I was shocked at the proximity of special interests to the rulemaking process, their obfuscation techniques, and how near they came to staining President Trump's deregulatory program. The efforts of the Health Department to cover its mistakes related to the opioid epidemic are covered in Chapter 4. The maritime industry's proximity is discussed in Chapter 11. This chapter explains how two other regulations, which I call the "rebate rule" and the "car rule," proceeded through the regulatory process. That process begins when the Administration writes, and internally deliberates about, a proposed rule. The proposal then is published for the public to see and provide comments as to how the rule should be edited or rejected entirely. Finally, the Administration considers the public comments and either rejects the proposal or edits it before making the final rule the law of the land.

Both processes illustrate how special interests have long been the primary authors of the rules for their industry. Under the guise of "industry expertise," they deliberately obscure how they have written the regulations in their own interest. With some assistance from their advisers, both President Trump and Vice President Pence saw through the smokescreens and took historically unusual steps to help the general public understand the essence of their personal stakes in the rules. One of the rules was withdrawn before going into effect and the other rewritten in a compromise with the companies.

CORPORATE WELFARE

"We are going to blow up the way the industry does business!" These are the first words I heard in my first regulatory meeting. They came from Health Department staff sent to the White House by Secretary Azar to introduce his proposed "rebate rule," which is officially known as the "Removal of Safe Harbor Protection for Rebates Involving Prescription Pharmaceuticals." How could I be hearing this in an administration dedicated to removing costly Federal constraints on business? Minutes before, I had been assembling the CEA's case against government central planning. The *Wall Street Journal* noted the contradiction between White House principles and Health Department practice, when reporting on it three months later.

"Rebates" are checks reluctantly written *by* drug companies *to* health insurance plans. Much in the same way that a food manufacturer asks a grocery store for scarce prominent shelf space, or a beverage manufacturer asks to be exclusively offered on a restaurant's menu, each drug manufacturer asks health insurance plans to give their product special placement (in terms of, say, percentage reimbursed by the plan). The store, or restaurant, or health plan may grant the manufacturer's request, but only in exchange for a steep rebate on the product, which are savings that ultimately benefit consumers. For health plans covering prescription drugs, the consumer savings come in the form of lower monthly premiums (the insurer's payment of claims needs less premium from consumers when there are more rebates from drug companies).

Naturally, drug companies would prefer not to write rebate checks, but they must write them to remain competitive. Unless, of course, they could convince the Federal government to end the practice. Secretary Azar's rebate rule was proposing to do exactly that, at least in the Medicare segment, which is about one third of the prescription-drug market. Drug companies would no longer be allowed to write rebate checks to Medicare drug plans. If legal, the proposed rebate rule would increase the profits of drug companies and increase the Medicare premiums paid by senior citizens and taxpayers.

The rule is properly understood as a business-to-business price control. It is business-to-business regulation because it restricts transactions between two businesses: a drug maker and a Medicare insurance plan. Business-to-business regulations are especially difficult to justify because, by virtue of operating a successful business, business people have shown that they can look out for themselves without micromanagement from the government. The rule is a price control because the rebate is an important part of the price that insurance plans pay for drugs.

Sheepishly (it was my first regulatory meeting), I inquired how the Health Department had determined whether these business-to-business price controls would operate as proposed, rather than collapsing under the weight of unintended consequences as so many other central-planning schemes had. They proudly recounted how they "showed this to the President of Pfizer [a major drug company] and he thought it was an excellent idea!" (In addition to a veteran of the Health Department, Mr. Azar is also former president of the U.S. division of another major drug company, and thereby personally acquainted with industry executives.) The culture of regulation is so ingrained at the Health Department that it did not occur to them that, in a room full of White House staff enthusiastic to help "drain the swamp," drug-company approval of a regulation helping protect it from competition would be seen as convincing evidence that the regulation contradicts administration priorities.

The special interests had additional strategies for writing this rule and concealing its costs. The Federal Register, which is the daily publication of the U.S. government agencies, is supposed to show estimates of the effects of major proposed regulations. For rules issued by the Health Department, its actuaries are tasked with preparing the estimates, known as "Regulatory Impact Analysis" (RIA). To their credit, the actuaries were not swayed by the Secretary's untactful objections (to be charitable to the Secretary) to their RIA estimating benefits for drug companies and $196 billion in costs to taxpayers. Secretary Azar therefore broke precedent and hired a consulting firm, also working in the drug industry, to prepare alternative estimates.

A sharply-dressed bearded man stood up near the door of the White House meeting room and bellowed, "HHS, you need to hear OMB loud and clear: your AKS RIA is DOA!" and exited the meeting. As several others filed out of the room behind him, I leaned toward CEA's General Counsel Joel Zinberg and whispered, "That must be a world record for number of acronyms in one sentence. What the hell does it mean?" Joel chuckled and said, "I have no idea, except that we're going to enjoy working with that guy."

That guy was Joe Grogan, who at the time was the Office of Management and Budget's (OMB) Associate Director of Health Programs. The leadership at OMB was appalled that the Health Department (HHS) would be proposing a single regulation that took $196 billion out of the Federal budget over ten years by increasing the premiums on Medicare plans, the majority of which are paid from the Medicare budget. AKS refers to "Anti-Kickback Statute," which is the law to be reinterpreted by the rebate rule and what DOA refers to as "Dead on Arrival" at the White House; the OMB would not give the rebate rule its required blessing. Either Secretary Azar would withdraw this rule or President Trump himself would settle the dispute.

SPECIAL POWERS?

A couple years before, Chicago graduate and Clemson University Professor Tsui called me with unpleasant news. "Are you aware of Spence's paper? His conclusion about price controls is the opposite of ours." Michael Spence, not to be confused with Vice President Mike Pence, is a Nobel Laureate in economics, whose article about price regulation has been cited over a thousand times. An error in our paper would mean a year's worth of work wasted. "I have not seen it, please send me a copy and I'll take a look," I said.

Normally there would be a pit in my stomach for the several (unscheduled) hours that it typically takes to reconcile two technical papers. But this time I was confident. In less than 30 minutes, I emailed Tsui back with the conclusion. "Take a look at Spence's long footnote on page 420, it has his crucial mistake." For light amusement, I let Tsui digest that for the afternoon and to wonder what special powers of mine resolved it so quickly.

I do not have special powers, but I did have brand new automated reasoning software, which I call *TheoryGuru*. *TheoryGuru* allows me to input economic assumptions, such as the assumptions in our paper, Spence's paper, or a government agency's rulemaking, and then pose various queries. The software, which I wrote to augment Stephen Wolfram's *Mathematica* computing system, takes a second or two to answer a query as "true," "false," or "maybe." Without the software, such answers might take hours or days to obtain "manually." *TheoryGuru* is for a technical economist what an electronic cash register is to a retail cashier. The more complicated the query, the greater is the software's advantage.

Our price control paper had been recently confirmed by *TheoryGuru*, which gave me confidence. Because the automated-reasoning machine had said "true," there is no way that Spence or anyone else could show otherwise. I quickly found Spence's mistake by feeding his assumptions to *TheoryGuru* and then querying the truth of his conclusions. Later, I called Professor Tsui to confess that it was a machine, rather than me, behind the emailed conclusion.

TheoryGuru proved to be well suited for the White House, where time pressures are high and economic questions can be mercilessly complicated. Automation also helps in the White House where there is only a tiny number of employees in comparison to the employment in the executive agencies it aspires to supervise. One of *TheoryGuru*'s first major uses would be to evaluate claims about the Health Department's proposed rebate rule coming from the drug industry.

"KEVIN SHOULD REWRITE THE RULE"

Shortly after Mr. Grogan's parade of acronyms communicated OMB's disapproval, Director Mick Mulvaney was in the Oval Office telling President Trump how expensive the proposed rebate rule would be. Secretary Azar tried to refute this with the consulting company's alternative estimate. Secretary Azar pointed out that the Medicare program and the business-to-business transactions related to it are complicated, so that the government actuary's estimates are fallible.

Under pressure from President Trump to "do something about drug prices," Secretary Azar had found a genuine distortion related to rebates. However, the rebate distortion reflects a more fundamental problem with Medicare's "reinsurance" formula. He was proposing regulations of business-to-business pricing that were excessively complicated and lucrative for drug companies. The distortion would be fixed better at its source, as does the Medicare modernization proposal in the President's budget. As President Trump would later explain in Green Bay, "But prescription drugs, look, it's a rigged system, OK, if I told you how crazy it is, the Web, it's the Web, you need 193 I.Q. to even understand. This web of geniuses, they put this thing to lower drug prices. It has 19 effects here and 27 …."

Referring to CEA's Chairman, President Trump said, "Kevin should rewrite the rule." Legally the proposed rule had to be written by the Health Department, but what he meant is that CEA would be the internal referee in the technical aspects of the dispute. (POTUS knows the policy instruments well, reminding staff often in 2019 with otherwise promising ideas that "We cannot do that with regulation. It requires Congress and therefore will not happen.") Refereeing would not be easy because, among other things, the Medicare prescription drug program has longstanding price controls, complicated subsidy formulas, to which the rebate prohibition would be adding. Kevin gulped and headed back to set Tom and me to work. Although he is a computer aficionado and had to approve the Federal purchase of my *Mathematica* license, Kevin probably did not know what *TheoryGuru* would do for us.

Tom and I conducted multiple technical interviews with the government actuaries, OMB Medicare experts, the Secretary's adviser, and the private consulting company hired by the Health Department. The latter two regularly reminded me that, unlike them, I had zero prescription-drug-industry work experience. The Secretary's adviser also privately asserted to the various White House components that Tom and I had no clue how the Medicare prescription-drug program works.

In parallel, I built a computer model of the prescription-drug supply chain and its regulation. Both the government and private consultants confirmed that the rebates vary dramatically across products, with some drugs sold with high rebates and others sold with none. Asking the consulting company why this happened, I was told that manufacturers found variable rebates to be more profitable than uniform rebates. So, I told *TheoryGuru* that manufacturers were maximizing profits. *TheoryGuru* returned a contradiction between that assumption and the private consultants' conclusion that manufacturer pricing would be uniform after the rebate rule went into effect. On the next call with the private actuaries, I asked them why we should expect the drug companies to use uniform pricing after the rule went into effect, when that pricing would not be maximizing their profits. Despite their industry knowledge, the consultants had no answer.

The logical mistake (I do not know their intent) helped the consulting company to conclude, contrary to the government actuaries and pleasing to their client (Secretary Azar), that the rebate rule would not result in particularly high profits for drug companies or particularly high premiums for senior citizens. CEA prepared its referee memo on the rebate rule, putting the mistake at about $50 billion.

The various White House components hoped that, aided by CEA's finding, President Trump would reject the rebate rule at the next Oval Office meeting. Secretary Azar was unphased, dismissing the nonuniform pricing projected by CEA as "borderline illegal." (Mr. Azar is an experienced lawyer and knows what is legal; his "borderline" qualifier is an acknowledgement that nonuniform pricing is legal and would occur.) As described in Chapter 1, at this point POTUS did not follow the advice of either side. The proposed rule would instead be taken to the next stage of the rulemaking process, which is to publish the proposal on the internet for public comment. Later the White House would reconvene with Secretary Azar to write a final rule considering the public comments.

Remembering how President Trump said, "Kevin should rewrite the rule," I insisted that the Health Department eliminate inaccuracies before publishing its proposed rule. First on my list was its estimate of the costs of the rule's unintended consequences. The department was saying that its rule, designed to "blow up the way the industry does business," would have unintended consequences limited only to wasting a bit of time for businesspeople to read the rule and reread their contracts and then for consumers to read the revised contracts. The department's estimate of the associated costs was a mere $56 million per year in a $150 billion industry segment, or less than 0.05 percent. Both the character and amount of their estimate were absurd. They were also contrary to the directives of the Office of Management and Budget's Circular A-4, and contrary to the department's own internal guidelines. I edited the proposed rule to replace their cost estimate with mine, which turned out to be about 200 times larger. The OMB rejected my edits, saying that it was not a good time (the government was shut down over a funding dispute with Congress) to ask the Health Department to perform better. The department's indefensible practices, which contribute to obscuring how rules benefit special interests at the expense of the general public, had endured for decades. It would be a long journey, OMB said, to shepherd it to compliance with OMB directives. OMB would later begin the journey by seeking public comment on "Marginal Excess Tax Burden as a Potential Cost Under EO 13771," which outlined the simple procedure I had used earlier that year to better estimate the costs of the proposed rebate rule. OMB is now recommending that all agencies follow it.

Although the rebate rule's numerical estimates would not change, OMB did back me up on editing its prose, such as false and misleading statements about why the consulting company's estimate was purportedly superior to the government actuaries. The adviser, who Secretary Azar put in charge of writing the rule on behalf of the Department, fought me on every edit. One set of false statements appears in the table on the third page of the proposed rule, which has an incorrect formula because the adviser (the same aspiring central planner accusing Tom and me of technical ignorance) did not account for the placement of rebates in the requirements for reconciling Medicare payments to prescription drug plans. Despite my repeated explanations and citations to Medicare rules, he still refused to fix the formula and the numbers in the table because they provide an impression that is opposite of the conclusions of the government actuaries and CEA. The compromise was to add a footnote to the table explaining what the table omits, which was a cryptic way of saying that the table does not illustrate what happens to rebates in the actual marketplace.

He also refused to delete one of the Secretary's false talking points about drug price inflation, so the compromise was for me to insert a truthful sentence after it (as explained in Chapter 9, echoing one of the President's tweets). The first page of the published proposed rule therefore has this mutual contradiction: "Since 2010, the prices of existing drugs have been rising in the United States much more rapidly than warranted either by inflation or costs. Since 2016, the prescription drug part of the consumer price index grew 2 percent less than inflation, and one official measure of drug price inflation was actually negative in

2018, for the first time in almost 50 years." Other false (and internally contradictory) statements, such as "The Rebate-Based System Harms Beneficiaries," remained in the published version despite my protests.

POTUS DECIDES

The public gave 25,905 comments on the rebate rule. The Congressional Budget Office also prepared a budgetary estimate for the rule, which was close to the estimate by the government actuaries. Secretary Azar then acknowledged that his proposed rule would increase Medicare premiums shortly before the presidential election. At the April 3 meeting cited in Chapter 2, President Trump sat with arms folded while he listened to Secretary Azar concoct a scheme to temporarily offset the premium increase with a Federal "risk corridor" subsidy for Medicare prescription-drug plans. (The complicated scheme further strained the relationship between Secretary and CMS Administrator because it used, for political rather than scientific purposes, her authority to conduct a "demonstration.")

Then Vice President Pence walked in, unscheduled. While Brian Blase offered his chair at the Resolute Desk to VPOTUS, POTUS said, "Why don't you guys explain that all again for Mike?" Brian and Secretary Azar obliged. To my relief, VPOTUS conveyed his understanding by summarizing, "It looks like this rule is corporate welfare for both drug companies and insurance companies."

However, the President's experiment was still incomplete. He said, "I want you 'young geniuses' to put your heads down and move ahead with this." We understood that as an expression of appreciation for our skills and an acknowledgement of our disappointment. Three months later, President Trump unequivocally ended the rebate rule.

In an interesting epilogue, the Health Department thought that it might still have the authority to publish a final rule without any cooperation from the White House. Secretary Azar's adviser called OMB to ask what would happen if the department, contrary to POTUS' instructions, failed to withdraw the rebate rule. OMB explained that it would have no choice but to issue a "return letter" that, despite its sanitized language, would be a stern public rebuke of the department. The rule was withdrawn. As Tom and I predicted, drug manufacturers were upset, including the manufacturer where Secretary Azar had been president.

CAR COMPANIES DON'T WANT YOU TO READ THIS

Eighty-six dollars is the number that car companies do not want you to see because it shows how they profit by overcharging consumers for environmental protection. The protection is delivered through regulations on automobile manufacturing that were authored by the Obama Administration and then revised by the Trump Administration while I was there. In the pages that follow, I explain how the $86 was discovered and how car companies succeeded in keeping it hidden, until now.

To help fight climate change, Federal "CAFE and GHG" regulations require vehicles (cars and light trucks) sold in the U.S. to abate carbon dioxide emissions (i.e., emit less greenhouse gas or "GHG"). Eighty-six dollars per ton of GHG is what the consumers were paying on vehicles bought between 2012 and 2016 in order to comply with the regulations. The worldwide benefit of GHG abatement has been studied extensively and by all accounts is far less than the $86 per ton. Simply put, as of 2016, the vehicle regulations needed to be relaxed and climate policy to adopt alternative methods with costs that do not exceed benefits.

The Obama Administration did the opposite in the vehicle regulations it set for the coming decade. Consumers would be forced to abate more tons, which would prove to be more expensive (i.e., more than the $86) per ton abated than the already expensive abatement that occurred under earlier regulations. Why would the Obama Administration elevate consumer costs far beyond the environmental value? One answer is that the ruling class would not pay much of the $86 because they live in big cities and drive less. They are also more likely to buy an electric car that, unlike the average car, would not see much of a price increase as a result of President Obama's restrictions on vehicle emissions. A considerable number of them are content with any carbon reduction paid for by other people.

Eighty-six dollars may not seem like much until we look at it per car rather than per ton. The average new car emits more than 40 tons of carbon during its lifetime, and each ton would cost progressively more as the regulations become stricter. As a result, President Obama's regulations would have added $2,900 to the average price of a new car. The corresponding environmental benefit would be worth only $600 to the world and even less to the United States. The following figure shows these added costs and worldwide benefits on a per car basis.

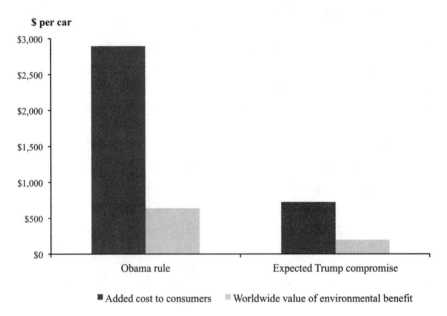

President Obama's rule had consumers overpaying $1,700 per car for an environmental benefit, even under the liberal assumption that each ton of carbon dioxide abated is worth $50.

It is not just the environmental lobby that is content to fight climate change regardless of what it costs the consumer. The American car companies (Ford and General Motors) favor regulation too. Recall from Chapter 8 that all presidents since Johnson have used the chicken tax to protect them against foreign competition. President Reagan also protected them with a quota on Japanese imports. In effect, President Obama protected them with a quota on European imports, because

European companies tend to specialize in selling the higher-emissions vehicles whose sales are especially limited by the CAFE/GHG regulations. As a result, the emissions regulations would have them paying fines either to the government or to other car companies. Yes, Ford and GM would incur some costs to reduce the emissions of the vehicles they sell, but the reduced European competition is expected to more than compensate for that.

To the horror of the ruling class, Trump won the 2016 Presidential election. Reversing President Obama's plan to have vehicle consumers overpay for carbon abatement was expected to be the crown jewel in President Trump's historic deregulatory portfolio. Indeed, one of the star lawyers in the Trump Administration, Jeffrey Rosen, first served on the presidential transition planning team to help begin the regulatory budget (Chapter 7). Rosen then became Deputy Secretary of Transportation to help write the proposed "SAFE rule" reversing the Obama CAFE/GHG regulations. When that was complete, President Trump moved him to Deputy Attorney General where he will, among other things, be overseeing litigation about the SAFE rule.

Even as late as 2018, the $86 per ton was still unknown. An estimate like that was implicit in the Preliminary RIA jointly prepared by DOT and EPA, but the car companies could rest assured that the public (and most experts) would never understand the RIA's 1,625 pages, let alone the regulation of which it was a part. The thick cloud of mystery gave the car companies room to have the SAFE rule significantly rewritten if they could only convince President Trump.

CEA discovered that 1,625 pages are unnecessary to see that vehicle consumers were overpaying for carbon abatement. The shortcut is to look at the market for carbon credits that the Obama Administration created among car companies. Like most other markets, the carbon-credit market supplies quantitative information as to what are the net private costs of adjustments in the behavior of producers and consumers. The price of carbon credits thereby quantifies the private cost of reducing vehicle emissions by, for example, engineering or by skewing sales toward lower-emission models. Comparing the private costs with the environmental benefits is just a matter of a small bit of arithmetic that can be proved in half a page, or in a simple chart.

The $86 is revealed from transactions among the companies during the years 2012 through 2016 and reflects the extra cost to consumers of changing the composition and engineering of vehicles so that less GHG is emitted per vehicle. The $86 is very much in the spirit of OMB's Circular A-4, which strongly recommends the use of market or "revealed preference" information in regulatory impact analysis. There is no substitute for seeing what people do when they are spending their own money, as they do in real-world markets. I confirmed this with OMB/OIRA experts in February 2019, including one of them who is both an expert on transportation regulation and an author of Circular A-4 (OIRA is the part of OMB that tracks regulations). Jeremy Weber and I also visited DOT to get some of their economists' reactions to CEA's approach. They had no fundamental objection either on principle or with our results, which turned out to be similar to the bottom line of the 1,625-page Preliminary RIA DOT prepared with EPA.

Although the $86 is the result of simple arithmetic, precisely connecting it with the economic effects of regulation was not easy. There was confusion among economists in the administration whether the extra fuel cost of operating a high-emissions vehicle had to be added to the cost of GHG credits (at $86 each). The veteran macroeconomists in the administration were dubious that CAFE/GHG regulations would have any effect on GDP. They are among the most knowledgeable in the world as to the formulas used in the national accounts to calculate Gross Domestic Product (GDP) and other measures of national economic performance and had been looking at such measures for decades as the regulations evolved. *TheoryGuru* was essential here too, especially for clarifying my own thinking and ensuring that conclusions were robust to various real-world complications. I then used it to construct a concise proof that, according to the official government formulas, relaxing the GHG emissions standard by one ton would increase real GDP by exactly $86 per vehicle. Relaxing the standard by a larger tonnage, as the Trump Administration is doing, would increase GDP even more.

Encouraged by most White House components, I continued with the preparations of an estimate of the total value of President Trump's deregulatory portfolio. Once the deregulations were finished and had their full effects on the economy, they would increase annual real household incomes by about $4,000, I estimated by adding the effects of twenty-one of some of the most consequential rules. The car rule was the crown jewel of the twenty-one. Breaking protocol (I'm not complaining!), one senior staff member marched straight out of our meeting in the Roosevelt Room, across the hall, and into the Oval Office to tell President Trump about CEA's draft report. Not much later, POTUS mentioned in at least one speech that deregulation would be increasing real incomes by at least "$3,000" per family. But there was not yet any public report giving the details.

TRUTH CAPTURED BY SPECIAL INTERESTS

I always knew that a simple demonstration would be a problem for the domestic car companies. I told my CEA colleagues as much, but naively assumed that the companies were too far away to know what CEA was preparing. In fact, they or their allies in the administration saw the draft report circulating internally for comments and edits.

The first objections I misunderstood to be merely technical. The objections had rigorous technical answers (some produced by *TheoryGuru*), which I supplied. Then the correspondence got weird.

As huge fans of deregulation, Larry Kudlow and his National Economic Council (NEC) presumably wanted the concise demonstration of its value that was contained in CEA's draft report. Although CEA never heard Larry's opinion, others at NEC said that they would not allow the report to be released. Nobody at NEC answered my emails (Brian Blase had just returned to private life). So, I went over to the West Wing and Larry's office, where I was cryptically referred to another NEC staff member back in the Eisenhower Executive Office Building.

He also did not answer my emails or phone calls.

With the Federal government lacking so much knowledge about how the world works, I knew that NEC serves a legitimate function of interfacing with the business community. Larry knows many CEOs personally. This was my first clue that objections might be coming from car companies.

The acting OIRA Administrator, who had requested CEA to produce the report, was also not answering my emails or calls. His deputies did not answer either. Obviously, there was a problem under the surface that was sufficiently embarrassing that OIRA and NEC did not want CEA to know about it. Curious with this unprecedented behavior, I waited in the hall outside the acting Administrator's office until he exited. Although surprised, he did not divulge anything. I did the same with the NEC staff, who also did not divulge anything but put me in touch with an attorney who would arrange a conference call between DOT, EPA, OIRA, CEA, and the Department of Justice (DOJ).

The first part of the call consisted of misinformed proclamations from DOT (not the same people that Jeremy and I met) that the $86 was fundamentally inaccurate. But then DOJ expressed an understandable concern. CEA was using the $86 to evaluate the proposed car rule, but it would be better if CEA waited to see the final car rule to be released later in the year. This was a controversial rule and, predictably, there would be attempts to overturn it in court, putting billions of consumer dollars at risk. One of the tactics of a rogue judge might be to point to analysis from CEA that was not described in the proposed rule, even though legally CEA has nothing to do with writing or enforcing the rule (that is the job of DOT and EPA). Although frustrated that we could not assume that judges would follow the law, I agreed that a CEA report was not worth risking billions of consumer dollars. They half-heartedly accepted what I proposed, that CEA would rewrite its report to quantify the costs of President Obama's rule, without any mention of rules from the Trump Administration.

We rewrote the report. Without looping in DOT or EPA, DOJ let slip that it approved. CEA's revised report would not impair DOJ's ability to defend President Trump's car rule in court. More importantly, the revised report clearly showed how President Obama's rule was forcing consumers to far overpay for carbon abatement. This would pry loose the true secret.

The true secret was that the car companies want consumers to overpay for carbon abatement. In their view, the overpayment is a feature of President Obama's rule, not a bug. They thought that President Trump's rule needed, at the very least, to be revised so that consumers would continue to overpay to some degree. The car companies, I believe, communicated this to DOT, EPA, or NEC; or all of them. Despite DOJ's concurrence, DOT and EPA refused to let CEA's deregulation report say anything about car rules. CEA's "interim" deregulation report was officially released without mentioning the President's single biggest deregulation, or the Obama regulation that preceded it.

It was clear to me that the car companies were rewriting the car rule. Other White House staff insisted that the signature deregulation would be finalized with little modification. Then in August 2019, @realdonaldtrump broadcast, "My proposal to the politically correct Automobile Companies would lower the average price of a car to consumers by more than $3000 while at the same time making the cars substantially safer. Engines would run smoother. Very little impact on the environment! Foolish executives!" To the untrained eye, POTUS appeared to reject the car companies' request to rewrite the rules. To the contrary, this tweet, which was his first ever on the car rule, meant that he was considering more than one option. President Trump is an experimenter (Chapter 1 of this book), and the tweet was part of an experiment to determine what would be the political cost and benefits of standing up to the car companies versus compromising with them.

In case there was any doubt which car companies were pressuring, hours later @realdonaldtrump tweeted, "The Legendary Henry Ford and Alfred P. Sloan the Founders of Ford Motor Company and General Motors are 'rolling over' at the weakness of current car company executives willing to spend more money on a car that is not as safe or good and cost $3000 more to consumers. Crazy!" This was followed by a pivot to an anti-California theme: "Henry Ford would be very disappointed if he saw his modern-day descendants wanting to build a much more expensive car that is far less safe and doesn't work as well because execs don't want to fight California regulators. Car companies should know that when this Administration's alternative is no longer available California will squeeze them to a point of business ruin. Only reason California is now talking to them is because the Feds are giving a far better alternative which is much better for consumers!"

Two months later, the *Wall Street Journal* broke the news that the administration was revising its car rule. The emissions standards would be tightened from what they are now. On the other hand, the revised rule would only be about one-third of the way to President Obama's standard in terms of miles per gallon and about one-fourth in terms of costs to vehicle consumers (recall the figure). The car companies continue to be one of a dwindling number of creatures that survive in the Washington DC swamp, sustained in part by concealing the consumer harms that result from regulations of their industry.

FURTHER WATCHING AND READING

The economics of rebates is examined in a 2008 article by Klein and Murphy and in Chapter 13 of *Chicago Price Theory*. The fact that drug companies vary rebates across their products is known in economics as "Ramsey pricing," which I refer to as "nonuniform pricing" in this chapter. Ramsey pricing is the topic of a 1992 article by William G. Shepherd and dates back to a query posed to the Cambridge University economics guru Frank P. Ramsey by one of his teachers. If the rebate rule had gone into effect, I expect that drug companies would have offered discounts to pharmacies that vary across drugs (rebates to insurance plans or their "pharmacy benefit manager" representatives would not be allowed). President Trump's discussion of the rebate rule is in the Green Bay rally video cited in the social media bibliography.

TheoryGuru has a bit in common with the 2016 election: it defied repeated expert predictions. Referring to the quantifier-elimination technique driving *TheoryGuru*, mathematician Charles Steinhorn predicted that "quantifier elimination is something that is do-able in principle, but not by any computer that you and I are ever likely to see." In 2014, a group of artificial intelligence experts warned that the "practical limit to obtain a solution would be at most five variables." *TheoryGuru* shows instead that quantifier elimination works in the real world, where my typical application involves about 20 variables. I have been working with computer scientists James Davenport and Matthew England to figure out why it works so easily. Part of the reason is the ingenuity of Stephen Wolfram's *Mathematica* software, which includes Adam Strzeboński's algorithms. Nikolaj Bjorner and Leonardo de Moura wrote *Z3* software that can answer many of the same questions with an entirely different algorithm, which means that *TheoryGuru* and *Z3* can mutually assure anyone who suspects that one or the other has a software bug. Stephen Wolfram's 2017 book is an enjoyable introduction to *Mathematica*, and available free online with hands-on demonstrations. Computer scientist Christopher W. Brown has published accessible explanations of the jargon in the field.

Undistorted by passion, automated reasoning may serve another purpose. If the often-cited "Trump Derangement Syndrom" has any truth to it, some of President Trump's opponents are so upset by the 2016 election that they can no longer think or reason cogently. Likewise, President Obama's communication director concluded that "Barack Obama drove Republicans insane." Controversy tends to go unresolved in such an environment. Gottfried Leibniz, one of the legends in the history of mathematics, envisioned "calculators" that would provide the resolution. He wrote in 1688, "if controversies were to arise, there would be no more need of disputation between two philosophers than between two calculators. For it would suffice for them to take their pencils in their hands and to sit down at the abacus, and say to each other (and if they so wish also to a friend called to help): Let us calculate" [translated from German].

More resources on this topic are available at my web site http://help. economicreasoning.com/. It includes a three-minute video exposing a fundamental logical error in Paul Krugman's analysis of the recession. Another example disproves commentary about the 2017 tax cut by Obama economists Jason Furman and Larry Summers. Is it unfair that they do not have a Leibniz calculator? I provide *TheoryGuru* free on the internet, but cannot force anyone to use it.

Environmental benefits are not enough by themselves to justify the CAFE/GHG regulations for vehicles. By most accounts, the worldwide benefit of abating a ton of carbon is $50 or less. The Environmental Protection Agency (EPA) and Department of Transportation (DOT) estimate that the benefit to the U.S. is far less than $50. As illustrated in a 2018 *Science* article, President Obama's EPA/DOT instead asserted *private* benefits. As an article by Sanstad and Howarth put it, consumers are purportedly "not merely ill-informed about energy technologies but also have trouble determining how to make 'correct' choices when provided with full and complete information. Thus, policies of various kinds are justified to ensure that consumers reap the benefits of energy-efficient technologies as identified by technical experts." According to EPA/DOT, stricter vehicle regulations would confer personal benefits, well beyond any estimate of the environmental benefit.

The paternalistic vehicle rule is proof of real substance behind populism. There really are Federal employees who think that the public cannot be trusted with choices such as buying the correct type of vehicle for their family. The Trump Administration's proposed SAFE rule rejected paternalistic justifications for stricter regulations.

As I write this, the Trump Administration has not yet publicized its final car rule or how it will justify regulations that are in between what they are now and what the Obama Administration had proposed. My estimates for that rule (e.g., the previous figure) are therefore estimated from the requirements described in the October 2019 *Wall Street Journal* article. The $86 private cost per ton cited in this chapter is calculated as the ratio of revenue received by Tesla for its sale of GHG credits, as reported on its website, to the number of credits it sold as reported by the EPA.

It is widely known in economics that vehicle-emissions standards are an excessively costly method of fighting climate change; see the articles by Crandall, Morris & Wardle, and Levinson. But it is increasingly politically incorrect to oppose climate policies, not to mention to support President Trump, so this result often goes unmentioned these days.

11

"DO I HEAR A CRY FOR HELP OUT THERE?"

SWAMP CREATURES PROTECT PUTIN'S BOOTLEGGERS

"…the best transportation secretary ever for the U.S. maritime industry."
AMERICAN MARITIME PARTNERSHIP, JUNE 5, 2019

"HELP … HELP…." As a foggy sunrise approached on August 10, 1981, he had been floating in Long Island Sound for more than five hours, his body temperature had dropped below 95 degrees, his energy was completely spent, and he had given up hope.

But Richard K. Lublin was about to have a stroke of luck at the end of the tragic evening. When the birds began chirping in the morning twilight, Lublin guessed that he was near enough land that a person there might hear even though he was not capable of yelling that loud.

"Do I hear a cry for help out there?!" Reggie Tuthill was accustomed to rising early on Monday mornings, but not to hearing voices from the

Sound. "Help, I'm drowning" was the reply.

Tuthill's wife called 911. Their shore has no piers or marinas, but the Tuthills did have a small rowboat pulled up on the rocks. Reggie got in the rowboat with his teenage son, issuing the warning, "Drowning people can be dangerous … if this man tries to pull us into the water, beat him with an oar." But Lublin was terribly weak and "did not have the strength for one more swimming stroke." The Tuthills slumped Lublin's torso over the stern and rowed him the 125 yards to shore where the Orient Fire Department would later treat him for hypothermia.

KILLED BY THE JONES ACT

Richard K. Lublin would survive, but his wife and three neighbors with Lublin on his 36-foot pleasure craft *Karen E* did not. Lublin's three neighbor children were left orphaned. The vessel *Karen E* was named after daughter Karen E. Lublin, who was ten years old when she too perished that night. All five were killed, in an instant likely, when the *Karen E* was smashed by an unmanned 300-foot barge loaded with 6,400 tons of cargo pulled by the tug *David McCallister*. The collision occurred more than 5 miles away from the spot where the Tuthills found Lublin.

With 1,100-foot tow lines, the *David McCallister*'s towing arrangement resembled that shown in the following figure. Single ships would better perform the same shipping tasks, as they do in other countries. But the dangerous tug-barge operation has become dominant in the United States because of a 100-year-old Federal law known as the Jones Act.

The uniquely American, and uniquely dangerous, tug-barge towing operation. 2019 image credit Casey B. Mulligan.

The 1920 Jones Act requires that all domestic shipping occur on ships that are U.S. built, U.S. crewed, U.S. registered, and owned by U.S. companies that are controlled by U.S. citizens. As an outright prohibition on the import of crews or vessels for the purpose of coastal shipping, the Jones Act is the ultimate act of protectionism that is far more harmful to consumers than a tariff or quota would be (recall Chapter 8). Customers of domestic shipping, who are primarily businesses that want to move cargo between various destinations in the U.S., are captive to the domestic maritime industry. As a result of the Jones Act's protection, the domestic maritime industry has been overcharging its customers by a factor of five to eight in comparison to the cost of foreign crews and vessels, if they were allowed. As explained in the pages that follow, these costs are passed onto American households in the form of higher prices for energy and other commodities, added pollution and mortality, and lower real wages.

By increasing costs by a factor of five to eight, the law has by now all but ended domestic coastal shipping and U.S. ship building. The unmanned barges like the one that sank the *Karen E* are the least-expensive work arounds that remain. Transporting the cargo shown in the previous figure with a single ship, as other countries do, and staying compliant with the Jones Act would require more crew expense than is needed with the unmanned barge. Such a ship would also have to be bought in the U.S., where it is prohibitively expensive.

PAYING RUSSIA TO BE OUR BOOTLEGGERS

A sizable amount of the cargo that, without the Jones Act, would be shipped on coastal waters ends up on trucks congesting our highways and polluting our atmosphere, especially near large cities where many people live and breathe. Other cargo ends up on circuitous international routes.

Natural gas is one of the products taking the circuitous route. Natural gas is consumed all over the world, but most of the natural gas reserves are in Russia, the Middle East, and the United States. Russia was once part of the Soviet Union, whose socialist government owned nearly all property, which was later sold off corruptly when the Soviet Union collapsed in 1991. Corruption continues in Russia today, with Russian President Vladimir Putin at its center. Russia's natural gas company, Gazprom, is the largest in the world. One would think that Gazprom would serve customers in the Eastern Hemisphere while American companies served customers in the Western Hemisphere, but the Jones Act upends transportation logistics and further enriches Gazprom.

Take the shipping of natural gas to consumers in Massachusetts, where winters are cold and overland gas pipelines rare. American businesses and Massachusetts consumers would gain tremendously if natural gas could be shipped from coastal terminals in Maryland or Georgia (less than 1,000 miles), especially in the winter. However, the Jones Act currently prohibits coastal shipments of natural gas because all of the world's ships equipped to carry natural gas are foreign built and therefore cannot operate on routes along the U.S. coasts. As with the alcohol prohibition of the 1920s, the prohibition of natural gas shipments creates profit opportunities for bootleggers.

Here is how it works. Foreign ships bring Russian natural gas thousands of miles across the Atlantic Ocean (the Jones Act does not apply to international routes), where they unload it in Massachusetts for almost $9 per thousand cubic feet in liquified form (known as LNG). The empty ships then make a short trip down the east coast where they refill with LNG at bargain prices as low as $3 per thousand cubic feet and then cross the ocean again to deliver to their final customers in Pakistan. From the point of view of the consumers in Massachusetts and Pakistan, and from producers in Russia and the U.S., this transport system is hardly different from running illegal bootlegging routes up the American east coast while delivering natural gas directly from Russia to Pakistan. Either way, the Russians get to pocket $6 per thousand cubic feet ($9 in Massachusetts minus $3 in Maryland or Georgia) at America's expense. The circuitous international route makes it all legal. You're welcome, Gazprom! You're welcome, international shippers!

The 1920 Jones Act's tragedies of life and economy have occurred for decades, with no Republican or Democrat administration making any sincere effort to stand up to the special interests supporting it. The anecdotes on the following pages are specific to the Trump Administration only because of my proximity to it. One way or another, the entrenched special interests have been firmly established in every administration (and Congress) in our lifetimes, or else the Jones Act would have been overturned long ago. Indeed, Presidential candidate Barack Obama wrote to the Seafarers International Union that "your members can continue to count on me to support the Jones Act ... and the continued exclusion of maritime services in international trade agreements." Presidents Reagan, George H.W. Bush, Clinton, and George W. Bush also expressed enthusiastic support for this prohibition of maritime (coastal shipping) services imports.

President Donald Trump and Russian President Vladimir Putin take press questions in Helsinki, July 16, 2018. Kremlin.ru photo licensed under the Creative Commons Attribution 4.0 International license.

President Trump hates the Jones Act. It is the type of harmful regulation that he has succeeded in ending in health insurance, telecommunications, farming, and many other industries. He hates that America has fallen so far behind shipbuilders in China, Korea, and Japan. He and others on his staff find it ridiculous that nowhere on earth is there a single LNG carrier that fits the Jones Act criteria. Quite literally Massachusetts consumers must rely on international shippers to do the bootlegging on their behalf. On top of all of that, standing next to Russian President Vladimir Putin on July 16, 2018, with the world watching, President Trump was pointedly asked by a journalist why the U.S. was buying "Russian gas for Boston" (the first half of the "bootleg" transaction).

The Jones Act includes a waiver process, which in principle could be applied to the Massachusetts, Puerto Rican, and other situations where the lack of a land transport option is enriching foreign shippers too. With an LNG waiver, Americans would be getting the $6 profit per thousand cubic feet that is now paid to the Russians for selling gas in Massachusetts for $9 and buying back for $3 further south on the U.S. east coast. The LNG-waiver process culminated in an April 22, 2019, Oval Office meeting attended by Department of Transportation (DOT) Secretary Chao, Peter Navarro, Kevin Hassett, National Economic Council (NEC) Director Larry Kudlow, Kevin Harrington (a senior director in the National Security Council), and a few others. Chao and Navarro were the only ones favoring the status quo: a Jones Act without waivers and thereby continued "bootlegging" by international shippers. In their view, all of the LNG carriers on earth, which are foreign built, should be prohibited from transporting natural gas from U.S. producers to consumers in Massachusetts, Puerto Rico, or anywhere else in the country, even if it means enriching Russian gas companies.

I am unable to confirm what Navarro's interests may be in supporting the Jones Act. However, in an attempt to dissuade CEA from concluding that the Jones Act has costs far outstripping its benefits, he provided a report from a fake think tank (with the address of the parking lot of the Washington DC Seafarers International Union, which is the labor union for workers in the maritime industry). Chief of Staff General Kelly was also annoyed with Navarro's persistent attempts to defend such flawed protectionism.

Special interests are more entrenched at DOT (see also Chapter 10).

It is public knowledge that Secretary Chao's family is in the international shipping business (Foremost Maritime Group), which is a potential conflict of interest for her because the Jones Act induces domestic shipping customers to hire international shippers to take their cargo on the circuitous international routes. She and her husband, Mitch McConnell, who holds the most powerful position in the U.S. Senate, received millions of dollars of gifts from the Chao shipping family. Senator McConnell had also been named a "Champion of Maritime" by a lobbying group whose stated purpose is to defend the Jones Act. But President Trump resisted the appeals from Chao and Navarro. He asked his staff to take the next step, which was to arrange a White House meeting with members of Congress.

Key Republican Senators, including the two Senators from Louisiana, Mississippi, and Alaska came in the next week. Also attending was a Congressman from Louisiana who won the 2017 "Champion of Maritime" award. All of them are well funded by the sea transport industry yet came remarkably uninformed about the Jones Act's harm to the safety and livelihoods of the people in their states or the rest of the country. President Trump was taken aback by their willingness to spend political capital to perpetuate such a broken system. He decided, for the time being, not to pick a fight with them.

The special interests could not have gotten any closer to the President's Resolute Desk than they did on April 22. Anyone doubting this must be unaware of the next chapter in the story. A month later, Secretary Chao was named the inaugural "American Maritime Hero" by the same lobbying group that earlier honored her husband and the Congressmen who pressured POTUS to, in effect, let the Russian bootlegging continue. Secretary Chao, they gushed, "is widely recognized as the best transportation secretary ever for the U.S. maritime industry."

MORE CRIES FOR HELP

Mr. Navarro, Secretary Chao, and their allies in Congress continue a long tradition of plugging holes in protectionism for the maritime industry. Before the Jones Act, the International Seamen's Union (the precursor to the Seafarer's International Union) lobbied for—and wrote much of—the 1915 Seaman's Act. Officially known as the Merchant Marine Act of 1915, the law imposed a set of featherbedding work rules (requiring an excessive number of maritime workers) on "all merchant vessels of the United States." With the luxury liner *Titanic* sinking shortly before, the Seaman's Union added an appealing tagline, "Lifeboats for All" (today's "Medicare for All" tagline is not entirely new). This addition to the bill included detailed specifications for numbers, dimensions, and arrangement of lifeboats. Although an articulate anti-protectionist, President Wilson could not resist the pressure by the Seaman's Union to sign its "Lifeboats for All" bill.

Once the Seamen's Act went into effect, the Seaman's Union was discouraged by the exploitation of loopholes for using foreign vessels. They demanded stricter prohibitions of foreign vessels and crews from domestic shipping services, which they got five years later with the Jones Act. But the Seamen's Act had another predictable, and tragic, consequence. A shipping manager testified to Congress in 1914 that the lifeboat requirements were unnecessary (coastal shipping routes are quite different from the *Titanic*'s) and probably dangerous. If a lake passenger ship followed every requirement enumerated in the law, "[t]he extra weight of lifeboats and rafts would make them top-heavy and unseaworthy ... some of them would turn turtle...," he predicted. Months later, on July 24, 1915, the *SS Eastland* capsized at its dock in the Chicago River (the following figure). As with the Lublin tragedy, the *Eastland* disaster was the predictable result of following Federal regulations in the real world where people also make mistakes and are sometimes even negligent. Having followed the requirements of the Seaman's Act, the top-heavy Eastland had no margin for operator error. Eight hundred forty-four people, primarily workers and families from the same Hawthorne factory cited in Chapter 1, drowned that day. Although my city of Chicago has famously suffered from fire, riots, and flooding, none of these come close to the death toll of that "Blue

Collar Titanic."

View of the Eastland taken from the Fire Tug in the Chicago River, showing the hull resting on its side on the river bottom. Image credit: Max Rigot Selling Company, Chicago [Public domain via Wikipedia Commons]

Natural gas is not the only market in which both domestic businesses and households are harmed by the Jones Act. Oil producers in Texas and elsewhere near the Gulf Coast are outcompeted for East Coast business by foreign producers from Nigeria, Saudi Arabia, and Canada. As shown in the following figure, the Congressional Research Service calculated that oil shipping rates are three to five times greater when originating in the Gulf Coast as compared to an international origin. Perversely, it can be cheaper for the Gulf Coast producers to ship their oil out of the country and then bring it back to our east coast than to ship it by the direct coastal route.

The pattern of simultaneous import and export of oil (see also the following figure) is repeated for other commodities because domestic companies can use foreign crews and vessels only when they are shipping to or receiving from a foreign port. The Congressional Research Service reports that annually millions of tons of ammonia, sulfur, nonferrous scrap, and nonferrous ore are both imported to, and exported from, the U.S. by ship. Yet none of these commodities is shipped between domestic Great Lake ports because the Jones Act, and the prohibitive shipping costs it requires, applies to those domestic routes. A 2013 report by the Government Accountability Office explains how, because of the Jones Act, Puerto Rico "generally does not purchase [fuel] from U.S. suppliers because the total cost is higher" and will instead "typically import fuel to the island from foreign countries, such as Venezuela, rather than from Gulf Coast refineries."

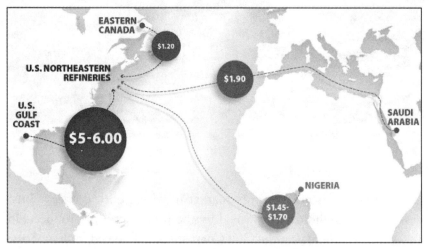

Ocean Oil Shipping Rates to U.S. Northeastern Refineries. Image credit comptroller.texas.gov.

Recall the (inaccurate) conventional wisdom that most regulation protects the environment. The reality is that regulations protect special interests, of which environmental groups are just a small fraction. The Jones Act's artificially high coastal shipping costs are at the behest of a domestic maritime industry that does not want to compete with foreign crews or vessels. The industry protection provided by the Jones Act ends up harming the environment by encouraging land transportation rather than cleaner but artificially expensive coastal shipping routes. Jones Act ships (i.e., those that are U.S. built, U.S. crewed, U.S. registered, etc.) only see any demand "serving Alaska, Hawaii, and Puerto Rico ... where shippers have little alternative," explains the Congressional Research Service. Otherwise shipments are diverted to land, where more fuel is consumed, roads are congested, and air pollution is aggravated near large population centers. An article by Stacy Yuen explains how even the cows may travel by the environmentally dirtiest mode: "Big Island ranches must charter a weekly 747 out of Keahole Airport [Hawaii] to get their cattle to the mainland because that's cheaper than Jones Act shipping. There's something wrong with that picture."

Protectionism usually comes with excuses attached. For the Jones Act, national security is offered as the excuse. In theory, the act creates a larger fleet of American-owned ships that our military could use in case of emergency. But the opposite has happened. The number of ocean-going ships compliant with the Jones Act fell below 100 in 2015 after exceeding 400 in 1950. The annual tonnage of U.S. coastwise cargo carried by ship has fallen from about 250 million in 1980 to about 70 million in 2016. The fact that coastwise cargo carried in other countries, which eliminated their versions of the Jones Act decades ago, more than doubled suggests that the Jones Act has not increased the number of American-owned ships. The U.S. now has zero LNG carriers, zero project cargo vessels, and zero heavy-lift vessels, which is contrary to the stated objective of the Jones Act to "have a merchant marine of the best equipped and most suitable types of vessels."

The act also fails to expand capacity for building large government vessels because different types of builders manufacture large vessels and Jones Act ships. Also because of the Jones Act, our nation is less secure as its east coast is consuming foreign fuels, rather than fuels from Florida, Texas, or other locations on the U.S. Gulf Coast. President Trump's

National Security Council believes that the Jones Act does even more harm to our national security than it does to our economy. Time will tell if the oars of the maritime special interests are big enough to beat back President Trump's historic agenda for deregulation and energy dominance.

FURTHER WATCHING AND READING

No research was needed to discover harm from the Jones Act; the Tuthills are my beloved in-laws. In addition to their memories of the incident, I also reviewed U.S. Coast Guard reports; charts; news articles from UPI, *The New York Times*, and others; and two August 1981 letters from the surviving Lublin family to the Tuthills. All but the Lublin letters are available online.

More explanation of the *Eastland* disaster is available in George W. Hilton's two books *Eastland: Legacy of the Titanic* and *Lake Michigan Passenger Steamers*. Page 11 of the former has the quote from the Senate testimony. The former book also explains how many shipowners in both Britain and the U.S. understood the dangers of the "Lifeboats for All" requirement driving the Seamen's Act's passage. The January 13, 1914, *New York Times* described the bill as "written for the Seamen's Union." The YouTube video cited in the social media bibliography shows original footage of removal of victims' bodies from the Chicago River. A Smithsonian.com article by Susan Q. Stranahan further describes the lifeboats-for-all movement. President Wilson's opposition to protectionism is described in an article by William Poole. "Shipping Under the Jones Act," published by the Congressional Research Service, describes the early regulatory history of coastal shipping in the U.S., as well as the trends for the size and cargos of the Jones Act fleet.

Centuries ago, Britain's Navigation Acts also prohibited, for the purposes of national defense, the import of foreign crews and vessels. Book IV of Adam Smith's *Wealth of Nations* acknowledged the trade-off between national income and defense, but concluded that the Navigation Acts "very properly endeavor[] to give the sailors and shipping of Great Britain the monopoly of the trade of their own country, in some cases, by absolute prohibitions...." Seven decades after Smith wrote, Gibson and Donovan's maritime history book explains, Britain's naval warfare looked more like the U.S. today in terms of scarcely using private vessels. In that environment, as John Lewis Ricardo wrote, "the impolicy and mischievous tendency of the maritime laws" were obvious and Britain repealed its Navigation Acts. (This is the nephew of the Ricardo cited by Mr. Navarro in Chapter 8.) The Gibson and Donovan book describes an entire portfolio of Federal policies currently protecting the maritime industry as well as their unintended consequences.

University of Chicago graduate Bill Browder was an early shareholder in the Russian gas company Gazprom. The shares he bought were soon worth 100 times what he paid for them, in part because he exposed some of Gazprom's corruption, making it more difficult for management to steal company assets from the shareholders. For more, see his thrilling memoir, *Red Notice: A True Story of High Finance, Murder, and One Man's Fight for Justice*.

The economics of liquified natural gas (LNG) and other energy production was an active subject of research at CEA, resulting (among other things) in energy chapters in the *2019 and 2020 Economic Reports of the President*. As part of that effort I prepared a last-minute monthly crude oil production chart for our March 18, 2019, meeting with the President. It showed U.S. production surging past Saudi Arabia and thereby exceeding every other country in the world. This chart was deep in a stack of materials for him but, as I expected, President Trump read ahead (while Kevin Hassett was reviewing findings for Lou Dobbs on speaker phone—recall Chapter 2) and declared the chart to be his favorite in all of the 700-plus page *2019 Economic Report of the President*.

The Cato Institute hosts a seven-minute podcast in which Colin Grabow explains how U.S. producers of LNG export to locations around the world, except U.S. locations. The Jones Act makes the domestic shipping literally impossible because none of the world's LNG carriers are compliant with the Jones Act. The podcast further explains how the Jones Act burdens Puerto Rico, which harms national security and protects no U.S. jobs.

NEC Director Larry Kudlow was actively engaged with improving energy trade. I learned a lot on the subject from Larry and his staff, the military detailee to the NSC who led maritime policy coordination, Andrew Rollo (on detail from U.S. Customs and Border Patrol), and Kevin Harrington (introduced above). Because the aforementioned military officer had the audacity to speak truth about the Jones Act's harms to safety, industry, and national security, Peter Navarro tried to use his influence to have the USCG intervene in this officer's planned rank promotion. It would appear White House staff are not the only ones keenly aware of Navarro's rudeness, ignorance, and dishonesty because the military did the opposite: despite Navarro's efforts to intervene on a military promotion on political grounds, this officer was promoted to the senior officer ranks in a White House Rose Garden ceremony.

The lobbying group conferring the "Champion of Maritime" awards is the American Maritime Partnership, which states its purpose as defending the Jones Act requirement that "any vessel transporting goods or passengers between two points in the United States ... must be U.S. owned, U.S. built, and U.S. crewed," asserting that the requirement is "in the best interests of the nation." *Forbes*, the *New York Times*, *Politico*, and *Vanity Fair* reported Secretary Chao's receipt of multimillion-dollar gifts. The *Politico* article cited a spokesman for Senator McConnell as confirming it. When asked by *The Intercept* about a possible conflict of interest between Secretary Chao's international shipping connections and her role at DOT, a

DOT spokesperson responded that "there is no conflict of interest" because DOT does not regulate foreign-flagged ships. With that response noted, a layperson might still notice an appearance of a conflict of interest because the Secretary is in the Oval Office opposing waivers to the Jones Act, which is driving shipping business toward the international shipping market, as it has with the delivery of LNG to Massachusetts and several other commodities cited in this chapter.

I found that, in contrast to Mr. Navarro, Secretary Chao is a kind and gracious person. Her agency hosts a web page full of complements that she has received from maritime union officials. That page also confirms that her designation as American Maritime Hero occurred in the month following the Oval Office meeting where she discouraged POTUS from even granting a waiver to the Jones Act. Her files at the Ronald Reagan Library and Museum show that she has collaborated with the Seafarers International Union and on issues related to the Jones Act during the Reagan Administration too. Candidate-specific tabulations of political donations can be found at opensecrets.org.

WHAT WE LEARN ABOUT OUR PRESIDENT AND OUR GOVERNMENT

"Yet, in holding scientific research and discovery in respect, as we should, we must also be alert to the equal and opposite danger that public policy could itself become the captive of a scientific-technological elite."

PRESIDENT DWIGHT D. EISENHOWER, JANUARY 17, 1961

THIS IS POPULISM

Populism is a reaction to flawed governing by a small, unelected, and insulated ruling class. The small class size is evident from the number and range of lead characters, both Democrat and Republican, that I had met in my professional life well *before* arriving at the White House. They include (but are not limited to) Ben Bernanke, Jeb Bush, Rich Clarida, Mitch Daniels, Martin Feldstein, Austan Goolsbee, Jonathan Gruber, Larry Kudlow, Nellie Ohr, George P. Shultz, Larry Summers, and Cass Sunstein. Even the Trump White House has one of the highest concentrations of Harvard alumni anywhere in America (Harvard alumni are less than 0.1 percent of the population). It's only a slight exaggeration to say that we all know each other. The White House, or at least parts of it, became so insulated during the previous administration that it reached a point at which the leading official justification for new regulations would, remarkably, be the numerous Harvard connections of the administration's experts.

Members of the ruling class, which include many in the journalism profession, care about their country and want to serve. But they also make real mistakes, a few of which are documented in this book. Lacking vigorous competition, the ruling class has little incentive to find its mistakes, or to acknowledge others who find them. Challenging fellow members of the ruling class carries personal risks and takes energy that could be directed in other ways. Political correctness can be comfortable, but handicaps clear thinking. Meanwhile, the ruling class too often mocks and dismisses populism as nothing more than a primitive "us-versus-them mentality."

The gulf between the ruling class and the rest of America is the accidental star of *The Final Year*. The intent of the film was to highlight the 2016 activities and achievements of "30 people setting the direction for the entire U.S. government and in that way the entire world." Those officials display little interest in the everyday concerns of Americans during the film. Neither the opioid crisis nor the recession is mentioned. Creating jobs for international refugees gets more screen time than creating jobs for American workers. By late on election night, the best that they can discern is that the "retrenchment forces got their hands on the levers of power."

The self-correction incentive is increasingly absent as the ruling class has become less accountable to elected officials. Independent agencies have grown in responsibility and been created anew. Take the Consumer Financial Protection Bureau (CFPB) discussed in Chapters 7 and 8. Career staff at the CFPB sued to prevent President Trump's appointee from sitting in the leadership position, merely because he was appointed by POTUS. Another lawsuit, which has now made it to the

Supreme Court, alleges that POTUS cannot remove a CFPB director.

Even the executive agencies, such as the Department of Justice or the Department of Health and Human Services, are insulated from elected officials by a growing web of technical, managerial, and legal complications. How could an outsider ever succeed in leading such a complex organization without the sympathy and cooperation of the veteran staff? It's only natural that a new president, including President Trump, would often appoint Cabinet Secretaries who had previously worked as a Secretary or Deputy-Secretary.

Voters paying for the ruling-class mistakes elected President Trump to disturb this state of affairs. Three attributes of the President are helping him obtain the requested results. The first is his extraordinary communication skill. He, or any populist for that matter, must bypass those journalists who prefer the ruling class to continue undisturbed. As documented in this book, my repeated experiences have shown me that any fact that is favorable to President Trump and not already in plain sight is unacknowledged.

President Trump successfully uses Twitter to bring more issues to the attention of the general public. Unconstrained by political correctness, he has drawn attention to illegal immigration, the opioid epidemic, the enforcement of intellectual property rights in China, the (formerly) high taxes on business, the movement to prohibit private health insurance, criminal justice reform, (formerly) rising prescription drug prices, and excesses of the climate change movement. Earlier administrations either ignored most of these problems or made them worse.

President Trump's political incorrectness makes it more difficult for the ruling class to see any real substance in populism. As they dismiss populism as racist, fascist, etc., they fan the populist flames that they wish to extinguish. Denying and obfuscating the President's obvious successes does not help. The other side of the coin is that President Trump's support comes almost exclusively from the voting public. If and when the voters say, "You're fired!", neither political party will have a place for him.

Historically, the policy influence of populism was limited because of the fractured populist movement. Dueling populist factions continue today, but so far candidate and President Trump's communication skills have succeeded in holding them enough together to achieve his policy goals. Just as significant, President Trump keeps his opponents divided too. Drawing attention to Medicare for All, issues of international trade, and the "rigged" 2016 Democratic primary have served this purpose.

RUNNING THE GOVERNMENT LIKE A BUSINESS

Second, President Trump remembers business practices that can be usefully applied to the Federal government. He no longer allows a Federal agency to make regulations merely because it unilaterally decides them to be beneficial. Each agency also must show that the costs of its regulatory portfolio remain within a budget determined by the White House. For the first time, the independent agencies must also have their regulations reviewed by the President's team.

Another one of those practices is deal making, by which I mean changing a bundle of business practices at the same time. Although "trade deals" with Mexico, Japan, China, and other countries receive much attention, the biggest deal of all has been with citizens and businesses within our own country. Many of us previously benefitted from a regulation protecting our own industry or occupation, while far more costs were paid due to the thousands of regulations protecting others. As illustrated in this book, nobody wants to disarm unilaterally in the battle for special interest favors. President Trump achieved mutually beneficial disarmament when he implemented the regulatory budget and ended hundreds of the special-interest regulations.

Regulatory budgeting and deal making also fits well with the President's communication strategies. It is too much to ask the public to engage with each of the thousands of individual regulations that needs to be removed. Although the sum of regulation is important to everyone, few of the regulations are glamorous or sizeable by themselves. But President Trump does communicate with voters about the totals as summarized in the regulatory budget and by the analysis of CEA. At the same time, he brings life to the summary totals with significant illustrations such as prescription drugs or automobiles.

Another business practice is to recognize the staff's talents and how they fit into the trajectory of the organization. The leader of a business, or division, is often a different person during the start-up phase than in a mature market phase. This turnover pattern is clear in the Trump Administration, as discussed in Chapter 5 in connection with Brian Blase, Andrew Bremberg, and General Kelly. Should we admire an administration that keeps its personnel for a full eight years because those staff are slow at doing their work?

Third but not least is President Trump's skill with experimentation. Smart people have occupied the White House before, trying incremental policy adjustments that did not deliver results. President Trump's typical experiment is deliberately disruptive, as demanded by his supporters and often needed for progress. As with the individual mandate, the rebate rule, competing in the 2016 election, and much more, the benefits from disruption are in monitoring the feedback.

In my meetings with major university presidents and top executives of large companies, I have been impressed by their rare talents. It is not surprising that they would reach the highest levels in their profession. Donald Trump's talents are even rarer. Although I am an avid fan of the National Football League's Chicago Bears, it was not until the 1990s that I first attended a game. The running back on the other team, Barry Sanders (not to be confused with U.S. Senator Bernie Sanders), ran through, around, and over my team like they were amateurs. Sanders' exceptional abilities were plain watching him in person on the field in a way that I had never appreciated on television. Yes, he was human but an example rare enough that I may never see again. What I saw that day was not enough for me to declare that Sanders is the best running back ever. But it was enough to pity the teams that had to play against him. Seeing President Trump in person conveys the same general impression as to how he compares with his competition.

How well does President Trump understand economics? As described in Chapter 6, without prompting or preparation, he arrived at the conclusion, for example, that (absent political considerations) immigrants should be charged a large fee for U.S. citizenship. He readily recognized that companies could profit in the face of rising wages if productivity were also increasing. He articulated the controversial Bennett hypothesis that college tuition increases over time because of increases in Federal assistance. He understands economic charts, often before we supply any added explanation. He often sees and probes genuine weak spots in arguments from his economic advisers. President Trump may express clear disagreement with an economic conclusion, but we learned that a deliberative process was behind his objections. He would spend a few days considering our materials and conclusion and update his opinion as needed.

In prepared settings, he recites CEA findings exactly as written, at least the first time; if "fake news" failed to accurately report the point, then later iterations may require deliberate exaggeration, as with the episodes described in this book. He has proven to be a capable speaker on "difference in differences" analysis of the economic effects of "fracking" and related techniques for extracting oil and gas from underground (Chapter 8).

Mr. Trump is a proficient experimenter, whom I saw privately testing ideas before making them public proclamations. These are reasons to conclude that so-called economics "mistakes" in his public proclamations are just as deliberate as the exaggerations about economic performance. His job as leader, statesman, and politician is more difficult than reciting the answers to an economics test.

POLICY SUCCESSES AND FAILURES

President Trump has had notable policy successes, many of them underreported, if reported at all. The 2017 tax reform law brought business-tax rates in line with the rest of the world. President Trump's Food and Drug Administration reduced prescription drug prices by removing regulations protecting special interests. President Trump's Department of Labor increased employment and wages by removing costly regulations on employers. Obamacare's individual mandate has been repealed. Hundreds of other regulations have been removed, some of which had been put in place at the behest of large banks, trial lawyers, major health insurance companies, big tech companies, and labor unions. This is not an exhaustive list.

There are policy failures, too. Other special interests, such as the automobile and maritime industries, have continued representation at the highest levels of the administration. These industries shift Federal policy in their favor, imposing wildly disproportionate costs on the rest of the country. Chapters 8, 10 and 11 provide inside accounts of how their influence continues.

The Federal government remains a massive, inept organization. No single person can understand all of what the government is doing. Although the President heads the executive branch, he cannot discover policy problems merely by directing the Federal bureaucracy to report up the chain of command. Lower-level employees have little incentive to become aware of such problems. To recall an example, the "benzo" provision in Obamacare (President Trump tried but failed to repeal the entire law) continues to subsidize half of the opioid-benzo cocktail that is a deadly favorite among opioid abusers. Even when unintended consequences come to a Federal agency's attention, its leadership may find suppressing facts to be in its personal interest (also in Chapter 4).

The ruling class does not want to be disrupted or to acknowledge policy failures. It knows from experience it can fight back and win. History will judge whether the populism personified by Donald Trump is a new beginning for Americans or a compelling historical anomaly.

LIST OF ACRONYMS

ACA	Affordable Care Act	**HCAHPS**	Hospital Consumer Assessment of Healthcare Providers and Systems
AKS	Anti-Kickback Statute	**HHS**	Department of Health and Human Services
AP	Associated Press	**IGM**	Initiative on Global Markets
CAFE	Corporate Average Fuel-Economy	**IP**	Intellectual Property
CBO	Congressional Budget Office	**IQ**	Intelligence Quotient
CC BY-SA	Creative Commons Attribute-ShareAlike	**LNG**	Liquified Natural Gas
CEA	Council of Economic Advisers	**MSNBC**	A network resulting from a partnership between Microsoft and the National Broadcasting Co.
CEO	Chief Executive Officer	**NAFTA**	North American Free Trade Agreement
CFPB	Consumer Financial Protection Bureau	**NEC**	National Economic Council
CMS	Centers for Medicare and Medicaid Services	**NLRB**	National Labor Relations Board
CNN	Cable News Network	**NSC**	National Security Council
CPI	Consumer Price Index	**OECD**	Organisation for Economic Co-operation and Development

DOA	Dead On Arrival	**OIRA**	Office of Information and Regulatory Affairs
DOC	Department of Commerce	**OMB**	Office of Management and Budget
DOI	Department of Interior	**POTUS**	President of the United States
DOJ	Department of Justice	**RIA**	Regulatory Impact Assessment
DOL	Department of Labor	**SAFE**	Safe Affordable Fuel Efficient vehicles
DOT	Department of Transportation	**SCIF**	Sensitive Compartmented Information Facility
DPC	Domestic Policy Council	**SS**	Steamship
EO	Executive Order	**SSI**	Supplemental Security Income
EOP	Executive Office of the President	**STLDI**	Short-term Limited Duration Insurance
EPA	Environmental Protection Agency	**TCJA**	Tax Cut and Jobs Act of 2017
FAQ	Frequently Asked Questions	**TPP**	Trans-Pacific Partnership
FART	Fair And Reciprocal Tariff Act	**UPI**	United Press International
FCC	Federal Communications Commission	**UPU**	Universal Postal Union
FDA	Food and Drug Administration	**USCG**	United States Coast Guard
FERC	Federal Energy Regulatory Commission	**USMCA**	United States-Mexico-Canada Agreement
GDELT	Global Database of Events, Language, and Tone	**USSR**	Union of Soviet Socialist Republics
GDP	Gross Domestic Product	**VPOTUS**	Vice President of the United States
GHG	Greenhouse Gas	**WHC**	Office of White House Counsel
GM	General Motors	**WHSR**	White House Situation Room

ACKNOWLEDGMENTS

These experiences, and therefore this book, were possible only because of the efforts of many people working in the Trump Administration. CEA Chairman Hassett and Chief of Staff D.J. Nordquist assembled an amazing team of economists. Tom Philipson, Rich Burkhauser, and Brian Blase kindly "showed me the ropes" so that I could quickly integrate into the large and complicated organization known as the Federal government. OIRA's Anthony Campau at once got me involved with regulation, which proved to help the President trumpet OIRA's achievements even though a little disruptive for it. Tom Philipson's health economics knowledge was also critical for making CEA productive in a modern government very much dominated by health policy.

The efforts and advice of several people at the University of Chicago, including undergraduates, graduate students, and faculty, also helped. My collaboration with Kevin Murphy, Robbie Minton, and Sonia Jaffe on *Chicago Price Theory* could not have come at a better time. Other collaboration with Kevin Tsui, Yona Rubinstein, and Trevor Gallen proved invaluable already in my first days in Washington. I doubt that I would have adequately recognized the special interests if it were not for a lesson that Gary Becker repeatedly taught me when he was alive: "somebody benefits" (referring to public policies that seem to make no economic sense).

Several Mulligans read and commented on drafts of this book: Brian, Elaine, Jack, Marc, and Tom. Jack also got us an apartment in Washington. I also appreciate the advice and efforts of the publishers and editors, Al Regnery, Eric Kampmann, and Stephen Thompson. Before they were assembled into a book, components were improved and sometimes conceived because of feedback from Joel Zinberg, Eric Sun, Steve Powers, Patrick McLaughlin, Matt Kahn, Doug Irwin, Steve Hanke,

Dora Costa, and University of Chicago students in the "Economics of Socialism" and in "Public Sector Economics." The Thomas W. Smith Foundation has supported much of my academic research that informs parts of this book, including analysis of health insurance, opioid markets, and the Samaritan's Dilemma in labor markets.

My year in Washington was a sacrifice by my wife and children. Mom did all of the work, while a year naturally seems like a long time in the life of a kid. Four of them were attending the University of Chicago Laboratory Schools at the time. For some context, this is the same school where President Obama's children attended grammar school (in the same grades as two of our children), as did Chicago Mayor Rahm Emanuel's children. Parents commonly have graduate degrees. The Pledge of Allegiance is not a regular activity there. It is a school that prides itself on teaching diversity and independent thinking, but by now you can guess that opinions about President Trump are not so diverse. Some of our children's classmates may have heard older family members curse about him; it is not so secret because the younger ones tend to repeat such things at school. Without any coaching, our 39-pound kindergartener would respond, "My dad doesn't like that!" I see this part of the experience as an ideal demonstration that conventional wisdom has flaws, even when it is commonly held by educated people. But I doubt that any of the kids would have voluntarily enrolled.

Finalizing the 2019 Economic Report of the President. Clockwise around the Resolute Desk: President Trump, Casey B. Mulligan, Richard Burkhauser, Kevin Hassett, Tomas Philipson, and D.J. Nordquist. Official White House Photo by Shealah Craighead. Used with Permission.

BIBLIOGRAPHY OF SOCIAL MEDIA

CHAPTER 1 NO LAFFING MATTER

Video about "Trump's Changing Stances on Health Care" by TimesVideo on 4/6/2016.

https://www.nytimes.com/video/us/politics/100000004315557/trumps-changing-stances-on-health-care.html

Tweet about weak auto executives by @realdonaldtrump on 8/21/2019.

https://twitter.com/realdonaldtrump/status/1164308814759260161

Tweet about foolish auto executives by @realdonaldtrump on 8/21/2019.

https://twitter.com/realdonaldtrump/status/1164169890917433346

CHAPTER 2 "I WISH THAT HE WOULD STAY OFF TWITTER"

Tweet about GDP growth by @realdonaldtrump on 3/18/2019.

https://twitter.com/realDonaldTrump/status/1107673256268623872

Video about "FULL RALLY: President Trump Rally in Greenville, North Carolina" by Fox 10 Phoenix on 7/17/2019.

https://www.youtube.com/watch?v=6qvB5tHRNOI&start=3330

Video about "Watch Live: President Trump's MAGA Rally in Green Bay (Full)" by NBC News on 4/27/2019.

https://www.youtube.com/watch?v=oWlLZZ8pcp8&start=4085

Video about "Lou Dobbs Tonight: FBC: March 18, 2019 7:00pm EDT" by Lou Dobbs Tonight on 3/18/2019.

https://archive.org/embed/
FBC_20190318_230000_Lou_Dobbs_Tonight?start=1080&end=1164

Tweet about Obamacare already taxing the middle class by @paulkrugman on 11/3/2019.

https://twitter.com/paulkrugman/status/1190996068168871936

CHAPTER 3 "AMERICA WILL NEVER
BE A SOCIALIST COUNTRY"

Video about "Trump's 2019 State of the Union address | Full Speech" by Fox News on 2/5/2019.

https://www.youtube.com/watch?v=TXep_uf-ESY

Tweet about CNN opining on Medicare for All, without reading it, by @Acosta on 10/10/2018.

https://twitter.com/Acosta/status/1050025395280642049

Video about "California Senate Passes Single-Payer Healthcare" by The Young Turks on 6/2/2017.

https://www.youtube.com/watch?v=ykT-cPcQMhs

Video about "Kamala Harris keeps shifting her health care position" by Washington Post on 1/29/2019.

https://www.youtube.com/watch?v=CiKwLv_hJAw

CHAPTER 4 "NO ONE IN OHIO CARES ABOUT BURMA"

Video about "Eric Holder mandates lesser penalties for minor drug crimes" by NBC News on 8/12/2013.

http://www.nbcnews.com/video/the-cycle/52737799

Video about "Five-Point Strategy to Combat Opioid Crisis" by HHS on 9/25/2018.

https://www.youtube.com/watch?v=DwZNEwQ7eGQ

Video about "Breaking the Taboo - Official Trailer" by docuphile on 12/6/2012.

https://www.youtube.com/watch?v=NW1XkSBCsP8

CHAPTER 5 "WE HAVE A LOT OF LOVE
IN THE ADMINISTRATION"

Video about "Interview: Pete Hegseth of Fox Interviews Donald Trump at Rally in Billings - September 6, 2018" by Factbase Videos on 9/7/2018.

https://www.youtube.com/watch?v=BVshIJVdnJY&start=133

Video about "Prescription Drug Prices" by C-SPAN on 10/15/2018.

https://www.c-span.org/video/?452944-1/
hhs-secretary-azar-speaks-prescription-drug-prices-forum

Video about "Larry Kudlow calls to 'put socialism on trial' during CPAC" by Fox News on 3/1/2019.

https://www.youtube.com/watch?v=UGoHALrUarY

CHAPTER 6 "OUR COMPANIES NEED HELP"

Podcast about "Is Migration a Basic Human Right?" by Freakonomics on 12/17/2015.

http://freakonomics.com/podcast/
is-migration-a-basic-human-right-a-new-freakonomics-radio-podcast/

CHAPTER 7 RUNNING THE GOVERNMENT LIKE A BUSINESS

Video about "Trump meets Kenyan president, ignores questions on McCain" by CBS News on 8/27/2018.

https://www.youtube.com/watch?v=wP99vAM9MkM

CHAPTER 8 "I AM A TARIFF MAN"

Tweet about "I am a Tariff Man" by @realdonaldtrump on 12/4/2018.

https://twitter.com/realDonaldTrump/status/1069970500535902208

Video about "President Reagan's Radio Address on Canadian Elections and Free Trade on November 26, 1988" by Reagan library on 11/26/1988.

https://www.youtube.com/embed/Tp1T7kPEdDY?start=221&end=235

Video about "Trump rips 'far-left energy nightmare' during fiery PA speech" by Fox Business on 8/13/2019.

https://www.youtube.com/watch?v=hqzOYF_NwmQ

Video about "Lecture segments" by Chicago Price Theory on 8/1/2019.

http://videos.chicagopricetheory.com

CHAPTER 9 "FAKE NEWS SHOULD BE TALKING ABOUT THIS"

Tweet about "Drug prices declined in 2018...." by @realdonaldtrump on 1/11/2019.

https://twitter.com/realdonaldtrump/status/1083866566314389504

Video about "President Trump Participates in a Fair and Honest Pricing in Healthcare Roundtable" by The White House on 1/23/2019.

https://www.youtube.com/watch?v=YZLbvQCfTQ4

Video about "President Trump Meets with Conservative Leaders on his Immigration Proposal" by The White House on 1/23/2019.

https://www.youtube.com/embed/04AF8VMf2Co?start=596&end=645

Video about "President Trump Holds a Cabinet Meeting" by The White House on 10/21/2019.

https://www.youtube.com/watch?v=lLpltkmBM1M&start=3385

Video about "President Trump Delivers the State of the Union Address" by The White House on 2/5/2019.

https://www.youtube.com/watch?v=BYU5VE2c6Ps

CHAPTER 10 INDUSTRY LOBBYISTS EXPOSED BY A ROBOT

Video about "Automated Economic Reasoning" by Becker Friedman Institute at Uchicago on 2/16/2017.

https://www.youtube.com/embed/Ewd_V8YodQg?start=2264&end=2635

Video about "Watch Live: President Trump's MAGA Rally in Green Bay (Full)" by NBC News on 4/27/2019.

https://www.youtube.com/watch?v=oWlLZZ8pcp8&start=4085

CHAPTER 11 "DO I HEAR A CRY FOR HELP OUT THERE?"

Video about "Trailer" by EASTLAND: Chicago's Deadliest Day on 6/18/2019.

https://www.youtube.com/watch?v=h1cCXh5uYRk

Podcast about "The Jones Act, Liquified Natural Gas, and Russia" by Colin Grabow on 11/1/2019.

https://www.cato.org/multimedia/cato-daily-podcast/
jones-act-liquid-natural-gas-russia

BIBLIOGRAPHY OF BOOKS

AND ARTICLES

THE BIBLIOGRAPHIES ARE AVAILABLE ONLINE
AT BIBLIO.YOUREHIREDTRUMP.COM.

CHAPTER 1 NO LAFFING MATTER

Cline, Andrew. "How Obama Broke His Promise on Individual Mandates." *The Atlantic*, June 29, 2012.

Council of Economic Advisers. *Deregulating Health Insurance Markets: Value to Market Participants.* Executive Office of the President, February 2019.

Council of Economic Advisers. *Economic Report of the President.* Executive Office of the President, March 2019.

Draper, Robert. "The Man Behind the President's Tweets." *The New York Times Magazine*, April 16, 2018.

"Executive Order 13890 of October 3, 2019, Protecting and Improving Medicare for Our Nation's Seniors." *Federal Register* 84, no. 195 (October 2019).

Gillespie, Richard. *Manufacturing knowledge: A history of the Hawthorne experiments.* Cambridge University Press, 1991.

Hayek, Friedrich A. "The Use of Knowledge in Society." *American Economic Review* 35, no. 4 (September 1945): 519-30.

Kessler, Glenn. "How many pages of regulations for 'Obamacare'?" *Washington Post*, May 15, 2013.

Keynes, John Maynard. *The Economic Consequences of the Peace*. London: Martins Press, 1919.

Kirkpatrick, Scott, C. Daniel Gelatt, and Mario P. Vecchi. "Optimization by simulated annealing." *Science* 220 (1983): 671–680.

Larson, Erik. *Thunderstruck*. New York: Crown Publishers, 2006.

Lipton, Eric. "Trump's Choice to Bring G7 to His Own Resort Would Violate Conflict-of-Interest Law, if He Weren't President." *New York Times*, October 18, 2019: A15.

Marconi, Guglielmo. "Wireless telegraphic communication." *Resonance* (Nobel Lecture) 7 (1909).

Mulligan, Casey B. *Side Effects and Complications: The Economic Consequences of Health-care Reform*. Chicago: University of Chicago Press, 2015.

Noonan, Peggy. "Trump's Defenders Have No Defense." *Wall Street Journal*, November 21, 2019.

Pfeiffer, Dan. *Yes We (still) Can: Politics in the Age of Obama, Twitter, and Trump*. New York: Hachette Book Group, 2018.

Rago, Joseph. "Casey Mulligan: The Economist Who Exposed ObamaCare." *Wall Street Journal*, February 7, 2014.

Rhodes, Ben. *The world as it is: A memoir of the Obama White House*. New York: Random House Trade Paperbacks, 2018.

Scott, Dylan. "A requiem for the individual mandate." *vox.com*. April 13, 2018. https://www.vox.com/policy-and-politics/2018/4/13/17226566/obamacare-penalty-2018-individual-mandate-still-in-effect.

Trump, Donald J. "Healthcare Reform to Make America Great Again." *donaldjtrump.com*. March 2, 2016. https://web.archive.org/web/20160303021149/https://www.donaldjtrump.com/positions/healthcare-reform.

—. "Remarks by President Trump at Presentation of the Medal of Freedom to Dr. Arthur Laffer." *whitehouse.gov*. June 19, 2019. https://www.whitehouse.gov/briefings-statements/remarks-president-trump-presentation-medal-freedom-dr-arthur-laffer/.

CHAPTER 2 "I WISH THAT HE WOULD STAY OFF TWITTER"

Ballard, Jerel. "Thousands attend Trump rally in Green Bay." *wsaw.com.* April 27, 2019. https://www.wsaw.com/content/news/Thousands-attend-Trump-rally-in-Green-Bay-509166801.html.

Consult, Morning. "National Tracking Poll #180545, May 23-29, 2018, Crosstabulation Results." *morningconsult.com.* May 2018. https://morningconsult.com/wp-content/uploads/2018/05/180545_crosstabs_POLITICO_1_20.pdf.

Council of Economic Advisers. *Economic Report of the President.* Executive Office of the President, March 2019.

Council of Economic Advisers. *The Administration's FDA Reforms and Reduced Biopharmaceutical Drug Prices.* Executive Office of the President, October 2018.

Dorn, Sara. "A history of Joe Biden's most touchy-feely moments." *New York Post,* March 30, 2019.

Draper, Robert. "The Man Behind the President's Tweets." *The New York Times Magazine,* April 16, 2018.

http://www.trumptwitterarchive.com/archive. 2019.

Leetaru, Kalev. "Measuring the Media's Obsession With Trump." *realclearpolitics.com.* December 6, 2018. https://www.realclearpolitics.com/articles/2018/12/06/measuring_the_medias_obsession_with_trump_138848.html.

Michels, Holly K. "Tester highlights pre-existing conditions as Trump rallies Bozeman." *helenair.com.* November 3, 2018. https://helenair.com/news/state-and-regional/govt-and-politics/tester-highlights-pre-existing-conditions-as-trump-rallies-bozeman/article_3253e213-45ac-5366-a782-1c1ee7e69216.html.

Newport, Frank. "Deconstructing Trump's Use of Twitter." *gallup.com.* May 16, 2018. https://news.gallup.com/poll/234509/deconstructing-trump-twitter.aspx?version=print.

Paletta, Damian, Erica Werner, and Josh Dawsey. "Ryan, McConnell try to coax Trump away from shutdown—using props and flattery." *The Washington Post,* September 7, 2018.

Parker, Ashley. "Manners Fit Jeb Bush, if Not an Uncouth Race." *New York Times*, January 16, 2016.

Real Clear Politics. "2016 Republican Presidential Nomination." *realclearpolitics.com*. 2016. https://web.archive.org/web/20150715022058/http://www.realclearpolitics.com/epolls/2016/president/us/2016_republican_presidential_nomination-3823.html.

Working, Holbrook. "Note on the correlation of first differences of averages in a random chain." *Econometrica* 28 (1960): 916–918.

CHAPTER 3 "AMERICA WILL NEVER BE A SOCIALIST COUNTRY"

American Psychiatric Association. "Goldwater Rule's Origins Based on Long-Ago Controversy." *psychiatry.org*. 2019. https://www.psychiatry.org/newsroom/goldwater-rule.

Appelbaum, Binyamin, and Jim Tankersley. "What Could Kill Booming U.S. Economy? 'Socialists,' White House Warns." *New York Times*, October 23, 2018.

Burrell, Ian. "Cenk Uygur's The Young Turks: This YouTube news bulletin is challenging the fogeys of US TV." *The Independent*, September 28, 2014.

Chicago Booth IGM Economic Experts Panel. "Economic Stimulus (revisited)." *igmchicago.org*. July 29, 2014. http://www.igmchicago.org/surveys/economic-stimulus-revisited.

Cillizza, Chris, and Harry Enten. "Here come the 2020 dropouts." *cnn.com*. December 5, 2019. https://www.cnn.com/2019/12/05/politics/2020-democratic-presidential-candidates-ranked/index.html.

—. "Why Kamala Harris is the new Democratic frontrunner." *cnn.com*. November 12, 2018. https://www.cnn.com/2018/11/12/politics/2020-rankings-democrats/index.html.

Council of Economic Advisers. *Economic Report of the President*. Executive Office of the President, March 2019.

Council of Economic Advisers. *Economic Report of the President*. Executive Office of the President, February 1992.

Council of Economic Advisers. *The Opportunity Costs of Socialism*. Executive Office of the President, October 2018.

BIBLIOGRAPHY OF BOOKS AND ARTICLES

"Employment Act of 1946." Public Law 304, February 20, 1946.

Marx, Karl. *Capital: A critique of political economy, Volume I.* Translated by Samuel Moore and Edward Aveling. Moscow: Progress Publishers, 1867/1887.

Marx, Karl, and Friedrich Engels. *The communist manifesto.* Moscow: Progress Publishers, 1848/1969.

Matthews, Dylan. "The White House, definitely not scared of socialism, issues report on why socialism is bad." *vox.com.* October 23, 2018. https://www.vox.com/policy-and-politics/2018/10/23/18013872/white-house-socialism-report-cea-mao-lenin-bernie-sanders.

Ohr, Nellie Hauke. *Collective farms and Russian peasant society, 1933-1937: The stabilization of the kolkhoz order.* PhD Dissertation, Stanford University, 1991.

Resnick, Stephen A., and Richard D. Wolff. *Class theory and history: Capitalism and communism in the USSR.* Routledge, 2013.

The SMT-LIB Initiative. *The Satisfiability Modulo Theories Library.* 2018. http://smtlib.economicreasoning.com/.

Trump, Donald J. "2019 State of the Union Address." Speech, Washington, DC, February 5, 2019.

—. "Donald Trump: Democrats 'Medicare for All' plan will demolish promises to seniors." *USA Today*, October 10, 2018.

U.S. Congress. House. "Expanded & Improved Medicare For All Act." HR 676, 115th Congress, January 24, 2017.

U.S. Congress. House. "Medicare For All Act." HR 2034, 110th Congress, April 26, 2007.

U.S. Congress. House. "Medicare For All Act." HR 4683, 110th Congress, February 17, 2006.

U.S. Congress. House. "Medicare for All Act of 2019." HR 1384, 116th Congress, February 27, 2019.

U.S. Congress. Senate. "American Health Security Act of 2009." S 703, 111th Congress, March 25, 2009.

U.S. Congress. Senate. "American Health Security Act of 2011." S 915, 112th Congress, May 9, 2011.

U.S. Congress. Senate. "American Health Security Act of 2013." S 1782, 113th Congress, December 9, 2013.

U.S. Congress. Senate. "Medicare for All Act." S 1218, 110th Congress, April 25, 2007.

U.S. Congress. Senate. "Medicare for All Act of 2017." S 1804, 115th Congress, September 13, 2017.

U.S. Congress. Senate. "Medicare for All Act of 2019." S 1129, 116th Congress, April 10, 2019.

CHAPTER 4 "NO ONE IN OHIO CARES ABOUT BURMA"

Adams, Jerome, Gregory H. Bledsoe, and John H. Armstrong. "Are pain management questions in patient satisfaction surveys driving the opioid epidemic?" *American Journal of Public Health* 106 (2016): 985.

Adler, Jeremy A., and Theresa Mallick-Searle. "An overview of abuse-deterrent opioids and recommendations for practical patient care." *Journal of Multidisciplinary Healthcare* 11 (2018): 323.

Bambauer, Kara Zivin, James E. Sabin, and Stephen B. Soumerai. "The exclusion of benzodiazepine coverage in Medicare: simple steps for avoiding a public health crisis." *Psychiatric Services* 56 (2005): 1143–1146.

Becker, Gary S. "Irrational behavior and economic theory." *Journal of political economy* 70 (1962): 1–13.

Centers for Medicare and Medicaid Services. "Medicare Program: Changes to Hospital Outpatient Prospective Payment and Ambulatory Surgical Center Payment Systems and Quality Reporting Programs." *Federal Register*, November 21, 2018: 58818-59179.

—. "Medicare Program: Medicare Prescription Drug Benefit." *Federal Register*, January 28, 2005: 4194-4585.

—. "Medicare Program; Changes to the Medicare Advantage and the Medicare Prescription Drug Benefit Programs for Contract Year 2013 and Other Changes." *Federal Register*, April 2012: 22072-22175.

—. "HCAHPS Update Training." *cms.gov*. February 2019. HCAHPS Update Training.

Centers for Disease Control and Prevention. "Drug Overdose Deaths." *cdc.gov*. June 27, 2019. https://www.cdc.gov/drugoverdose/data/statedeaths.html.

Cicero, Theodore J., Matthew S. Ellis, and Hilary L. Surratt. "Effect of abuse-deterrent formulation of OxyContin." *New England Journal of Medicine* (Mass Medical Soc) 367 (2012): 187–189.

Cooper, Marta. "A leading historian on why liberalism failed—and what we can do to start rescuing it." *qz.com*. January 14, 2017. https://qz.com/882209/a-leading-historian-on-how-liberalism-can-be-rescued-in-2017/.

Council of Economic Advisers. *Economic Report of the President*. Executive Office of the President, February 2010.

Council of Economic Advisers. *Economic Report of the President*. Executive Office of the President, February 2020.

Council of Economic Advisers. *The Role of Opioid Prices in the Evolving Opioid Crisis*. Executive Office of the President, April 2019.

Council of Economic Advisers. *The Underestimated Cost of the Opioid Crisis*. Executive Office of the President, October 2019.

Cumming-Bruce, Nick. "U.S. Will Remain in Postal Treaty After Emergency Talks." *New York Times*, September 25, 2019.

Dale, Helen. "White Trash." *The Spectator*, August 20, 2016.

Diamond, Dan. "Meet Alex Azar's new chief of staff." *politico.com*. January 26, 2018. https://www.politico.com/newsletters/politico-pulse/2018/01/26/meet-alex-azars-new-chief-of-staff-084324.

e.Republic. "Federal Employees By State." *governing.com*. January 2019. Federal Employees By State.

Easterly, William. *The tyranny of experts: Economists, dictators, and the forgotten rights of the poor*. New York: Basic Books, 2014.

Express Scripts. "2018 Drug Trend Report." *express-scripts.com*. February 6, 2019. https://web.archive.org/web/20191216173635/https://www.express-scripts.com/corporate/drug-trend-report.

Food and Drug Administration. "Safety Labeling Change Notification." *fda.gov*. August 21, 2016. https://www.fda.gov/media/107603/download.

Food and Drug Administration, Center for Drug Evaluation and Research. "Data and Methods for Evaluating Impact of Opioid Formulations with Properties Designed to Deter Abuse in Postmarket Setting." *fda.gov*. July 11, 2017. https://www.fda.gov/media/107603/download.

—. "Summary Review for Regulatory Action, Application Number 22-272." *fda.gov*. December 30, 2009. https://www.accessdata.fda.gov/drugsatfda_docs/nda/2010/022272s000MedR.pdf.

Governor's Task Force on Drug Enforcement, Treatment, and Prevention. "Final Report." *in.gov*. Fall 2016. https://www.in.gov/recovery/files/2016finalreportrevised.pdf.

Greene, Jan. "Naloxone 'Moral Hazard' Debate Pits Economists Against Physicians." *Annals of Emergency Medicine* 72, no. 2 (August 2018): A13-A16.

Groppe, Maureen. "Who is Alex Azar? Former drugmaker CEO and HHS official nominated to head agency." *USA Today*, November 13, 2017.

Hayes, Christal. "Don McGahn has officially left his position as White House counsel, official says." *USA Today*, October 17, 2018.

Higham, Scott, Sari Horwitz, and Katie Zezima. "The Fentanyl Failure." *The Washington Post*, March 13, 2019.

Holder, Eric. "Department Policy on Charging Mandatory Minimum Sentences and Recidivist Enhancements in Certain Drug Cases." *justice.gov*. August 12, 2013. https://www.justice.gov/sites/default/files/oip/legacy/2014/07/23/ag-memo-department-policypon-charging-mandatory-minimum-sentences-recidivist-enhancements-in-certain-drugcases.pdf.

Horwitz, Sari. "Holder Seeks to Avert Mandatory Minimum Sentences for Some Low-Level Drug Offenders." *The Washington Post*, August 12, 2013.

LeTourneau, Nancy. "Eric Holder: 'The Drug War…Is Over.'" *Washington Monthly*. February 26, 2016. https://washingtonmonthly.com/2016/02/26/eric-holder-the-drug-war-is-over/.

Mandell, Brian F. "The fifth vital sign: A complex story of politics and patient care." *Cleve Clin J Med* 83 (2016): 400–401.

Mulligan, Casey B. "Prices and Federal policies in Opioid Markets." *NBER working paper*, no. 26812 (February 2020).

National Academies of Sciences, Medicine, and others. *Pain management and the opioid epidemic: balancing societal and individual benefits and risks of prescription opioid use.* National Academies Press, 2017.

National Institute on Drug Abuse. "Benzodiazepines and Opioids." *drugabuse.gov.* March 2018. https://www.drugabuse.gov/drugs-abuse/opioids/benzodiazepines-opioids.

—. "Opioid Overdose Reversal with Naloxone (Narcan, Evzio)." *drugabuse.gov.* April 2018. https://www.drugabuse.gov/related-topics/opioid-overdose-reversal-naloxone-narcan-evzio.

Office of Management and Budget. "2019 Budget Fact Sheet: Lower the Price of Drugs by Reforming Payments." *whitehouse.gov.* February 2018. https://www.whitehouse.gov/wp-content/uploads/2018/02/FY19-Budget-Fact-Sheet_Reforming-Drug-Pricing-Payment.pdf.

Office of Management and Budget. "Circular A-4: Regulatory Analysis." (OMB, Office of Information and Regulatory Affairs) 2003.

Pfeiffer, Dan. *Yes We (still) Can: Politics in the Age of Obama, Twitter, and Trump.* Hachette UK, 2018.

Physicians for Responsible Opioid Prescribing. "Citizen Petition to the Centers for Medicare and Medicaid Services (CMS) requesting changes to the HCAHPS Survey." *supportprop.org.* April 13, 2016. http://www.supportprop.org/wp-content/uploads/2014/12/HCAHPS-Letter-Final-04-11-16.pdf.

Powell, David, Rosalie Liccardo Pacula, and Erin Taylor. "How increasing medical access to opioids contributes to the opioid epidemic: evidence from medicare part d." *NBER working paper*, no. 21072 (April 2015).

President's Commission on Combating Drug Addiction and the Opioid Crisis. "Final Report." *whitehouse.gov*. November 1, 2017. https://www.whitehouse.gov/sites/whitehouse.gov/files/images/Final_Report_Draft_11-1-2017.pdf.

Quinones, Sam. *Dreamland: The true tale of America's opiate epidemic*. New York: Bloomsbury Publishing USA, 2015.

Rhodes, Ben. *The world as it is: A memoir of the Obama White House*. Random House Trade Paperbacks, 2018.

The Final Year. Directed by Greg Barker. Performed by Ben Rhodes, Samantha Power, John Kerry and others. 2017.

Schnell, Molly. "The Economics of Physician Behavior." *Princeton University PhD Dissertation*, 2018.

Silver, Nate. "Election Update: Leave The LA Times Poll Alone!" *FiveThirtyEight.com*. August 23, 2016. https://fivethirtyeight.com/features/election-update-leave-the-la-times-poll-alone/.

Stevenson, Peter. "'Morning Joe' has blacklisted Kellyanne Conway. And that's not all." *The Washington Post*, February 15, 2017.

Sun, Eric C., Anjali Dixit, Keith Humphreys, Beth D. Darnall, Laurence C. Baker, and Sean Mackey. "Association between concurrent use of prescription opioids and benzodiazepines and overdose: retrospective analysis." *BMJ* 356, no. 8097 (March 2017).

Tefera, Lemeneh, William G. Lehrman, and Patrick Conway. "Measurement of the patient experience: clarifying facts, myths, and approaches." *JAMA* 315 (2016): 2167–2168.

Tetlock, Philip E. *Expert Political Judgment: How Good Is It? How Can We Know?* Princeton, NJ: Princeton University Press, 2017.

"The Patient Protection and Affordable Care Act." Public Law 148, March 23, 2010.

The World Staff. "How the deadly drug fentanyl is making its way to the US." *pri.org*. July 19, 2019. https://www.pri.org/stories/2019-07-19/how-deadly-drug-fentanyl-making-its-way-us.

Trump, Donald J. *The Inaugural Address.* Washington, D.C.: The White House, 2017.

U.S. Department of Health and Human Services. "Alex M. Azar II." *hhs.gov.* January 29, 2017. https://www.hhs.gov/about/leadership/secretary/alex-m-azar/index.html.

—. "Better Research." *hhs.gov.* May 15, 2018. https://www.hhs.gov/opioids/about-the-epidemic/hhs-response/better-research/index.html.

U.S. Department of Health and Human Services, Office of the Assistant Secretary for Planning and Evaluation. "Guidelines for Regulatory Impact Analysis." *aspe.hhs.gov.* 2016. https://aspe.hhs.gov/system/files/pdf/242926/HHS_RIAGuidance.pdf.

U.S. Drug Enforcement Agency. "Fentanyl." *dea.gov.* 2019. https://www.dea.gov/factsheets/fentanyl.

Vance, J. D. *Hillbilly Elegy–A Memoir of a Family and Culture in Crisis. 2016.* New York: Harper, 2016.

CHAPTER 5 "WE HAVE A LOT OF LOVE IN THE ADMINISTRATION"

Allen, Mike, and Jonathan Weisman. "Bush Ousts O'Neill and a Top Adviser." *The Washington Post*, December 7, 2002.

Anonymous. *A Warning.* New York: Hatchette Book Group, 2019.

Baker, Peter. "U.S. to Restore Full Relations With Cuba, Erasing a Last Trace of Cold War Hostility." *New York Times*, December 17, 2014.

Barro, Robert J., and Jason Furman. "Macroeconomic effects of the 2017 tax reform." *Brookings papers on economic activity*, 2018: 257–345.

BBC News. "Philip Hammond plans to quit if Johnson becomes PM." *bbc.com.* July 21, 2019. https://www.bbc.com/news/uk-politics-49062514.

Cancryn, Adam, and Dan Diamon. "White House to name Grogan top policy aide." *politico.com.* January 22, 2019. https://www.politico.com/story/2019/01/22/white-house-grogan-policy-aide-1105122.

Congressional Budget Office. "Regulatory Impact Analysis: Costs at Selected Agencies and Implications for the Legislative Process." *cbo.gov*. March 1997. https://www.cbo.gov/sites/default/files/105th-congress-1997-1998/reports/1997doc04-entire.pdf.

Council of Economic Advisers. *Deregulating Health Insurance Markets: Value to Market Participants.* Executive Office of the President, February 2019.

Council of Economic Advisers. *Economic Report of the President.* Executive Office of the President, February 2011.

Council of Economic Advisers. *Economic Report of the President.* Executive Office of the President, February 2018.

Council of Economic Advisers. *Economic Report of the President.* Executive Office of the President, March 2019.

Council of Economic Advisers. *Expanding Work Requirements in Non-Cash Welfare Programs.* Executive Office of the President, July 2018.

Council of Economic Advisers. *The Economic Effects of Federal Deregulation since January 2017: An Interim Report.* Executive Office of the President, June 2019.

Council of Economic Advisers. *The Role of Opioid Prices in the Evolving Opioid Crisis.* Executive Office of the President, April 2019.

Cunningham, Paige Winfield. "The Health 202: The Trump appointee you've never heard of who's reshaping health policy." *The Washington Post*, November 13, 2017.

DeYoung, Karen, Nick Miroff, and Juliet Eilperin. "Obama Begins Historic Visit to Cuba." *The Washington Post*, March 20, 2016.

Diamond, Dan, Rachana Pradhan, and Adam Cancryn. "Trump pulled into feud between top health officials." *politico.com*. December 5, 2019. https://www.politico.com/news/2019/12/05/trump-pulled-into-feud-between-top-health-officials-076861.

Feinberg, Ashley. "The New York Times Unites vs. Twitter." *slate.com*. August 15, 2019. https://slate.com/news-and-politics/2019/08/new-york-times-meeting-transcript.html.

Gerstenzang, James. "Bush Fires His Top Economic Advisors." *Los Angeles Times*, December 7, 2002.

Gordon, Michael R., and David E. Sanger. "Deal Reached on Iran Nuclear Program; Limits on Fuel Would Lessen With Time." *New York Times*, July 14, 2015.

Grice, Andrew. "Boris Johnson's triumph of populism comes straight from the Trump playbook." *independent.co.uk.* December 13, 2019. https://www.independent.co.uk/voices/boris-johnson-general-election-december-2019-a9244811.html.

Hassett, Kevin. "Tax Policy and the Economy: An Early Look at the Economic Impact of TCJA." *Special Session of the Annual Meeting.* American Economic Association, 2019.

Jaffe, Sonia, Robert Minton, Casey B. Mulligan, and Kevin M. Murphy. *Chicago Price Theory.* Princeton University Press (ChicagoPriceTheory.com), 2019.

Milbank, Dana. "'CEA You Later,' Bush Says." *The Washington Post*, March 6, 2003.

Mulligan, Casey B., and Tomas J. Philipson. "A Turnabout on Corporate Taxes." *Wall Street Journal*, October 24, 2017.

Niskanen, William A. *Reaganomics: An insider's account of the policies and the people.* New York: Oxford University Press, 1988.

Oakeshott, Isabel. "Britain's man in the US says Trump is 'inept': Leaked secret cables from ambassador say the President is 'uniquely dysfunctional and his career could end in disgrace.'" *Daily Mail*, July 6, 2019.

Rampell, Catherine. "After Shock: A Recession is Coming. Trump Will Make It So Much Worse." *The Washington Post*, December 20, 2018.

Rhodes, Ben. *The world as it is: A memoir of the Obama White House.* Random House Trade Paperbacks, 2018.

Summers, Lawrence H. "Trump's top economist's tax analysis isn't just wrong, it's dishonest." *The Washington Post*, October 17, 2017.

Swan, Jonathan, and Caitlin Owens. "Scoop: Trump and Pence intervene in clash between top health officials." *axios.com.* December 5, 2019. https://www.axios.com/trump-pence-alex-azar-seema-verma-2e7f7cbf-e167-4e29-9688-b401e5976a3c.html.

Trump, Donald J. "Remarks by President Trump to the 73rd Session of the United Nations General Assembly." *whitehouse.gov.* September

25, 2018. https://www.whitehouse.gov/briefings-statements/
remarks-president-trump-73rd-session-united-nations-general-assembly-new-york-ny/.

Wead, Doug. *Inside Trump's White House: The Real Story of His Presidency.* New York:
Hachette Book Group, 2019.

CHAPTER 6 "OUR COMPANIES NEED HELP"

Angrist, Joshua D., and Jörn-Steffen Pischke. *Mostly harmless econometrics: An empiricist's
companion.* Princeton, NJ: Princeton University Press, 2008.

Anonymous. *A Warning.* New York: Hatchette Book Group, 2019.

Becker, Gary S. *The Challenge of Immigration: A Radical Solution.* London: Institute for
Economic Affairs, 2011.

Bennett, William J. "Our Greedy Colleges." *New York Times*, February 18, 1987.

Council of Economic Advisers. *Economic Report of the President.* Executive Office of the
President, March 2019.

Editorial Board. "President Obama needs to push for a law change to address crisis on the
border." *The Washington Post*, July 10, 2014.

Edsall, Thomas B. "Trump Has a Gift for Tearing Us Apart." *New York Times*, December
11, 2019.

Frey, William H. "US population growth hits 80-year low, capping
off a year of demographic stagnation." *brookings.edu.* December
21, 2018. https://www.brookings.edu/blog/the-avenue/2018/12/21/
us-population-growth-hits-80-year-low-capping-off-a-year-of-demographic-stagnation/.

Friedman, Milton. *Capitalism and Freedom.* Chicago: University of Chicago Press, 1962.

Jenkins, Holman W., Jr. "Border Dilemmas Are the Same for Trump or Obama." *Wall
Street Journal*, November 29, 2019.

Marx, Karl. *Capital: A critique of political economy, Volume I.* Translated by Samuel Moore
and Edward Aveling. Moscow: Progress Publishers, 1867/1887.

McPherson, Michael S., and Morton Owen Schapiro. *Keeping college affordable: Government and educational opportunity.* Washington, DC: Brookings Institution Press, 2010.

Mulligan, Casey B. *Side Effects and Complications: The Economic Consequences of Health-Care Reform.* Chicago: University of Chicago Press (acasideeffects.com), 2015.

—. *The Redistribution Recession.* New York: Oxford University Press (redistributionrecession. com), 2012.

Oroho, Steven. "GOP lawmaker says it's not moral to entice immigrants to make a hazardous trip to N.J." *nj.com.* December 14, 2019. https://www.nj.com/opinion/2019/12/gop-lawmaker-says-its-not-moral-to-entice-immigrants-to-make-a-hazardous-trip-to-nj.html.

Pasour, E.C. "The Samaritans Dilemma and the Welfare State." *fee.org.* June 1, 1991. https://fee.org/articles/the-samaritans-dilemma-and-the-welfare-state/.

Rampell, Catherine. "After Shock: A Recession is Coming. Trump Will Make It So Much Worse." *The Washington Post,* December 20, 2018.

Robb, Greg. "White House economist says forecasts of recession don't make sense." marketwatch.com. February 28, 2019. https://www.marketwatch.com/story/white-house-economist-says-forecasts-of-recession-dont-make-sense-2019-02-28.

Robinson, Jenna A. "The Bennett Hypothesis Turns 30." *James G. Martin Center for Academic Renewal* (ERIC), 2017.

Tankersley, Jim. "Fed, Diminishing Its Economic Outlook, Predicts No Rate Increases This Year." *New York Times,* March 20, 2019.

Timiraos, Nick, and Alex Leary. "Trump to Fed Chairman Powell: 'I Guess I'm Stuck With You'." *Wall Street Journal,* April 2, 2019.

Trump, Donald J. "Remarks by President Trump on Modernizing Our Immigration System for a Stronger America." *whitehouse.gov.* May 16, 2019. https://www.whitehouse.gov/briefings-statements/remarks-president-trump-modernizing-immigration-system-stronger-america/.

Wong, Tom K. "Statistical Analysis Shows that Violence, Not Deferred Action, Is Behind the Surge of Unaccompanied Children Crossing the Border." *americanprogress.org.* July

8, 2014. https://www.americanprogress.org/issues/immigration/news/2014/07/08/93370/statistical-analysis-shows-that-violence-not-deferred-action-is-behind-the-surge-of-unaccompanied-children-crossing-the-border/.

Zandi, Mark, Chris Lafakis, Dan White, and Adam Ozimek. *The macroeconomic consequences of Mr. Trump's economic policies.* Moody's Analytics, 2016.

CHAPTER 7 RUNNING THE GOVERNMENT LIKE A BUSINESS

Allison, Bill, Mira Rojanasakul, Brittany Harris, and Cedric Sam. "Tracking the 2016 Presidential Money Race." *bloomberg.com.* December 9, 2016. https://www.bloomberg.com/politics/graphics/2016-presidential-campaign-fundraising/.

"An Act to promote the welfare of American seamen in the merchant marine of the United States [Merchant Marine Act of 1915]." Public Law 302, March 4, 1915.

Chait, Jonathan. "'We Do That All the Time, Get Over It,' Mulvaney Boasts About Ukraine Plot." *nymag.com.* October 17, 2019. http://nymag.com/intelligencer/2019/10/mulvaney-ukraine-get-over-it.html.

Clinton, William J. "Presidential Documents: Executive Order 12866 of September 30, 1993." *Federal Register,* October 4, 1993: 51735.

Council of Economic Advisers. *Deregulating Health Insurance Markets: Value to Market Participants.* Executive Office of the President, February 2019.

Council of Economic Advisers. *Economic Report of the President.* Executive Office of the President, February 1994.

Council of Economic Advisers. *Economic Report of the President.* Executive Office of the President, February 2020.

Crews, Clyde Wayne. "Less than 1 Percent of Federal Regulations Get Cost-Benefit Analysis." *cei.org.* November 17, 2015. https://cei.org/blog/less-1-percent-federal-regulations-get-cost-benefit-analysis.

Department of Health and Human Services. "Removal of Safe Harbor Protection for Rebates Involving Prescription Pharmaceuticals and Creation of New Safe Harbor

Protection for Certain Point-of-Sale Reductions in Price on Prescription Pharmaceuticals and Certain Pharmacy Benefit Manager Service Fees." *Federal Register*, February 6, 2019: 2340-63.

Departments of Treasury, Labor, and Health and Human Services. "Excepted Benefits; Lifetime and Annual Limits; and Short-Term, Limited-Duration Insurance." *Federal Register*, October 31, 2016: 75316-75327.

Ellig, Jerry. "Evaluating the Quality and Use of Regulatory Impact Analysis: The Mercatus Center's Regulatory Report Card, 2008-2013." (Mercatus) 2016.

Ellig, Jerry, Patrick A. McLaughlin, and John F. Morrall III. "Continuity, change, and priorities: The quality and use of regulatory analysis across US administrations." *Regulation & Governance* 7 (2013): 153–173.

"Emission standards for new motor vehicles or new motor vehicle engines." U.S. Code, Title 42, Section 7521, 2019.

George Washington University Regulatory Studies Center. "Economically Significant Final Rules Published by Presidential Year." *www.regulatorystudies.gwu.edu.* June 27, 2019. https://regulatorystudies.columbian.gwu.edu/reg-stats.

Guida, Victoria, and Katy O'Donnell. "Battle over CFPB leadership ends as Mulvaney challenger resigns." *politico.com.* July 6, 2018. https://www.politico.com/story/2018/07/06/consumer-financial-protection-bureau-leadership-battle-674254.

Massachusetts et al. v. Environmental Protection Agency et al. 05-1120 (Supreme Court of the United States, April 2, 2007).

McLaughlin, Patrick A. and Casey B. Mulligan. *Three Myths about Federal Regulation.* Arlington, VA: Mercatus Center, 2020.

Mulligan, Casey B. "Prices and Federal policies in Opioid Markets." *NBER working paper*, no. 26812 (February 2020).

Office of Management and Budget. "Circular A-4: Regulatory Analysis." (OMB, Office of Information and Regulatory Affairs) 2003.

Office of Management and Budget, Office of Information and Regulatory Affairs.

"Information Collection Budget of the United States Government." *obamawhitehouse. archives.gov.* 2016. https://obamawhitehouse.archives.gov/sites/default/files/omb/inforeg/icb/icb_2016.pdf.

Renda, Andrea. "One step forward, two steps back? The new US regulatory budgeting rules in light of the international experience." *Journal of Benefit-Cost Analysis* 8 (2017): 291–304.

Sunstein, Cass R. *The cost-benefit revolution.* Cambridge, MA: MIT Press, 2018.

Swan, Jonathan. "Government workers shun Trump, give big money to Clinton." *thehill.com.* October 26, 2016. https://thehill.com/homenews/campaign/302817-government-workers-shun-trump-give-big-money-to-clinton-campaign.

Taub, Amanda, and Max Fisher. "As Leaks Multiply, Fears of a 'Deep State' in America." *New York Times*, February 16, 2017.

The White House. "Declassified Memorandum of Telephone Conversation." *whitehouse. gov.* September 24, 2019. https://www.whitehouse.gov/wp-content/uploads/2019/09/Unclassified09.2019.pdf.

Trnka, Daniel, and Yola Thuerer. "One-In, X-Out: Regulatory offsetting in selected OECD countries." *OECD Regulatory Policy Working Paper*, no. 11 (2019).

Trump, Donald J. "Presidential Documents: Executive Order 13771 of January 30, 2017." *Federal Register*, February 3, 2017: 9339-9341.

U.S. AID. "Kenya." *usaid.gov.* December 18, 2019. https://www.usaid.gov/kenya.

U.S. Congress. House. "Medicare for All Act of 2019." HR 1384, 116th Congress, February 27, 2019.

U.S. Department of Commerce. "Modification of Regulations Regarding Benefit and Specificity in Countervailing Duty Proceedings." *reginfo.gov.* November 2019. https://www.reginfo.gov/public/do/eAgendaViewRule?pubId=201910&RIN=0625-AB16.

U.S. Department of Labor. "Defining and Delimiting the Exemptions for Executive, Administrative, Professional, Outside Sales and Computer Employees [Overtime Rule]." *Federal Register*, May 23, 2016: 32391-32552.

Wead, Doug. *Inside Trump's White House: The Real Story of His Presidency*. New York: Hachette Book Group, 2019.

Webb, Romany. "Six Important Points About BLM's Revised Methane Waste Prevention Rule." *columbia.edu*. September 18, 2018. http://blogs.law.columbia.edu/climatechange/2018/09/18/ six-important-points-about-blms-revised-methane-waste-prevention-rule/.

Wong, Edward, Annie Karni, and Emily Cochrane. "Trump Administration Drops Proposal to Cut Foreign Aid After Intense Debate." *New York Times*, August 22, 2019.

CHAPTER 8 "I AM A TARIFF MAN"

AftermarketNews Staff. "Number of SUVs, Pickup Trucks on the Road Holds Strong, According to Experian Automotive." *aftermarketnews. com*. November 4, 2008. https://www.aftermarketnews.com/ number-of-suvs-pickup-trucks-on-the-road-holds-strong-according-to-experian-automotive/.

American Maritime Partnership. "Statements of Support." *mctf.com*. January 2015. https:// web.archive.org/web/20150111202441/http:/www.mctf.com/statements.html.

Barfield, Claude. "Amid inconclusive trade talks, the US must challenge China's heightened intellectual property theft." *aei.org*. August 14, 2019. https://www.aei.org/technology-and-innovation/intellectual-property/amid-inconclusive-trade-talks-the-us-must-challenge-chinas-heightened-intellectual-property-theft/.

Barro, Robert, and Xavier Sala-i-Martin. *Economic growth*. Cambridge, MA: MIT Press, 2004.

Boyd, Gerald M. "President Imposes Tariff on Imports Against Japanese." *New York Times*, April 18, 1987: 1.

Bravender, Robin. "Déjà vu for staff as Gorsuch makes headlines." *eenews.net*. February 1, 2017. https://www.eenews.net/stories/1060049378.

Congressional Budget Office. *How the 2017 Tax Act Affected CBO's Economic and Budget Projections*. Washington, DC: Congressional Budget Office, 2018.

Council of Economic Advisers. *Deregulating Health Insurance Markets: Value to Market Participants*. Executive Office of the President, February 2019.

Council of Economic Advisers. *Economic Report of the President*. Executive Office of the President, January 1987.

Council of Economic Advisers. *Economic Report of the President*. Executive Office of the President, January 1989.

Council of Economic Advisers. *Economic Report of the President*. Executive Office of the President, March 2019.

Council of Economic Advisers. *Economic Report of the President*. Executive Office of the President, February 2020.

Council of Economic Advisers. *The Administration's FDA Reforms and Reduced Biopharmaceutical Drug Prices*. Executive Office of the President, October 2018.

Council of Economic Advisers. *The Economic Effects of Federal Deregulation since January 2017: An Interim Report*. Executive Office of the President, June 2019.

Council of Economic Advisers. *The U.S., the International Postal System, and the UPU: An Economic Framework*. Executive Office of the President, January 2019.

Council of Economic Advisers. *The Value of U.S. Energy Innovation and Policies Supporting the Shale Revolution*. Executive Office of the President, October 2019.

Cumming-Bruce, Nick. "U.S. Will Remain in Postal Treaty After Emergency Talks." *New York Times*, September 25, 2019.

Diggs, Keith E. "Tariffication of the coastwise trade laws." *Mich. L. Rev.* 112 (2013): 1507-17.

Dolan, Matthew. "To Outfox the Chicken Tax, Ford Strips Its Own Vans." *Wall Street Journal*, September 23, 2009.

Donnan, Shawn. "Trump's Trade 'Bad Cop' Thinks He Has Found a Winning Formula." *finance.yahoo.com*. December 1, 2019. https://web.archive.org/web/20191222150755/https://finance.yahoo.com/news/trump-trade-bad-cop-thinks-050100184.html.

Dornbusch, Rudiger. "Policy options for freer trade: the case for bilateralism." In *An American Trade Strategy: Options for the 1990s*, by Robert Z. Lawrence and Charles L. Schultze, eds. 124. Washington, D.C.: Brookings Institution, 1990.

Dudley, Susan E. "Documenting Deregulation." *forbes.com*. August 14, 2018. https://www.forbes.com/sites/susandudley/2018/08/14/documenting-deregulation/#35d3cd31d13f.

Editorial Board. "The High Cost of Steel Quotas." *Chicago Tribune*, February 19, 1989.

Farnsworth, Clyde H. "U.S. Raises Tariff for Motorcycles." *New York Times*, April 2, 1983: 1.

Federal Communications Commission. "Restoring Internet Freedom." *fcc.gov*. 2018. https://www.fcc.gov/restoring-internet-freedom.

Friedman, Milton. "Outdoing Smoot-Hawley." *Wall Street Journal*, April 20, 1987.

Frittelli, John. *Revitalizing Coastal Shipping for Domestic Commerce*. Tech. rep., Congressional Research Service, 2017.

—. *Shipping US crude oil by water: vessel flag requirements and safety issues*. Congressional Research Service, 2014.

Gallagher, John. "Trump Vows Not to Act on Jones Act." *freightwaves.com*. May 2, 2019. https://www.freightwaves.com/news/regulation/trump-vows-not-to-act-on-jones-act.

Golway, Terry. "Democrats take state Senate, returning Albany to one-party rule." *politico.com*. November 7, 2018. https://www.politico.com/states/new-york/albany/story/2018/11/06/democrats-take-state-senate-returning-albany-to-one-party-rule-684360.

Grossman, Gene M. "The theory of domestic content protection and content preference." *The Quarterly Journal of Economics* (MIT Press) 96 (1981): 583–603.

Hanke, Steve. "I've Seen The Horror Of Trump's Tariffs Before, With Reagan's Terrible Trade Policies." *Forbes*, March 2, 2018.

—. "President Trump Delivers Lifesaving Deregulation." *Forbes*, July 11, 2019.

—. "Reflections on Reagan the Intellectual." *Globe Asia*, August 2007.

Hanke, Steve, and Edward Li. "The Strange and Futile World of Trade Wars." *Journal of Applied Corporate Finance* 31 (2019): 59–67.

Hershey, Robert D., Jr. "Murray L. Weidenbaum, Reagan Economist, Dies at 87." *New York Times*, March 21, 2014.

Ikenson, Dan. "Ending the 'Chicken War': The Case for Abolishing the 25 Percent Truck Tariff." *cato.org*. June 18, 2003. https://www.cato.org/sites/cato.org/files/pubs/pdf/tbp-017. pdf.

Irwin, Douglas A. *Free trade under fire*. Princeton, NJ: Princeton University Press, 2009.

—. *Managed trade: The case against import targets*. Washington, DC: American Enterprise Institute, 1994.

Johnson, Lyndon B. "Proclamation 3564 [Chicken Tax]." *govinfo.gov*. December 4, 1963. https://www.govinfo.gov/content/pkg/STATUTE-77/pdf/STATUTE-77-Pg1034.pdf.

Kessler, Glenn. "Trump's claim his deregulatory actions are saving American households $3,000 a year." *The Washington Post*, August 15, 2019.

Krugman, Paul. "The Art of the Flail." *New York Times*, April 5, 2018.

Levinson, Arik. "The hidden American tax on imported cars: Fuel economy standards instead of tariffs." Edited by Chad P. Brown. *Economics and Policy in the Age of Trump*. London: CEPR Press, 2017. 79-84.

Lucas, Robert E., Jr. "Supply-side economics: An analytical review." *Oxford economic papers* 42 (1990): 293–316.

Lyons, Kate. "'It Stinks': Twitter Gets Wind of Oddly Named Trump Tariff Bill Draft." *theguardian.com*. July 1, 2018. https://www.theguardian.com/us-news/2018/jul/02/ trump-fart-act-report-blows-through-washington.

Miles, Martha A., and Caroline Rand Herron. "The Nation; Washington Puts a Large Tariff on Canadian Lumber." *New York Times*, October 19, 1986.

Mitchell, Josh. "White House Predicts Deregulation Will Boost Household Incomes." *Wall Street Journal*, June 28, 2019.

Mulligan, Casey B. *The Redistribution Recession.* New York: Oxford University Press (redistributionrecession.com), 2012.

Munk, Bernard. "The welfare costs of content protection: the automotive industry in Latin America." *Journal of Political Economy* 77 (1969): 85–98.

Niskanen, William A. *Reaganomics: An insider's account of the policies and the people.* New York: Oxford University Press, 1988.

Ortiz, Alfredo. "Trump Fights to Fix Shipping Rates That Favor China." *realclearpolitics.com.* April 4, 2019. https://www.realclearpolitics.com/articles/2019/04/04/trump_fights_to_fix_shipping_rates_that_favor_china_139960.html.

PWC. "The Trump administration wants to lower drug prices. Here's what they've already done." *pwc.com.* November 20, 2019. https://www.pwc.com/us/en/industries/health-industries/library/latest-thinking-on-drug-pricing.html.

Reagan Library Collections. "Dolan, Anthony 'Tony' R." reaganlibrary.gov. June 14, 2018. https://www.reaganlibrary.gov/sites/default/files/archives/textual/smof/dolan.pdf.

Reagan, Ronald. "Executive Order 12291—Federal Regulation." *archives.gov.* February 17, 1981. https://www.archives.gov/federal-register/codification/executive-order/12291.html.

Russakoff, Dale. "Policy Faltered; Term Popularized." *The Washington Post*, January 13, 1986.

Smith, Adam. *An Inquiry into the Nature and Causes of the Wealth of Nations.* Edited by Edwin Cannan. London: Methuen & Co., Ltd, 1776/1904.

Suwanto, Fabiola M. "Indonesia's New Patent Law: A Move in the Right Direction." *Santa Clara High Technology Law Journal* 9, no. 1 (January 1993): 265-85.

Tax Foundation. "Preliminary Details and Analysis of the Tax Cuts and Jobs Act." *taxfoundation.org.* December 18, 2017. https://taxfoundation.org/final-tax-cuts-and-jobs-act-details-analysis/.

The White House. "President Donald J. Trump Has Secured a Historic Phase One Trade Agreement with China." *whitehouse.gov.*

December 13, 2019. https://www.whitehouse.gov/briefings-statements/
president-donald-j-trump-secured-historic-phase-one-trade-agreement-china/.

—. "President Donald J. Trump Is Appointing a Historic Number of Federal Judges to
Uphold Our Constitution as Written." *whitehouse.gov*. November 6, 2019. https://www.
whitehouse.gov/briefings-statements/president-donald-j-trump-appointing-historic-number-
federal-judges-uphold-constitution-written/.

U.S. Customs and Border Protection. "Notice of proposed revocation of one ruling letter
and proposed revocation of treatment relating to tariff classification of the WorkMax 800
utility vehicle." *cbp.gov*. August 10, 2011. https://www.cbp.gov/bulletins/Vol_45_No_35_
Title.pdf.

U.S. Department of Commerce, Bureau of Economic Analysis. "Table 1.1.5. Gross
Domestic Product." *bea.gov*. December 20, 2019. https://apps.bea.gov/iTable/iTable.cfm?re
qid=19&step=2&isuri=1&1921=survey#reqid=19&step=2&isuri=1&1921=survey.

U.S. International Trade Commission. "Annual Tariff Data." *usitc.gov*. 2020. https://
dataweb.usitc.gov/tariff/annual.

Vance, J. D. *Hillbilly Elegy–A Memoir of a Family and Culture in Crisis. 2016*. New York:
Harper, 2016.

Varas, Jacqueline. "The Total Cost of Trump's Tariffs." *americanactionforum.
org*. December 16, 2019. https://www.americanactionforum.org/research/
the-total-cost-of-trumps-new-tariffs.

Volcovici, Valerie, and Catherine Ngai. "Oil companies rush to
exploit end of U.S. crude export ban." *reuters.com*. December 23,
2015. https://www.reuters.com/article/us-enterprise-products-exports/
oil-companies-rush-to-exploit-end-of-u-s-crude-export-ban-idUSKBN0U61Q920151223.

Whelan, Robbie. "'Chicken Tax' Hangs Over Pickup Truck Makers in Nafta Debate." *Wall
Street Journal*, February 15, 2017.

CHAPTER 9 "FAKE NEWS SHOULD BE TALKING ABOUT THIS"

Associated Press. "Trump hails drug price decline not supported by the evidence." *apnews. com.* January 11, 2019. https:/apnews.com/bce3a214039c4271b3f3337e0e522b2a.

Council of Economic Advisers. *Deregulating Health Insurance Markets: Value to Market Participants.* Executive Office of the President, February 2019.

Council of Economic Advisers. *Measuring Prescription Drug Prices: A Primer on the CPI.* Executive Office of the President, October 2019.

Council of Economic Advisers. *The Administration's FDA Reforms and Reduced Biopharmaceutical Drug Prices.* Executive Office of the President, October 2018.

Diamond, Dan, Anita Kumar, Rachana Pradhan, and Adam Cancryn. "'They're all fighting him': Trump aides spar with health secretary." *politico.com.* June 18, 2019. https://www.politico.com/story/2019/06/18/alex-azar-health-care-hhs-trump-cabinet-1538651.

Editorial Board. "Sound, Fury, and Prescription Drugs." *New York Times*, July 6, 2019.

Express Scripts. "2018 Drug Trend Report." *express-scripts.com.* February 6, 2019. https://web.archive.org/web/20191216173635/https://www.express-scripts.com/corporate/drug-trend-report.

Food and Drug Administration. "Scott M. Gottlieb, MD." *fda.gov.* April 19, 2019. https://www.fda.gov/node/373545.

—. "What We Do." *fda.gov.* March 28, 2018. https://www.fda.gov/about-fda/what-we-do.

Holden, Dominic. "Inside the Trump Administration's Secret War on Weed." *buzzfeednews. com.* August 29, 2019. https://www.buzzfeednews.com/article/dominicholden/trump-secret-committee-anti-marijuana.

Kessler, Glenn. "Can Trump Claim Credit for $26 Billion in Savings on Prescription Drugs?" *The Washington Post*, January 16, 2019.

Levin, Mark R. *Unfreedom of the Press.* New York: Simon and Schuster, 2019.

Lynch, Sarah. "Mueller report shows evidence Trump committed crimes, House Judiciary chairman says." *reuters.com*. July 21, 2019. https://www.reuters.com/article/us-usa-trump-nadler/mueller-report-shows-evidence-trump-committed-crimes-house-judiciary-chairman-says-idUSKCN1UG0IK.

Ornstein, Charles, and Katie Thomas. "Generic Drug Prices Are Falling, but Are Consumers Benefiting?" *New York Times*, August 8, 2017.

Paavola, Alia. "Top PBMs by Market Share." *beckershospitalreview.com*. May 30, 2019. https://www.beckershospitalreview.com/pharmacy/top-pbms-by-market-share.html.

Pear, Robert. "Trump Spurns Medicaid Proposal After Furious White House Debate." *New York Times*, July 30, 2018.

Pfeiffer, Dan. *Yes We (still) Can: Politics in the Age of Obama, Twitter, and Trump*. Hachette UK, 2018.

Sheetz, Michael. "Teva stock plummets 18% after rough quarter in US generic drug market." *finance.yahoo.com*. August 3, 2017. https://finance.yahoo.com/news/teva-stock-plummets-18-rough-135334052.html.

Terlep, Sharon, and Joseph Walker. "Generic-Drug Trends Squeeze Walgreens Profit." *Wall Street Journal*, April 2, 2019.

Teva Pharmaceutical Industry Ltd. "Company Profile." *tevapharm.com*. 2019. https://www.tevapharm.com/about/profile/.

Trump, Donald J. *Letter to the Honorable Nancy Pelosi*. Washington, DC: The White House, December 17, 2019.

U.S. Department of Labor, Bureau of Labor Statistics. "Consumer Price Index - December 2018." *bls.gov*. January 11, 2019. https://www.bls.gov/news.release/archives/cpi_01112019.pdf.

CHAPTER 10 INDUSTRY LOBBYISTS EXPOSED BY A ROBOT

Arai, Noriko H., Hidenao Iwane, Takua Matsuzaki, and Hirokazu Anai. "Mathematics by Machine." *ISSAC '14 Proceedings of the 39th International Symposium on Symbolic and Algebraic Computation*. New York: ACM, 2014. 1-8.

Bento, Antonio M., et al. "Flawed analyses of US auto fuel economy standards." *Science* 362 (2018): 1119–1121.

Brown, Christopher W. "Companion to the Tutorial Cylindrical Algebraic Decomposition Presented at ISSAC 2004." June 30, 2004. http://www.usna.edu/Users/cs/wcbrown/research/ISSAC04/handout.pdf.

Brown, Christopher W. "Improved Projection for Cylindrical Algebraic Decomposition." *Journal of Symbolic Computation* 32, no. 5 (2001): 447-465.

Centers for Medicare and Medicaid Services. "Guidance Regarding Part D Bids." *archive. org.* April 5, 2019. https://web.archive.org/web/20190526042144/https:/www.cms.gov/ Research-Statistics-Data-and-Systems/Computer-Data-and-Systems/HPMS/Downloads/ HPMS-Memos/Weekly/SysHPMS-Memo-2019-Apr-5th.pdf.

Congressional Budget Office. *Incorporating the Effects of the Proposed Rule on Safe Harbors for Pharmaceutical Rebates in CBO's Budget Projections.* Washington, DC: Congressional Budget Office, 2019.

Crandall, Robert W. "Policy watch: corporate average fuel economy standards." *Journal of Economic Perspectives* 6 (1992): 171–180.

De Moura, Leonardo, and Nikolaj Bjørner. "Z3: An efficient SMT solver." *International conference on Tools and Algorithms for the Construction and Analysis of Systems.* 2008. 337–340.

Editorial Board. "Why are Drugs Cheaper in Europe?" *Wall Street Journal*, October 28, 2018.

eRulemaking Program Management Office. "Fraud and Abuse Removal of Safe Harbor Protection for Rebates Involving Prescription Pharmaceuticals." *regulations.gov.* 2019. https://www.regulations.gov/docket?D=HHSIG-2019-0001.

Foldy, Ben, and Timothy Puko. "White House Backing Off Proposed Fuel-Efficiency Freeze." *Wall Street Journal*, October 31, 2019.

"Gottfried Leibniz." *wikiquote.com.* November 8, 2019. https://en.wikiquote.org/wiki/ Gottfried_Leibniz.

Jaffe, Sonia, Robert Minton, Casey B. Mulligan, and Kevin M. Murphy. *Chicago Price Theory*. Princeton University Press (ChicagoPriceTheory.com), 2019.

Japsen, Bruce. "Trump's Aborted Drug Price Rule Spares 'Middlemen' And The Drug Industry." *Forbes*, July 11, 2019.

Klein, Benjamin, and Kevin M. Murphy. "Exclusive Dealing Intensifies Competition for Distribution." *Antitrust Law Journal* 75, no. 2 (2008): 433-466.

Levinson, Brian. "Cost Benefit Analysis of Cafe Standards compared to the Alternative Fuel/Carbon Tax." *Journal of Environmental and Resource Economics at Colby* 2 (2015): 126.

Morris, Julian, and Arthur R. Wardle. *CAFE and ZEV Standards: Environmental Effects and Alternatives*. Policy Brief, Reason Foundation, 2017.

Mulligan, Casey B., James H. Davenport, and Matthew England. "TheoryGuru: A Mathematica Package to apply Quantifier Elimination Technology to Economics." Edited by James H. Davenport, Manuel Kauers, George Labahn and Josef Urban. *Mathematical Software—ICMS 2018*. Cham, Switzerland: Springer, 2018. 369-78.

Office of Management and Budget. "Circular A-4: Regulatory Analysis." (OMB, Office of Information and Regulatory Affairs) 2003.

Office of Management and Budget. "Marginal Excess Tax Burden as a Potential Cost Under E.O. 13771." *regulations.gov*. 2019. https://www.regulations.gov/document?D=OMB-2017-0002-0055.

Owermohle, Sarah, and Sarah Karlin-Smith. "Will dropping rebates raise premiums? Azar says, No." *politico.com*. March 18, 2019. https://www.politico.com/newsletters/prescription-pulse/2019/03/18/will-dropping-rebates-raise-premiums-azar-says-no-548269.

Pfeiffer, Dan. *Yes We (still) Can: Politics in the Age of Obama, Twitter, and Trump*. Hachette UK, 2018.

PhRMA. "Members." *phrma.org*. 2019. https://www.phrma.org/en/About/Members.

Plumer, Brad. "Trump Put a Low Cost on Carbon Emissions. Here's Why It Matters." *New York Times*, August 23, 2018.

Ramsey, Frank P. "A Contribution to the Theory of Taxation." *Economic Journal* 37, no. 14 (1927): 47–61.

Roehrig, Charles. *The impact of prescription drug rebates on health plans and consumers.* Washington: Altarum, 2018.

Rosen, Jeffrey A., and Brian Callanan. "The Regulatory Budget Revisited." *Admin. L. Rev.* (HeinOnline) 66 (2014): 835.

Sanstad, Alan H., and Richard B. Howarth. "Consumer rationality and energy efficiency." *1994 ACEEE Summer Study on Energy Efficiency in Buildings: Human dimensions of energy consumption* (ACEEE) 1 (1994): 175.

Shepherd, William G. "Ramsey pricing: Its uses and limits." *Utilities Policy* 2 (1992): 296–298.

Spence, A. Michael. "Monopoly, Quality, and Regulation." *Bell Journal of Economics* 6, no. 2 (Autumn 1975): 417-29.

Steinhorn, Charles. "Tame Topology and O-Minimal Structures." In *Computational Aspects of General Equilibrium Theory*, by Donald J. Brown and Felix Kubler, 165-91. Berlin: Springer-Verlag, 2008.

Strzeboński, Adam. "Computation with semialgebraic sets represented by cylindrical algebraic formulas." *ISSAC '10 Proceedings of the 35th International Symposium on Symbolic and Algebraic Computation.* New York: ACM, 2010. 61-68.

Strzeboński, Adam. "Cylindrical algebraic decomposition using local projections." *Journal of Symbolic Computation* 76 (September-October 2016): 36-64.

Svab, Petr. "Senate Panel Approves Trump Nominee Jeffrey Rosen as Deputy AG." *The Epoch Times*, May 9, 2019.

U.S. Department of Health and Human Services. "Removal of Safe Harbor Protection for Rebates Involving Prescription Pharmaceuticals and Creation of New Safe Harbor Protection for Certain Point-of-Sale Reductions in Price on Prescription Pharmaceuticals and Certain Pharmacy Benefit Manager Service Fees." *Federal Register*, February 6, 2019: 2340-63.

—. "Trump Administration Proposes to Lower Drug Costs by Targeting Backdoor Rebates and Encouraging Direct Discounts to Patients." *hhs.gov.* January 31, 2019. https://www. hhs.gov/about/news/2019/01/31/trump-administration-proposes-to-lower-drug-costs-by-targeting-backdoor-rebates-and-encouraging-direct-discounts-to-patients.html.

U.S. Department of Health and Human Services, Office of the Assistant Secretary for Planning and Evaluation. "Guidelines for Regulatory Impact Analysis." *aspe.hhs.gov.* 2016. https://aspe.hhs.gov/system/files/pdf/242926/HHS_RIAGuidance.pdf.

U.S. Dept. of Transportation, National Highway Traffic Safety Administration and U.S. Environmental Protection Agency. "Preliminary Regulatory Impact Analysis: The Safer Affordable Fuel-Efficient (SAFE) Vehicles Rule for Model Year 2021—2026 Passenger Cars and Light Trucks." *nhtsa.gov.* July 2018. https://www.nhtsa.gov/sites/nhtsa.dot.gov/files/documents/ld_cafe_my2021-26_pria_0.pdf.

Wolfram, Stephen. *An Elementary Introduction to the Wolfram Langauge.* Wolfram Media, Incorporated, 2017.

CHAPTER 11 "DO I HEAR A CRY FOR HELP OUT THERE?"

American Maritime Partnership. "About American Maritime Partnership." *americanmaritimepartnership.com.* 2018. https://www.americanmaritimepartnership.com/about/who-we-are/.

—. "American Maritime Partnership Announces Centennial Celebration of American Maritime Heroes." *americanmaritimepartnership.com.* June 5, 2019. https://www. americanmaritimepartnership.com/press-releases/american-maritime-partnership-announces-centennial-celebration-of-american-maritime-heroes/.

—. "American Maritime Partnership Names Congressman Steve Scalise 'Champion of Maritime' for Steadfast Commitment to Domestic Maritime Industry." *americanmaritimepartnership.com.* December 13, 2017. https://www. americanmaritimepartnership.com/press-releases/american-maritime-partnership-names-congressman-steve-scalise-champion-maritime-steadfast-commitment-domestic-maritime-industry/.

—. "Sen. Mitch McConnell Named Champion of Maritime." *americanmaritimepartnership. com*. October 15, 2014. https://www.americanmaritimepartnership.com/press-releases/ sen-mitch-mcconnell-named-champion-maritime/.

—. "Statements of Support." *archive.org*. January 2015. https://web.archive.org/ web/20150111202441/http://www.mctf.com/statements.html.

"An Act to promote the welfare of American seamen in the merchant marine of the United States [Merchant Marine Act of 1915]." Public Law 302, March 4, 1915.

Arthur J. Morris Law Library. "The Wreck of the Karen E in the Long Island Sound." *archives.law.virginia.edu*. 2017. https://archives.law.virginia.edu/dengrove/writeup/ wreck-karen-e-long-island-sound.

Barron, James. "Coast Guard Calls in Navy Divers in Search for Wreck of the Karen E." *New York Times*, September 20, 1981.

Browder, Bill. *Red Notice: A True Story of High Finance, Murder, and One Man's Fight for Justice*. New York: Simon and Schuster, 2015.

Council of Economic Advisers. *Economic Report of the President*. Executive Office of the President, February 2020.

Daly, Michael. "The Wreck of the Karen E." *New York Magazine*, November 23, 1981: 32-38.

Dunlap, David W. "A Search Sub is Believed to Have Found Karen E." *New York Times*, September 26, 1981.

Editorial Board. "Elaine Chao, Mitch McConnell and Questions of Conflict." *New York Times*, October 16, 2019.

Editors. "Able Seamen." *New York Times*, January 13, 1914: p. 8.

Fang, Lee, and Spencer Woodman. "Global Shipping Business Tied to Mitch McConnell, Secretary Elaine Chao Shrouded in Offshore Tax Haven." *intercept.com*. February 5, 2018. https://theintercept.com/2018/02/05/ mitch-mcconnell-elaine-chao-offshore-paradise-papers/.

Frittelli, John. *Revitalizing Coastal Shipping for Domestic Commerce.* Tech. rep., Congressional Research Service, 2017.

Frittelli, John. "Shipping Under the Jones Act: Legislative and Regulatory Background." Congressional Research Service Report, 2019.

—. *Shipping US crude oil by water: vessel flag requirements and safety issues.* Congressional Research Service, 2014.

Gallagher, John. "Trump vows not to act on Jones Act." *freightwaves.com.* May 2, 2019. https://www.freightwaves.com/news/regulation/trump-vows-not-to-act-on-jones-act.

Gibson, Andrew, and Arthur Donovan. *The Abandoned Ocean: A History of United States Maritime Policy.* Columbia, DC: University of South Carolina Press, 2000.

Hilton, George W. *Eastland: Legacy of the Titanic.* Stanford, CA: Stanford University Press, 1996.

Hilton, George Woodman. *Lake Michigan passenger steamers.* Stanford, CA: Stanford University Press, 2002.

Hoxie, Philip, and Vincent H. Smith. "The Jones Act Does Not Add to Our Nation's Defenses." *AEI Paper & Studies* (The American Enterprise Institute), 2019: 10.

Kogan, Rick. "New film remembers the SS Eastland and the day 844 died in the Chicago River." *Chicago Tribune*, July 17, 2019.

LeMoult, Craig. "Trump Was Asked About a Russian Gas Shipment To Boston. Here's What That Tells Us About Energy in New England." *wgbh.org.* July 17, 2018. https://www.wgbh.org/news/local-news/2018/07/17/trump-was-asked-about-a-russian-gas-shipment-to-boston-heres-what-that-tells-us-about-energy-in-new-england.

Loris, Nicolas, Brian Slattery, and Bryan Riley. "Sink the Jones Act: Restoring America's competitive advantage in maritime-related industries." *Heritage Foundation Backgrounder*, 2014.

"Merchant Marine Act of 1920." U.S. Code, Title 46, Section 50101, 1920.

Neufeld, Jennie. "Read the full transcript of the Helsinki press conference." *vox.com*. July 17, 2017. https://www.vox.com/2018/7/16/17576956/transcript-putin-trump-russia-helsinki-press-conference.

Obama, Barack. "Letter to the Seafarers International Union." August 28, 2008. https://web.archive.org/web/20110526083543/http://www.seafarers.org/HeardAtHQ/2008/Q3/Images/Seafarers%20Endorsement.pdf.

Poole, William. "Woodrow Wilson and the Tariff: Lessons for Today." *mises.org*. July 9, 2018. https://mises.org/wire/woodrow-wilson-and-tariff-lessons-today.

Raju, Manu, and John Bresnahan. "Members' fortunes see steep declines." *politico.com*. June 12, 2009. https://www.politico.com/story/2009/06/members-fortunes-see-steep-declines-023693.

Ricardo, John Lewis. *The Anatomy of the Navigation Laws*. London: Charles Gilpin, 1847.

Reagan Library Collections. "Chao, Elaine." *reaganlibrary.gov*. June 24, 2016. https://www.reaganlibrary.gov/sites/default/files/archives/textual/smof/chao.pdf.

Smith, Adam. *An Inquiry into the Nature and Causes of the Wealth of Nations*. Edited by Edwin Cannan. London: Methuen & Co., Ltd, 1776/1904.

Stranahan, Susan Q. "The Eastland Disaster Killed More Passengers Than the Titanic and the Lusitania. Why Has It Been Forgotten?" *Smithsonian.com*. October 27, 2014. https://www.smithsonianmag.com/history/eastland-disaster-killed-more-passengers-titanic-and-lusitania-why-has-it-been-forgotten-180953146/.

Tindera, Michela. "A $59 Million Will Sheds Light On Shipping Fortune Connected To Elaine Chao And Mitch McConnell." *Forbes*, June 10, 2019.

U.S. Coast Guard, New York Investigating Officer. "Findings of Fact [Barge and Pleasure Boat Karen E]." *wordpress.com*. February 26, 1982. https://towmasters.files.wordpress.com/2009/03/uscg_ir_karene_davidmcallister_collision.pdf.

U.S. Department of Transportation. "Secretary Elaine L. Chao Honored as American Maritime Hero." *transportation.gov*. June 11, 2019. https://www.transportation.gov/briefing-room/secretary-elaine-l-chao-honored-american-maritime-hero.

United Press International. "Yacht owner cited for negligence in death of family, neighbors." *upi.com.* June 3, 1982. https://www.upi.com/Archives/1982/06/03/ Yacht-owner-cited-for-negligence-in-death-of-family-neighbors/1665391924800/.

United States Government Accountability Office. *Puerto Rico: Characteristics of the Island's Maritime Trade and Potential Effects of Modifying the Jones Act.* Report to Congressional Requesters, Washington, DC: United States Government Accountability Office, 2013.

Yuen, Stacy. "Keeping Up with the Jones Act." *hawaiibusiness.com.* August 4, 2012. https:// www.hawaiibusiness.com/keeping-up-with-the-jones-act/.

EPILOGUE WHAT WE LEARN ABOUT OUR PRESIDENT AND OUR GOVERNMENT

Brooks, David. "The Populist Addiction." *New York Times,* January 25, 2010.

Eisenhower, Dwight D. "Farewell Address (1961)." *ourdocuments.gov.* January 17, 1961. https://www.ourdocuments.gov/doc.php?flash=false&doc=90&page=transcript.

Fearnow, Benjamin. "Bernie Sanders Rebukes NBC Host: If 2016 Wasn't Rigged I Would have 'Defeated Donald Trump'." *newsweek.com.* June 26, 2019. https://www.newsweek.com/ bernie-sanders-defeat-donald-trump-2016-rigged-primary-dnc-nbc-kasie-hunt-1446116.

Guida, Victoria, and Katy O'Donnell. "Battle over CFPB leadership ends as Mulvaney challenger resigns." *politico.com.* July 6, 2018. https://www.politico.com/story/2018/07/06/ consumer-financial-protection-bureau-leadership-battle-674254.

Harvard University. "Quick Facts." *harvard.edu.* 2019. https://www.harvard.edu/ media-relations/media-resources/quick-facts.

Leetaru, Kalev. "The Game of the Name: Media Bias and Presidents." *realclearpolitics.com.* October 15, 2018. https://www.realclearpolitics.com/articles/2018/10/15/the_game_of_the_ name_media_bias_and_presidents_138351.html.

Millhiser, Ian. "The Supreme Court will decide if Trump can fire the CFPB director. The implications are enormous." *vox.com.* October 18, 2019. https://www.vox.com/policy-and-politics/2019/9/18/20872236/ trump-justice-department-supreme-court-cfpb-unitary-executive.

The Final Year. Directed by Greg Barker. Performed by Ben Rhodes, Samantha Power, John Kerry and others. 2017.

ABOUT THE AUTHOR

The *Wall Street Journal* calls him "The economist who exposed Obamacare." Casey B. Mulligan, Professor of Economics at the University of Chicago, received his PhD in economics from the University of Chicago in 1993. Mulligan has been a visiting professor at Harvard University, Clemson University, and the Irving B. Harris Graduate School of Public Policy Studies. He served as Chief Economist of the White House Council of Economic Advisers during 2018 and 2019.

Casey has received awards and fellowships from the Manhattan Institute, the Fraser Institute for Public Policy, the National Tax Association, the National Science Foundation, Wolfram Research, the Alfred P. Sloan Foundation, the Smith-Richardson Foundation, and the John M. Olin Foundation. His research covers capital and labor taxation, the gender wage gap, health economics, regulation, Social Security, voting and the economics of aging.

Mulligan has written widely on discrepancies between economic analysis and conventional wisdom. Before *You're Hired!*, he wrote *Chicago Price Theory* (with Jaffe, Minton, and Murphy), *Side Effects and Complications*, *The Redistribution Recession*, and *Parental Priorities and Economic Inequality*. He has also written numerous op-eds and blog entries for the *New York Times*, the *Wall Street Journal*, the *New York Post*, the *Chicago Tribune*, http://blogsupplyanddemand.com, and other blogs and periodicals. Follow @caseybmulligan on Twitter.

INDEX

Note: *f* after page number indicates a figure.

A

@realdonaldtrump, 15–18, 23–27, 131, 135, 160
Acosta, Secretary of Labor Alex, xiv
Acronyms, 187–188
Affordable Care Act (ACA), xv, 3, 4, 8–10, 12
    inaccurate reporting on, 139
    individual mandates, 4*f*, 12–13
    opioid coverage, 46–47
    stimulus law, 30
    subsidies, 12
    tax penalty, 1, 4, 9, 12
Annual average to annual average growth rate, 27–28, 85–86
Apprentice, The, xi–xii
Automobile emissions standards and deregulation, 69–70, 96, 98, 110, 124, 127–128, 154, 155–157, 161, 164
Azar, Secretary of Health and Human Services Alex M. II, 5–6, 12-13, 17–19, 26, 51-55, 58, 63, 67, 69, 134, 139–140, 145–154

B

Ball, Krystal, 30
Barr, Attorney General William, 141
Barro, Robert J., 72, 128
Baxter, CEA Staff Economist Andrew, 81
Becker, Gary S., 54, 81-82, 87, 189
Benefits of immigration, 81–82
Bennett, William J., 86, 89, 185
Bennett hypothesis, 86, 89, 185
Bernanke, CEA Chairman Ben, xii
Biden, Joe, 22-23
Blase, Special Assistant Brian, xv, 18-19, 26, 74-75, 153, 158, 184, 189
"Blue Collar Titanic," 172–173, 173*f*
Bolton, National Security Advisor John, 66
Bremberg, Director of Domestic Policy Council Andrew, xv, 75, 139, 184
Browder, Bill, 177
Burkhauser, CEA member Rich, xiii, 20, 32, 73, 81, 133
Bush, George H.W., 63, 118, 169

Bush, George W. Administration, xii, 65, 103, 120, 131

Bush, John Ellis "Jeb," 25-26, 180

Business practices in Trump Administration, 90–104, 183–185

Butterfield, Senior Associate Staff Secretary Nick, 62

C

Cabinet meetings formats, 137–139

Car companies, 70, 70, 154–161

Carter Administration, 75, 119

Chao, Secretary of Transportation Ellen, 106, 170–171, 179

Chaos question evidence, 64–79

Chaos vs. predictability in Trump Administration, 68

Chicago Price Theory, xv, 71, 128, 161, 189

"Chicken tax," 112–113, 126–127, 155

China trade, 44–45, 106, 114–117, 183

Cipollone, White House Counsel Pat, 68

Clarida, Rich, 180

Climate change movement, 43–45, 59–61, 96, 124–125, 155, 164, 182

Comey, FBI Director James, 94

Conway, Kellyanne, 19, 55, 62

Corinth, Kevin, xiii, 54, 73

Corporate welfare, 145–147

Criminal justice reform, 59, 182

D

Darroch, British Ambassador Sir Kim, 78–79

Deep state, 93–95

Deregulation, xiii, xv, 11–12, 40, 68–70, 75, 96–98, 103, 105–106, 113–114, 117–119, 121–124, 128–129, 130–133, 141–142, 158–160, 176

Deregulation agenda in Trump Administration, 120–126, 156

Devaluation of US dollar, 86

Dobbs, Lou, 20-21, 28, 37, 177

Dore, Jimmy, 30

Dolan, Special Assistant to the President Anthony, 35, 106

Drug deregulation in Trump Administration, 130–143

Dukakis, 1988 Democratic Presidential nominee Michael, 24f

E

Economic experimenter, Trump as, 2–10, 15, 153, 160, 184–185

Economic experiments, 2–5

Economic forecasts, 17, 88

Economic growth, 17, 21, 80–81, 84–85, 88, 121

Economic growth and immigration, 83–85

Economic regulations, 125f

Economic research in policy arena, 33

Economic Report of the President
general, 17, 71
1947, 61
1987, 127
1989, 116
1992, 39
2010, 61
2011, 71
2012, 98
2019, 11, 16, 20, 28, 37, 39, 88, 103, 177, 190
2020, 59

Eisenhower, Dwight, 180

Ellig, Jerry, 103

Employment Act of 1946, xiii

Enjeti, Saagar, 30

Environmental costs and deregulation, 97–98, 100–101, 126, 154–155, 155f, 157, 163, 174–175

Environmental Protection Agency, 97

F

Fake news, 30–38, 86, 129, 130–144, 185

FDA deregulation, 131, 133, 142

Federal agency staff, Trump administration, xiii–

Federal regulation myths, 97–102

Fee system for immigration, 82, 87

Fentanyl, 43–50, 57, 126

Fiedler, Matthew, 135

Final Year, The 45, 60, 104, 181

Fitzgerald, CEA Chief International Economist
Tim, 138
Flood, Acting White House Counsel Emmet, 68
Ford Administration, 119
Ford, Henry, 160-161
Fracking, 86, 124, 185
Friedman, Milton, 87, 109
Furchtgott-Roth, Acting Assistant Treasury
Secretary Diana, 67
Furman, Jason, 72-73, 163

G
Gazprom (Russian natural gas company), 168,
177
Goldwater Rule of American Medical
Association, 38
Gottlieb, Commissioner of the FDA Scott, 67,
130, 131, 133
Goodwin, Michael, 20
Goolsbee, Austan, 36, 180
Grogan, Director of the Domestic Policy
Council Joe, 18-19, 63, 66-67, 147, 149
Gruber, Jonathan, 9, 180

H
Haley, Deputy Assistant to the President Vince,
34-35, 74
Hammond, Philip, 78-79
Hanke, Steve, 111, 123, 127
Harrington, Deputy Assistant to the President
for Strategic Planning Kevin, 170, 178
Harris, Kamala, 37
Harvard alumni in government, 72, 135,
180–181
Hassett, CEA Chairman Kevin, xiii, 16, 20–21,
20f, 32, 33, 36, 53, 63, 72-73, 81, 91, 95,
113, 133, 149-151
Hawthorne effect, 5–6, 11, 172
Health insurance, xv
health reimbursement accounts, 75
Short-Term Limited Duration Health
Insurance plans, 75
tax penalty, 1, 4, 9, 12
Holder, Eric, 47-48, 50, 61, 63, 126
Holder Memo, 50, 63, 126
Human capital project, 78

I
Illegal immigration, 81, 182
Immigration policy, 80–89
benefits for, 81–82
economic growth and, 83–85
fee system, 82, 87
merit-based system, 81, 82, 85, 88
points system, 82
Samaritan's Dilemma, 80, 83–84
unaccompanied children, 83
Impromptu economist, Trump as, 85–87
Inaccurate reporting on ACA, 139
Individual mandates of ACA, 4f, 12–13
Intellectual property theft, 117, 128, 169, 182
Interest rates, 85, 86, 105
International aid scrutiny, xvii, 90–92
Investigational drug deregulation, 123
Iraq War, xiii
Irwin, Douglas A., 113-114, 127

J
Jones Act, 166–175
Judicial reform, 125

K
Kelly, Chief of Staff General John, 68, 75, 76,
78, 170, 184
Kenkel, CEA Senior Economist Don, xiii, 54
Kennedy, Edward, 23, 31
Keynes, John Maynard, 13
Krugman, Paul, 41, 128
Kudlow, NEC Director Larry, 20f, 26, 65-66,
69, 85, 106, 158-159, 170, 178, 180
Kushner, Senior Advisor to the President Jared,
76, 81

L
Laffer, Arthur, 8-9, 13, 113
Laffer curve, 8–10, 13, 113
Larrimore, CEA Senior Economist Jeff, 81
Lerner Symmetry Theorem, 114
Levin, Mark R., 140-141
Lighthizer, US Trade Representative Robert, 105
Lobbyists and special interests, 144–164
corporate welfare, 145–147
TheoryGuru and true cost calculations,
148–150, 157–158, 162–163, 184

Lublin, Richard K., 165–166
Lucas Jr., Robert E., xiv, 128

M

Marconi, Nobel Prize Winner Guglielmo, 2, 3, 5, 8, 11
Marginal Excess Tax Burden, 152
Marginal tax rate cuts, xiii
Marginal way of thinking, 73
Marxism, 32, 36, 38
Matsumoto, CEA Senior Economist Brett, 142
McConnell, Senate Majority Leader Mitch, 22, 171, 178
McGahn, White House Counsel Don, 53, 68
Medicare, 13, 46, 67, 95, 146, 149–153, 187
    for all, 22–23, 28, 31–39, 32f, 95, 172, 183
    Part D, 49–55, 61
    rebate rule, 5–6, 94, 98, 101–102, 123–124, 144–153, 161
    reinsurance formula, 149
Menashi, Associate Counsel to the President Steven, 12, 53
Merit-based system for immigration, 81, 82, 85, 88
Miller, Senior Advisor to the President Stephen, 35, 37, 81
Mnuchin, Treasury Secretary Steven, 67
Mueller investigation and fake news, 141–142
Mulvaney, Acting White House Chief of Staff Mick, 20f, 23, 63, 68, 77, 78, 92, 122, 139, 149

N

Naloxone, 56, 58
Natural gas and federal regulations, 118
Natural Gas Policy Act, 118, 124, 167–175
Navarro, Director of the Office of Trade and Manufacturing Policy Peter, 66, 86, 108, 113–116, 170–171, 177–179
Neoclassical growth model, 71, 127–128
Niskanen, William A., 68, 77, 111, 119-122, 126
Nordquist, CEA Chief of Staff D.J., xiii, 20f, 36, 189, 190f

O

Obama Administration, 7, 9–11, 25, 44, 46, 48, 69, 71, 75, 83–84, 98, 101, 103, 125, 135, 154, 156, 164
Obamacare, xiii, 9, 22, 28, 186. See also Affordable Care Act (ACA)
Ocean oil shipping rates, 174f
Ohr, Nellie 40, 180
Opioid coverage of ACA, 46–47
Opioid epidemic, xiii, xviii, 10, 42–63, 68, 71, 74, 95, 98, 116, 126, 144, 181–182, 186, 190

P

Pandemic, 71
Parker, Senior Advisor to the Secretary for Health Reform Jim, 67
Pear, Robert, 139
Pelosi, Nancy, 29, 46, 143
Pence, VPOTUS Mike, 22, 57, 145, 148, 153
Pfeiffer, Dan, 11, 44-45, 59, 137
Philipson, CEA Member Tomas, xiii, 20f, 32, 34, 63, 68, 72, 73, 132
Points system, for immigration, 82
Populism, xviii, 2–6, 23, 44–46, 60, 79, 93, 122, 163, 180–183, 186
Populist experimenter, Trump as, 2–5
Populist metrics, 128
Postal service subsidies, 116
Powell, Chair of the Federal Reserve Jay, xv, 61, 84
Prescription drug prices, xiv, 5, 17,19, 28, 46, 49, 52, 57, 68–69, 86, 97–98, 120–121, 123, 130–143, 136f, 146, 149–153, 182, 184–185
Presidential rallies as form of communication, 19, 28, 35–36, 124, 161
Presidential speech writing, 35
Productivity metrics, 70, 128
Profit and supposed exploitation, 32
Protectionism, 107–109, 111, 168, 171, 175, 176
Purposefulness, 116–117
Putin, Russian President Vladimir, xviii, 168, 169f, 170

R

Raleigh, Helen, 42

Reagan Administration, 68, 71, 105, 106, 106*f*, 108–111, 116, 119, 122, 125–127, 140, 179

Regulatory budgeting, 95–97

Resistance passions, 73

Restoring Internet Freedom rule, 121

Rhodes, Ben, 43, 45, 59, 74

Ricardo, David, 115-116, 177

Rollo, Senior Director for International Trade Andrew, 178

Rosen, Deputy Attorney General Jeffrey, 156

Ross, Secretary of Commerce Wilbur, 20–21, 26–27, 34–36, 74

Ruling class, 22, 45–46, 60, 77, 101, 122, 154, 156, 180–182, 186

S

Samaritan's Dilemma, 80, 83–84

Sanders, Bernie, xvii, 23, 24*f*, 30, 31, 184

Sanders, White House Press Secretary Sarah, 19, 138

Scavino, Senior Advisor to the President for Digital Strategy Dan, 15, 17, 27, 134

Schlapp, Director of Strategic Communications Mercedes, 19

Seaman's Act, 102, 172

Shale production prohibition costs, 124, 128

Short-Term Limited Duration Health Insurance plans, 75

Silver, Nate, 60

Sloan, Alfred P., 160

Smith, Adam, 111, 176

Socialism, xiv, 23, 29–41, 69, 73–74, 95

Special interests, 92–94, 111, 119–122, 144–147, 151, 158–161, 169–171, 174, 176, 186

Spence, Michael, 148

Stimulus law and ACA, 30

Subsidies for ACA, 12

Subsidizing, 8, 9, 12, 25, 30, 46, 49–52, 80, 84, 116, 186

Sullivan, Joe, 116

Summers, Larry, 72-73, 163, 180

Sun, CEA Senior Economist Eric, xiii, 61

Sunstein, Cass, 100, 102, 104, 180

Supply-side economics, 127–128

Surprise medical billing, 138

T

Tariff-as-tax, 113–114

Tariff quotas, 110

Tariff retaliation, 108, 114

Tariffs, 105–129

"chicken tax," 112–113, 126–127, 155

definition, 108

protectionism, 107–109, 111, 168, 171, 175, 176

purposefulness, 116–117

tariff-as-tax, 113–114

tariff quotas, 110

tariff retaliation, 108, 114

and trade wars, 107–111

voluntary export restraints, 108, 127

Tax Cut and Jobs Act (TCJA), 113–114

Tax penalty for ACA, 1, 4, 9, 12

Tax reform, 185

Texas v Azar, 12

TheoryGuru, 148–150, 157–158, 162–163, 184

Trade wars, 107–111

Trial and error method, 2, 11

Trial and error method of Trump Administration, 2, 11

Trump, President Donald J. Administration

business practices, 90–104, 183–185

chaos vs. predictability, 68

as Communicator in Chief, 18–21

deregulation agenda, 120–126, 156

drug deregulation, 130–143

economic experimenter, 2–10, 15, 153, 160, 184–185

id, 7, 25

as impromptu economist, 85–87

persona, 25–26

populist experimenter, 2–5

prescription drug prices, xiv, 17, 28, 68–69, 130–143, 136*f*, 182, 185

tariffs, 105–129

trial and error method, 2, 11

Twitter, xvii, 7, 14–28, 16*f*, 40, 69, 77, 126, 182

Trump, Senior Advisor to the President Ivanka, 65, 66, 78

Tsui, Kevin, 148
Tuthill, Reggie, 165-166, 176
Twitter use, Trump, xvii, 7, 14–28, 16*f*, 40, 69,
    77, 126, 182

U
Ukraine call, 7, 92
Unaccompanied children and immigration, 83
United States Mexico Canada Agreement
    (USMCA), 38, 109, 127
Urbanowicz, HHS Chief of Staff Peter, 55

V
Vehicle emissions, 69, 98, 127–128, 156, 164
Voluntary export restraints, 108, 127
Vought, Acting OMB Director Russ, 18-19

W
Wall Street Journal, 13, 72, 84, 88, 109, 127,
    140, 145, 161, 164
Warning, A (Anonymous), 64, 70, 76–77, 87
Washington Bubble, xiv, 2, 10, 42–43, 47, 60,
    63, 93, 112
Wead, Doug, 77, 103
Weber, CEA Senior Economist Jeremy, 157, 159,
    178
Weidenbaum, Murray, 117-118
"White House in chaos" articles, xvi
White House staff, Trump administration,
    xiii–ix
Willems, Deputy Director of NEC Clete, 115
Winslett, Ben, 8-10, 13, 99
Wireless radio communication, 2, 3, 5, 8
Wolfram, Stephen, 148, 162
Wong, CEA Senior Economist Anna, xiii
Worthington, CEA Senior Economist Paula, xiii
Worthington, Deputy Assistant to the President
    and Advisor for Policy, Strategy, and
    Speechwriting Ross, 34-35, 74

Y
Yeltsin, Boris, 40
"Young Turks, The," 30

Z
Zinberg, CEA Senior Economist Joel, 147, 189